THE
CHICANO
HERITAGE

This is a volume in the Arno Press collection

THE CHICANO HERITAGE

Advisory Editor
Carlos E. Cortés

Editorial Board
Rodolfo Acuña
Juan Gómez-Quiñones
George F. Rivera, Jr.

*See last pages of this volume
for a complete list of titles.*

ON THE OLD WEST COAST

Being further Reminiscences of a Ranger

MAJOR HORACE BELL

Edited by

LANIER BARTLETT

ARNO PRESS
A New York Times Company
New York — 1976

Editorial Supervision: LESLIE PARR

Reprint Edition 1976 by Arno Press Inc.

Copyright © 1930 by William Morrow
& Company, Inc.
Renewed 1957 by Lanier Bartlett

Reprinted by permission of
William Morrow & Company, Inc.

THE CHICANO HERITAGE
ISBN for complete set: 0-405-09480-9
See last pages of this volume for titles.

Manufactured in the United States of America

Library of Congress Cataloging in Publication Data

Bell, Horace, 1830-1918.
   On the old west coast, being further reminiscences of a ranger.

   (The Chicano heritage)
   Reprint of the ed. published by Morrow, New York.
   1. Frontier and pioneer life--California, Southern. 2. California, Southern--Description and travel. 3. Bell, Horace, 1830-1918. I. Title. II. Series.
F867.B435   1976   979.4'9   76-1242
ISBN 0-405-09485-X

ON THE OLD WEST COAST

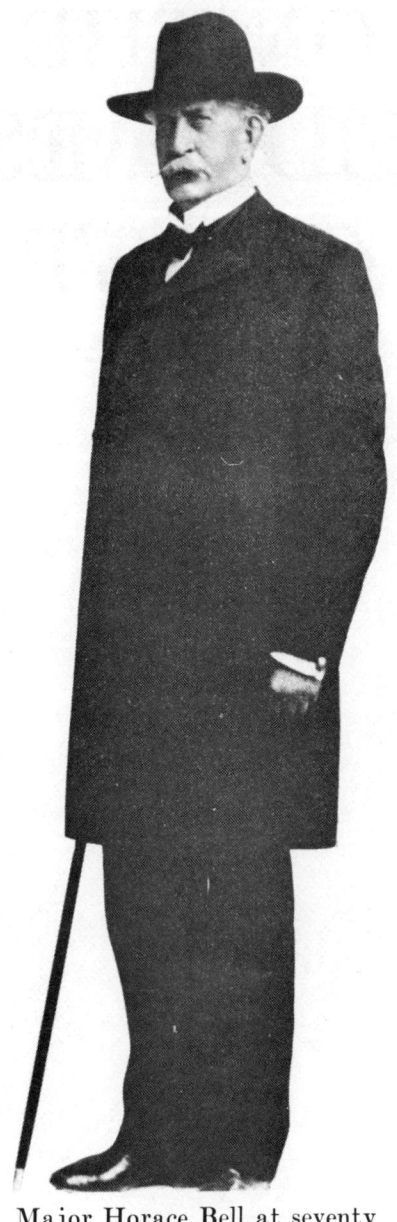

Major Horace Bell at seventy years of age.

ON THE
OLD WEST
COAST

Being further Reminiscences of a Ranger,

MAJOR HORACE BELL.

Edited by

LANIER BARTLETT

1930

NEW YORK

WILLIAM MORROW & CO.

COPYRIGHT - - - 1930
BY WILLIAM MORROW & COMPANY, INC.

All rights reserved. This book, or parts thereof, must not be reproduced in any form without permission of the publisher.

PRINTED IN THE U. S. A. BY
QUINN & BODEN COMPANY, INC.
RAHWAY, N. J.

"We deem it the duty of the truthful historian to show posterity life as it existed in the times of which he writes, and in doing this he must honor his enemies and spare not his friends."

HORACE BELL.

Contents

		PAGE
	INTRODUCTION	xi

CHAPTER		
1.	LOS CALIFORNIOS	1
2.	RUIN OF THE RANCHEROS	8
3.	A SERIOUS MATTER IS MEXICAN GRATITUDE	19
4.	BANDITS, DUELISTS AND FILIBUSTERS	32
5.	HOLY MASS AND THREE CARD MONTE	41
6.	HOW RAN RUNNELS DECORATED THE RAMPARTS OF PANAMA	53
7.	HISTORIC TREASURE BURIED IN CAHUENGA PASS	60
8.	LOS ANGELES DURING THE CIVIL WAR	72
9.	THE FELIZ CURSE	85
10.	TRAGIC FATE OF MEXICAN JOE	99
11.	THAT GRAND CALIFORNIAN, THE GRIZZLY BEAR	106
12.	THE LAST WORDS OF RAMON CARRILLO	114
13.	A TALE FROM NICARAGUA ABOUT TAILS IN KENTUCKY	127
14.	PEG-LEG SMITH, THE DEATH VALLEY PARTY AND JOHN GOLLER'S MINE	136
15.	REALLY IMPORTANT EVENTS	146
16.	A DEATH SENTENCE AT MONTEREY AND A SPORTING EVENT AT GILROY'S	153
17.	LIFE AND DEATH IN THE CITY OF THE ANGELS	164
18.	LEONIS THE BASQUE, KING OF CALABASAS	181
19.	SPIT IN THE MOUTH OF HELL	194
20.	A MALAY YANKEE AND THE GREAT PERALTA LAND FRAUD	207
21.	"THE LAW WEST OF THE PECOS"	218

CONTENTS

CHAPTER		PAGE
22.	SOME EARLY MAYORS	240
23.	MATRIMONIAL SHARKS AS BAD AS SHYLOCKS	255
24.	ORANGES ON JOSHUA TREES	267
25.	"KINGS OF THE COMMONWEALTH"	281
26.	IN PRAISE OF THE MORMONS	293
	NOTES	308
	INDEX	330

Andronico Sepúlveda

Illustrations

	PAGE
MAJOR HORACE BELL AT SEVENTY YEARS OF AGE	Frontispiece
DON YGNACIO DEL VALLE	2
DON JOSE DE LA GUERRA Y NORIEGA	2
CHURCH OF OUR LADY THE QUEEN OF THE ANGELS, LOS ANGELES	3
A NOTABLE MANSION	3
ABEL STEARNS	6
GENERAL MARIANO GUADALUPE VALLEJO	6
CALIFORNIAN MODE OF CATCHING CATTLE	7
REPRODUCTION OF A PAGE FROM MAJOR BELL'S MANUSCRIPT	9
A "BROADSIDE" OF THE CALIFORNIA GOLD DAYS	23
SAN FRANCISCO IN APRIL 1850, SHOWING CLAY STREET	24
THE POST OFFICE, CORNER OF PIKE AND CLAY STREETS	24
EMIGRANT TRAIN	25
SCENE IN THE GOLD MINES	25
JOAQUIN MURRIETA—FROM A PAINTING BY A PADRE	32
JOAQUIN MURRIETA AS PICTURED BY AN EARLY-DAY ARTIST	33
MEIGGS' WHARF	36
A PROCLAMATION OF JUNE 9TH, 1856	37
ESCORTING JUDGE TERRY AND OTHER PRISONERS TO THE VIGILANCE ROOMS	39
JUDGE SMITH TERRY	40
A HANGING	40

ILLUSTRATIONS

	PAGE
STABBING OF OFFICER HOPKINS BY JUDGE TERRY	41
FANCY BALL, CALIFORNIA EXCHANGE, SAN FRANCISCO	60
LODGING ROOM IN SAN FRANCISCO	60
SUFFERING IMMIGRANTS	61
FRENCH SHOEBLACKS	61
GENERAL WILLIAM WALKER OF NICARAGUAN FAME	65
PANORAMA OF LOS ANGELES IN THE '50'S	72
MAJOR HORACE BELL ABOUT THE TIME OF THE CIVIL WAR	73
GEORGIA HERRICK BELL	80
FAMOUS WINERY OF JEAN LOUIS VIGNES	81
REPRODUCTION OF A PAGE FROM MAJOR BELL'S MANUSCRIPT	97
GENERAL JOSE ANTONIO CARRILLO	120
JOSE SEPULVEDA	120
YOUNG NATIVE DANDIES OF 1850	121
THE BELLA UNION	164
"THE TWO FRIENDS"	164
CHINESE GAMBLING HOUSE, SAN FRANCISCO	165
DEAD CHINAMEN IN JAIL YARD AFTER THE LOS ANGELES MASSACRE	165
EDITORIAL IN THE LOS ANGELES STAR	167
LOS ANGELES STAR OF OCTOBER 25, 1871	169
LYNCHING OF LACHENAIS FOR THE KILLING OF JACOB BELL	176
FIRST HOUSE ON THE SITE OF THE PRESENT CITY OF PASADENA	177
SOME PRESS COMMENTS REPRINTED IN THE PORCUPINE	189
STEPHEN C. FOSTER	240
DON FRANCISCO SEPULVEDA	240

ILLUSTRATIONS

	PAGE
FAMOUS SADDLE AND BRIDLE OF GENERAL ANDRES PICO	241
THE PRESIDIO OF SAN FRANCISCO	256
SAN FRANCISCO BEAUTIES	256
INTERIOR OF EL DORADO, SAN FRANCISCO	257
FIRST PRESBYTERIAN CHURCH, SAN FRANCISCO	257
RUSH FOR THE GOLD REGIONS	296
SUTTER'S MILL	296
ANTONIA DE BANDINI	297
DON JUAN BANDINI AND DAUGHTER MARGARITA	297

The illustration facing page 7 is taken from an old print which has been reproduced in "A Pictorial History of California" published by the University of California.

Illustrations facing pages 2, 3, 6, 40, 120, 121, 165, 176, 177, 240, 241, and 297 are reproduced from the Ingersoll Historical Collection in the Los Angeles Public Library.

The endpapers, and illustrations facing pages 33, 36, 37 and 41 are reproduced through the courtesy of the California State Library.

Illustrations facing pages 24, 25, 60, 61, 165, 256, 257, and 296 are reproduced from engravings in "The Annals of San Francisco" by Soulé, Gihon, and Nisbet, published by D. Appleton & Company.

Concepción Palomares

Introduction

THROUGH a period of years following the publication of his now famous *Reminiscences of a Ranger* in 1881 it was the habit of Major Horace Bell to dictate to his secretary, as the spirit moved and as time permitted, further memories of tense events and original personalities that had spiced his adventurous years in California, Texas, Mexico and Central America.

As a gold miner in Hangtown while still in his 'teens, a Ranger in pursuit of the notorious Joaquín Murrieta when barely past his majority, a soldier of fortune in the forces of Benito Juárez in Mexico, an aide to General William Walker on the celebrated filibuster into Nicaragua, a Union officer throughout the Civil War and later stationed on the Texas border; still later a newspaper editor making war single-handed against dominant political groups in Los Angeles and an attorney who enjoyed the confidences of the old Spanish Californian families in those turbulent days of racial and political adjustment following the admission of California to the Union, Horace Bell surely had gathered an ample fund of memories of universal human interest when he chose to cast himself in the rôle of *This Truthful Historian,* as he liked to call his part as a chronicler of his contemporaries.

This appellation he emphasizes (sometimes, perhaps, with the gesture of the tongue in the cheek) because he was by nature an iconoclast. Webster's definition of an iconoclast is, I believe, *an image breaker; one who attacks superstitions or shams.* Possibly the first part of this definition conveys too severe an impression of the mental attitude of

Horace Bell when writing about the history he had seen in the making; but that he believed always in expressing his opinion fearlessly, whether unfavorable to a popular hero or propitious to a public villain, there can be no doubt. Certainly he was no iconoclast in the gloomy sense: he was rather a skilled caricaturist who could pick the essential motivating characteristic of a personality or an event, as he saw it, and with a few strokes of his pen exaggerate that feature just enough to give a new and startling interpretation to the subject of his sketch. Usually this new angle that he gives us is hugely amusing and sometimes it is disillusioning; but after all, is not the skillful caricature really the true portrait?

If Major Bell strikes at images it is more frequently with the weapons of satire, irony or broad humor than with heavy denunciation; and so he is always the successful entertainer whether or not we agree with his opinions. Friends or enemies, the rugged old Ranger loved to laugh at his contemporaries. He loved to laugh at himself and at the times in which he lived. And we laugh as we read the lines he left as the record of his iconoclasm, for certainly the spirit of his robust raillery still hovers, a chuckling wraith, over those precious delineations.

The thought that this self-declared *truthful* historian sometimes tells a story with his tongue in his cheek is in no wise a reflection on his veracity. It is a tribute to his ability to picture for us the spirit of the people and the times about which he writes, beyond relating the mere facts of events. Let the Chapter called *Spit in the Mouth of Hell* be an example. I doubt if there is to be found in modern literature a more delightful bit of quixotic writing than this rendition of the traditions of the Elizabeth Lake country. So quaintly blended are fact and fancy in the relation of the

INTRODUCTION

strange happenings interpreted for us by the significantly named Señor Embustero y Mentiroso that we get the feeling perfectly of a Catholic land where legend is more believed than history. Indeed, more believable than history.

Bell, the adventurous Indianan of Scotch-Irish ancestry, was not given over to smashing images only, but himself fashioned some both beautiful and noble. His American patriotism was a white flame within him; his admiration for the great West and its real pioneers was one of the governing ideals of his life; his championship of all whom he had reason to believe had been wronged was instinctive; his utterly unsentimental sentiment for California and its romantic history was his constant inspiration. But he was no hero worshiper. When he believed that a false image had been set up, or that an image was out of proportion, he felt no hesitancy in proclaiming it false or faulty, from his viewpoint.

The stalwart fighting gentleman of six feet two inches and pounds in perfect proportion was long a distinguished figure on the streets of Los Angeles; in the earlier years on a coal black stallion handsomely decked out in all the traditional Californian trappings of carved leather and silver mountings, later afoot with cane, long, tight-fitting frock coat and broad-brimmed black soft hat as he and the Pueblo of Our Lady of the Angels grew older together.

Usually our author, in the middle years, was engaged in fiery opposition to majority opinion or to privileged classes that had appropriated to themselves the power and the glory, as the files of his prickly and dreaded little paper, *The Porcupine,* will attest. In his determination to maintain his fixed opinions against all odds the Major sometimes had to fight his way through those very streets where he was so long prominent, and some of the exciting difficulties which he overcame are recorded in certain chapters of the following chronicle in a manner that is key to the character of the man.

Major Horace Bell died at Oakland, California, in 1918, in his eighty-eighth year and is buried in Los Angeles. Some years before his death he deeded his notes and manuscripts to a daughter, Mrs. J. A. Phillips (Virginia Herrick Bell) of Los Angeles, with the suggestion that they might be worth giving to the world in published form some day as records of events past but not always understood.

It has been my privilege to prepare from this material a book and to attempt to bring the people and events mentioned by the author closer to to-day's reader by a series of notes.

In reading it should be borne in mind that apparently none of the main text was dictated by Major Bell later than 1901, so that when he speaks of changes that have taken place "down to the present writing" allowance must be made for the approximate date at which he was recording his memories. It had been his intention to have his second volume of memories published during his life time, but the pressure of years and the increasing demand on his attention of other interests caused him to turn the material over to his posterity.

To the Californiana addict this volume will be a delight; to the lover of stories of adventure against historical backgrounds it will be absorbing; to the few who may be unable, for personal or traditional reasons, to accept the author's estimates of persons and events, it will undoubtedly prove provocative.

LANIER BARTLETT.

Los Angeles,
  March 15, 1930.

ON THE
OLD WEST
COAST

CHAPTER 1

Los Californios

THE native Spanish-speaking inhabitants of California prior to the American occupation designated themselves not as Spaniards nor as Mexicans but simply as Californios—that is, Californians. Hijos del pais—native sons—was an expression used by the young men further to emphasize their distinction as a race.

And indeed they were a distinct people. Territorially they were separated from the main body of Mexicans by long distances of burning desert or tedious and infrequent sea coast communications. They were Mexican in nationality only by the time the United States took over the province; that is, they were technically Mexicans but actually a separate entity. Politically California enjoyed an almost absolute independence towards the close of the Mexican régime. In those latter days the hijos del pais would no longer tolerate governors sent to them from below the border. They insisted they must have governors to the manor born. The last governor appointed from Mexico City, General Manuel Micheltorena, was expelled by the Californians in 1844 along with his army of cholos imported to enforce his rule. After that Mexico had to agree to California's own choice of an executive from among her native sons. Sometimes the northern and southern ends of the province could not agree on one. Then there had to be two governors, which was not always a satisfactory arrangement, either.

In manners, appearance and general make-up the Californians bore but slight resemblance to the bulk of the people of Mexico. Their isolation, their way of living, the concentration of lordly land holdings in the hands of a few families of pure Spanish origin, developed them into one of the most independent and happily self-sufficient people that ever lived on this earth. To Mexico they bore about the same relationship as did our American pioneers of the West to the American civilization east of the Alleghanies. The great stretch of country from San Diego to Sonoma, seven hundred miles long, was dominated by this small population scattered on wide-spreading ranchos with here and there a presidio,[1] pueblo or mission.

Los Angeles was the largest of the pueblos with a population, just prior to the raising of the American flag, of about fifteen hundred persons. But Santa Bárbara was the finest community, its people more refined, educated and aristocratic than those of any other settlement in the province. It was in all respects a stylish town, with a military background, for it was a presidio town.

Outside the pueblos and presidios the population (other than Indian) was composed of cattle-owning families that lived on ranchos measuring in area from one to eleven square leagues.* Each rancho maintained from one thousand to ten thousand or more head of cattle and an unbelievable number of horses.

A goodly people were these Californians. Generous to a fault, hospitable, rich in lands and herds. The ranchero was a prince in independence and a true gentleman, perhaps not always exactly as sophisticated society fixes the distinction, but as stamped by nature. An all around good fellow was this Spanish Californian chieftain of olden times. Nor

* A Spanish league was almost four miles.

Don José de la Guerra y Noriega.
Founder of a celebrated Santa Barbara family.

Don Ygnácio Del Valle.
Founder of a family still prominent in California. On his rancho of San Francisquito was made the first discovery of gold of positive record in California, in 1842.

Church of Our Lady the Queen of the Angels (Plaza Church), Los Angeles.
Pictured before the church was re-roofed in the early '60's. Note flat brea roof.

A Notable *Mansión*.
Home built by Alexander Bell, the author's uncle, in 1844, at Los Angeles and Aliso Streets. *From an old lithograph.*

was he wholly illiterate, by any means. In the most out-of-the-way places you would find somewhat of literature—most certainly copies of Gil Blas, Don Quixote and often Bernal Díaz's "History of the Conquest of Mexico." In the more pretentious households you would find a still wider collection of books.

And everywhere you would find music. There was always some one of the household who could play on the violin, guitar or harp, and all could dance superlatively.

As for horsemanship the Californian never had any equal anywhere. The Arabs, the Gauchos and the Comanches were his inferiors in this respect. All writers contemporaneous with the age of his glory agree on this point. They also agree that the women excelled in dancing to as striking a degree as did the men in horsemanship.

In the pueblos, Los Angeles and Santa Bárbara for instance, a good deal of elegance, refinement and culture existed. There were ladies here who would have graced the salons of Paris, who would have been ornaments in the society of Washington or New York.

The "adobe hovels" so often referred to by modern scribblers were inhabited by the servile Indian population or the lowest class of mestizos. The houses of the socially recognized Californians were comfortable, well furnished and sometimes elegant. When Capt. Alexander Bell[2] married a belle from Spain in 1844 he spent seventy thousand dollars in building and furnishing an adobe palace in Los Angeles. This building became the first capitol of California under American rule. Commodore Stockton occupied it for a time in 1846 as military governor, and General Frémont in 1847. The old building extended from Aliso to Commercial Street, on the east side of Los Angeles Street, and was quite an imposing structure. It was indeed the finest house in all California, but there were others of grand pretensions, notably the mansion of General Vallejo at Sonoma, of Antonio María Pico at San José, and the homes of the Carrillos, the Noriegas and the Ortegas at Santa Bárbara; of the Estudillos, the Arguellos and the Bandinis at San Diego. In Los Angeles houses of especial note were Governor Pío Pico's and Don Abel Stearns's, the latter a veritable one-story castle covering all the ground now occupied by the Baker Block and extending clear back from Main to Los Angeles Street.[3]

All the families above named and many others lived in comfort, some in sumptuous elegance; that is to say, they lived in fine houses, had good furniture, good kitchens and good cooks and wore fine clothing. These Californians were a dignified people, and it is the desire of this truthful historian, so far as able, to give them their proper standing in the history of the state they founded. They were rich, powerful and happy in ante-gringo times. They were not lazy, neither were they shiftless, dissolute nor dishonest. On the contrary they were a dashing, enterprising people. Their very manner of up-bringing of necessity developed a vigorous physical manhood and womanhood. The men from early boyhood to past middle-age were always in the saddle ranging the plains in care of their herds and always on the alert to repel incursions of hostile savages from the desert fastnesses; always in the open air, always on the go. How could the Californian be a lazy man? Indeed, he was quite the reverse. It was the rule on all the ranchos that with the *luzero* (morning star) every man had to be in the saddle and on the go until eleven o'clock, when he returned for breakfast.

How did it happen that these Californians lost their vast possessions?

LOS CALIFORNIOS

The opinion so often expressed by the modern gringo is that through gambling, profligacy and idleness these former grandees became impoverished. This is not true. Yet it is a fact that the majority of them did lose their possessions and were reduced to poverty. Why and how?

With but a few notable exceptions, they all became the meat of the Shylocks, after the American occupation.

They were so rich, potentially, that they never suspected that they could, by any possibility, become poor. But they had one weakness common to all Spanish-Americans. When they wanted cash they wanted it *immediately*. The Californian couldn't wait, neither would he; and with his ample security he could get all the money he wanted. But how he paid for it! He would pay interest as high as twelve and a half per cent. per day on each dollar borrowed, compounded daily! That was for small amounts. For large amounts he would pay the low (!) rate of five per cent. per month on the dollar, compounded monthly.

These rancheros were encouraged to run bills. Any of the alien population would credit them, especially the Jew peddler and shopkeeper. After the bill had run a certain time perhaps the creditor would take an order for cattle in payment, which he would probably hand over to an up-country cattle buyer. If that method was not agreeable a note would be taken at the usual rate of interest. The holder of the note would never present it for payment on the date due and the maker would perhaps forget about it until it had doubled or quintupled.

Then payment would be demanded.

Not being used to gringo methods the ranchero would not have money when called upon, and so he would go to El Boticario * (as we shall call him), who was the most

* Druggist, apothecary.

notorious of the Shylocks of the transition era. To El Boticario he would give his note, a note of hand, you understand, without any security other than that the maker of the note would have a league or two or three of land and a few thousand head of cattle worth twenty dollars a head. Ten per cent. a month compounded monthly would be the interest on this decoy. Assuming the note to be for one thousand dollars, it would never be presented for payment until the interest had run it up to five thousand. Then a new note would be written at five per cent. a month, compounded monthly, secured by a mortgage on "the old man's ranch."

The mortgage records of Los Angeles County are bloodstained and fearful. It makes one's hair stand on end to go through them. The Shylock practice was universal. All of the references herein, and hereafter made in this history so far as they relate to mortgage transactions, are sustained by the public records.

We deem it the duty of the historian to show to posterity life as it existed in the times of which he writes, and in doing this he must honor his enemies and spare not his friends. So it is here quite opportune and proper to moralize on the wholesale spoliation of the Californians, not through the active agency of the Government, but through its criminal toleration.

When in 1848 California was finally ceded by Mexico to the United States by the treaty of Guadalupe Hidalgo,[4] had our government then at one fell swoop confiscated every league of land owned by the transferred inhabitants and all their livestock it would have been an act of mercy as compared with what actually followed our acquisition of the province, to wit: turning loose on the unsuspecting popula-

Abel Stearns.
A Yankee who settled in California in 1830.

General Mariano Guadalupe Vallejo.
"The grand old man" of California. He was born in Monterey in 1808.

Californian mode of catching cattle.
From an old drawing.

tion a horde of sharpers and Shylocks from all lands under the dome of heaven.

The more enlightened Californians as a body welcomed the transfer to the American government as promising a new era of material prosperity and political security. But their education, civilization, manner of doing business, rendered them utterly unfit to cope with the powers arrayed against them—the sharpers licensed by the toleration of the Government. When it became evident that the natives were unable to protect themselves our Government ought to have protected them. Theirs was a civilization pertaining to the 16th century. They were three hundred years behind the forces of the 19th century.

Our Government did not protect them, but our laws did protect the Shylocks and sharpers, and thus wrought the ruin and desolation of a hitherto happy and prosperous people and brought a blight upon the country that has festered ever since. The Government's crime of omission in failing to protect these people was as great a crime as though it had actively engaged in the spoliation.

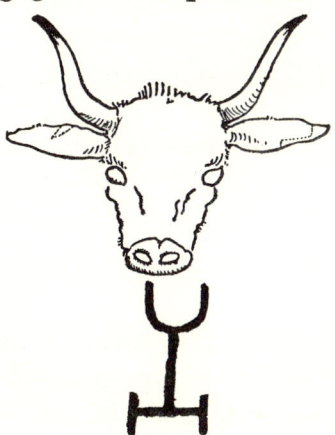

San Gabriél Arcángel

CHAPTER 2

Ruin of the Rancheros

EL BOTICARIO was mentioned in the preceding chapter and will be elaborated herein. A great man was El Boticario. He duly honored California with his coming in 1851, and shortly thereafter settled in Los Angeles.

He was an Irishman by birth, a Mexican by marriage and in religion a most ardent money-getter; indeed, a devoted worshiper of the Almighty Dollar. He was born and brought up in an ancient Irish castle built by that renowned old slugger, Brian Boru, about the time he slugged the Danes out of Ireland. In fact, El Boticario was a lineal descendant of Brian Boru himself.

Understand, I make this statement on the authority of El Boticario himself. On other authority than his this historian learns that the castle in Ireland was built of mud, had four walls and a thatched roof, two chimneys and two rooms, one door and two loopholes, that is to say, small windows without glass. El Boticario did not describe the ancestral castle this way, but a veritable Irish count did so describe it, a description which we accept as truthful, believing that Ireland is as full of this manner of castle as the other place is full of fiddlers.

El Boticario was not only a descendent of Munsterian royalty, or so claimed to be, but in Los Angeles he became a king—a money king, a financial dictator, Lord Paramount of this angelic land.

As related in "The Reminiscences of a Ranger" the truth-

Jose del Carmen Lugo gave his note to El Boticario, secured by a mortgage on valuable real estate, for the sum of $2720.00, dated, June 9th, 1854, interest five per cent a month, compounded monthly. Of course this was not a loan in full, or the odd numbered dollars would not have been in it, especially the twenty. It is fair to infer that it was interest compounded on prior small loans at the usual a per day interest, and so said the luckless Lugo.

By Reference to the records it shows that this $2720.00 grew to $13,127.54, and judgment was entered in the District Court for that amount, and the judgment to bear interest at the rate of five per cent a month to be compounded monthly; that is, the judgment followed the note, and of course there could be no redemption with interest piling up at such a rapid ratio. And the gentleman that permitted himself to enter this financial drag net died a pauper. El Boticario certainly died rich. So far as money went. But otherwise poor Ah! how very poor.

To close this pathetic chapter we will conclude by saying that the Californians struggled along under these mountains of usury, and many of them kept up so long as their cattle resources held out. But in 1863 '64 there came two years of successive drought and all of the cattle and all of the horses died and the ranchos began going to pay interest. And this ended their career of wealth.

Alas! Alas! How very sad! How very true!

No, El Boticario is not a fictious representation of the title of Shylocks, but taken for some time. Shylock or of California. His name is John G. Downey. Therefore will be found on an count of this many of the Shylocks State, he was King of the Shylocks. Sterling practice

Reproduction of a page from Major Bell's manuscript, with notes in his handwriting

ful historian who is penning these lines came to California in 1850 and after a try at mining around Hangtown hung up his hat on a Los Angeles peg in '52.

El Boticario had preceded our arrival here long enough to have sized up the country, to have taken the measure of the inhabitants, married and gone into business. He married into a native family that was poor in actual cash and unfortunately honest. With his wife he got five hundred dollars. That was his financial starter. From this small beginning he rounded up about two million dollars. He died highly honored; that is, the two millions were highly honored by his Munsterian descendants.

From the first El Boticario waxed richer and richer, while the Californians with whom he did business grew poorer and poorer. The first notable land owner to pay tribute to El Boticario was El Carpintero. Lemuel Carpenter, to be explicit.[1] A thoroughly Anglo-Saxon name, surely, but Lemuel was one of those Americans that had settled in the Land of Mañana in early days, when it was still Mexico, and his business sense had become numbed by that easy faith in his fellow man which characterized the Californians when they negotiated one with another over financial matters. Lemuel Carpenter had become El Carpintero and almost as native as his Spanish nickname implied. He owned forty thousand acres of the richest land in California, thousands of head of horned cattle and a corresponding number of horses. He had a good ranch house, a vineyard, corn fields, barley fields, springs, streams and lakes; also a family. He was of the most honorable standing, respected by all who knew him. His age was about fifty.

One unlucky day El Carpintero borrowed fifty dollars from El Boticario; this was about Christmas time, 1852, when he was having a good time among his friends in town and needed a little spending money instanter. For this sum he gave his note and forgot all about it for a year, when payment was demanded with interest. Lo, El Carpintero discovered he had signed a note bearing interest at the rate of 12½ per cent. a day, compounded daily! The note had grown from fifty dollars to five thousand dollars or thereabouts.

Then a new note was given Dec. 9, 1853, for five thousand dollars bearing interest at 5 per cent. a month, compounded monthly and payable in three months. This note was secured by the forty thousand acre ranch.

Oh, he was a broth of a boy, this sprig of Irish royalty, commonly known as El Boticario!

Did El Carpintero pay this five thousand dollars when due, with interest piled up? No, it ran on for a year and ten days. Then the interest was computed and another note given, this time for $9,154 at 5 per cent. a month, compounded monthly, secured by a second mortgage on the forty thousand acre ranch. This was in 1854. In 1856 the interest was again computed and another note was given for $4,000 with a reduced interest of 4 per cent. per month, compounded monthly. This note was given to secure an installment of interest due and unpaid, on the original note of fifty dollars with its accumulations.

El Carpintero having finally exhausted his mortgage security the $4,000 note was secured by the signature of good old Don Pío Pico, last governor of California under Mexico, who was a neighbor and compadre of El Carpintero. And let it here be explained in passing that one compadre never goes back on another. It is an endearing relationship between men that does not exist in gringo society.

It was in 1859 that El Boticario applied the thumbscrews of the law to El Carpintero and demanded his pound of flesh. He brought suit for the foreclosure of mortgage, and also sued on the Pico note.

El Carpintero squared up; he paid it all, principal, interest, compound interest and costs, except the $4,000 note with its four years' compound interest and its costs. That was paid by poor old Don Pío. It was the first step of this Californian grandee on the downward grade to poverty.

Of course El Carpintero paid the other notes not with cash but with his forty thousand acres, his cattle, horses, vineyards, cultivated fields; his springs, streams and lakes. More, he added his life's blood as further interest. He drove a bullet through his brain, and so passed the first of the great California private domains, and one of the richest, of that long list that was to go as tribute to the new business methods.

El Boticario was a pretty good sort of a man otherwise, possessed of many fine qualities, personally manly, a hater of other kinds of wrong, with a fair share of Irish nerve which would not let any man "tread on the tail of his shirt." His good qualities, however, too often fell down before the opportunities of raking in the dollars pertaining to his wife's country-people.

El Boticario and the Register of the U. S. Land Office in Los Angeles once had a tilt. This is the same Register mentioned in the author's former chronicle, who bit the nose off the U. S. District Attorney.

It was in '58 that the remarkable encounter occurred in which El Boticario figured. The Register was a fighter from way back. He was on the fight all the time. He was a pistol fighter, a knife fighter and away up in rough and tumble. The tale of the tilt above referred to is as follows:

Bruno Avila was the owner of El Rancho Centinela, now the manor of Dan Freeman; ten thousand acres worth a million dollars at present.[2] W. W. Jenkins, then a boy called "Bill" by everybody, now the "Baron of Alcatraz y Casteca," had a mustang racer. The Register discovered that Bruno Ávila longed to own that mustang so he went to Bill Jenkins, borrowed the plug and sold it to Bruno. That is, Bruno pledged the Rancho Centinela in payment until he had won enough cash racing his great steed to meet the price.

Bruno had now possessed himself of the horse but had no money to wager on the races. So he hied himself to El Boticario and on July 1, 1854, borrowed four hundred dollars at 6 per cent. per month, compounded monthly, secured by a mortgage on Rancho Centinela!

Now, at the time this mortgage was made the fee simple title was really vested in the Register, of course. Ascertaining this defect in his title after lending the four hundred El Boticario flew to the courts for redress. He brought suit to foreclose his mortgage and made the Register a party defendant with intent to subordinate title.

In court the case terminated in favor of the Register.

El Boticario appealed to the Supreme Court, which affirmed the original judgment; but not before the Register had been riddled with buckshot and sent to Kingdom Come by Uncle Billy Rubottom. But that is an entirely different story which will be taken up later.

Now as to the actual tilt: the Register and Bill Jenkins roomed on the west side of Spring Street opposite the present Bullard Block.* Their rooms were not far apart.

El Medico was a chum of El Boticario, as would seem natural enough in view of their more or less mutual professions.

* Site of the first Court House and of the present beautiful new City Hall.

The foreclosure fight was at white heat and the clans had on their war paint. As the early morning sun warmed the adobe walls of the Registerial residence El Medico passed by. The Register, coatless and in slippers, with suspenders dangling, stepped to the sidewalk and called: "Hello, Mac!"

Mac stopped and the Register said: "Mac, did you swear to that affidavit that was filed yesterday in the Ávila suit?"

Mac replied: "Why yes, what have you got to say about it?"

"This," replied the Register. "You swore to a damn lie."

Mac, the Medico, was six feet two inches in height and weighed two hundred pounds. The Register was six feet two inches and weighed two hundred pounds. Both were fighters from the Southern backwoods.

They clinched like two mighty grizzlies. Up and down, over and under, rough and tumble.

El Boticario came on the scene, revolver in hand; so did Bill Jenkins, who was still to be reckoned with in the transaction, and stood by to see fair play.

El Boticario tried to get in a shot but the Register kept El Medico so on the move that a shot was as likely to hit one as the other.

Then came the Town Marshal and the County Clerk. The Clerk was a lame man on horseback. The Marshal took the gun away from El Boticario just as the two giants let go of each other. The battle seemed a draw between these two; but the Register was still full of fight. He shook himself, hitched up his suspenders and charged on El Boticario. The latter was a little fellow, hardly a mouthful for the gigantic Register.

There was a little alley at the north end of the Court House, in front of which the fight took place, which led to the western hills. El Boticario concluded to go west via the alley. The Register followed in the wake of El Boticario.

Said Bill Jenkins to the Marshal: "For God's sake take Shore's (the County Clerk's) horse and catch the Register, or he'll eat El Boticario alive!"

The Marshal unhorsed the lame man, leaped onto the latter's steed and dashed away through the alley going west.

At the summit of the first hill El Boticario was far in the lead and the Marshal, overtaking the winded pursuer, prevailed on him to give up the chase, for the moment at least.

Having returned and breakfasted, the Register hied himself to the Ranger armory, borrowed a Mississippi rifle, went to his room, took a chair out onto the sidewalk, sat down comfortably tilted back against the adobe wall and waited for El Boticario, who was due to wend his way to the Court House to attend the trial of his suit.

El Boticario failed to wend. In the cool of the afternoon the Register paraded the town, rifle in hand, but failed to find his game.

The following day, which was steamer day to San Francisco, the hunter discovered that his would-be prey had registered at the stage office as a steamer passenger for the north. The Register decided to go north on the same steamer.[3]

At 4 P.M., the usual hour for the departure of the stage, the Register appeared, carpetbag in hand, and took his seat in the stage. The vehicle departed with the Register but without El Boticario.

The Register figured that his prey had dodged him by hiring a private conveyance in which to reach the harbor—which was in fact just what he had done.

But friends of the fleeing man despatched "Doctor" Jim Berry, a colored boy who was a light, fast rider, to San Pedro ahead of the stage to warn him that his nemesis was bound for the steamer.

The Register went north on the steamer and returned on the same vessel, just foaming with rage and disappointment. El Boticario had laid over at Banning's.[4] When the steamer sailed again he was aboard, safely bound north. He did not return to Los Angeles until a shooting scrape, that had nothing to do with this quarrel, caused the Register to be killed and decently buried.

All this time, however, the 5 per cent., the 6 per cent., the 10 per cent., all per month, went on working for him, so what difference did it make to El Boticario which end of the state he stood in?

In three years El Boticario became a capitalist of mighty caliber. Starting with five hundred dollars in 1852, in June, '55, he loaned José Sepúlveda,[5] Agustín Machado and Juan Avila, three of the richest hidalgos in California, $20,000 at $800 a month interest, compounded monthly in advance. Do not think he loaned this great sum in one lump. Most of it was interest on small sums previously loaned. This note ran four years and $81,000 interest was paid on it and all of the principal. Notwithstanding the payment in full, there was a mix-up in the accounting and suit was brought on the note, claiming an amount still due. Finally the matter was submitted to a referee, who reported $1,300 still due, which was paid with costs.

At this time there was one Miles, a Los Angeles store clerk, whose sole ambition was to make $5,000 out of California and then return to his old Kentucky home, "where," said he, "on five thousand I can live like a gentleman."

Having saved $500 he loaned it to this same Don José Sepúlveda at the rate of 10 per cent. per day, interest compounded every ten days: that is to say, the principal would double every ten days.

While fighting Sepúlveda and his partners on the $20,000 note, El Boticario heard of the $500 Miles note and bought it up for $5,000, paying in addition enough bounty money to land Miles on the wharf at Louisville, Ky.

Miles put his money in a sack and started home.

At San Pedro he boarded the tugboat *Ida Hancock* used in conveying passengers to the steamer in the offing. The tug burst her boiler, Miles was blown sky-high and his money was sifted into the mud of San Pedro Bay.

With his $500 assigned Miles note El Boticario went for his enemy hotter than ever. This note had grown to mammoth proportions. In ninety days note and interest together amounted to $256,000.

The "Baron of Casteca," Bill Jenkins, who was then a deputy sheriff, took a hand. To El Boticario he said: "If you persist in enforcing full payment you will be killed in less than a week." To Sepúlveda he said: "Compromise this note if you can. If you don't you will have to pay interest and all, though it takes every league of your property and your thousands of head of cattle, because it is the law of this land."

The note was compromised and Sepúlveda paid El Boticario on that $500 the enormous sum of $72,000.

To sum up, the loans of $20,000 and $5,000 realized the neat sums of $81,000 and $67,000 respectively, as clean-cut interest. In all, $148,000.

If the reader should wish to verify what is here written, and many other similar cases, he is referred to the records of Los Angeles County, California. Such cases are piled up in the archives of all our coast counties, but the very worst are recorded in this Angel City.

To close this pathetic chapter we will conclude by saying that the Californians struggled along under these mountains of usury as long as their cattle resources held out. But in 1863-4 there came two successive years of drought. The cattle and horses died and the ranchos—the land—began going to pay interest. That was the beginning of the end.

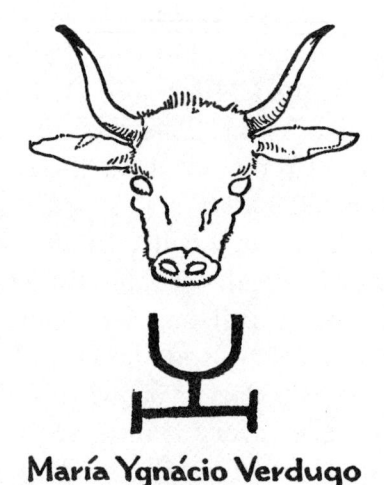

María Ygnácio Verdugo

CHAPTER 3

A Serious Matter is Mexican Gratitude

IN the autumn of '53 the author was stationed at San Gabriél Mission as a sort of military observer for the Rangers, keeping an eye open for any predatory remnants of Joaquín Murrieta's band. It was rather a pleasant berth; nothing to do but ride around in the daytime and keep run of the balls and fandangos at night.

One of these festive occasions happened to be a house-warming, or *bendición*—the christening of a domicile. While attending this party I was called out to meet an adventure which proved to be an amusing illustration of human nature as it crops out in the average Mexican. Bear in mind that when the word Mexican is used a Californian is not meant, but a cholo, the Californian's designation for all people from the interior of Mexico.

Over at the Mission a fandango was in full blast and at midnight, when everything was at fever heat, several Californians got into a row with a cholo, a stranger, and would have made tamales of him in short order had not this Ranger historian rescued the poor Mexican.

The next day El Cholo made his appearance to express his gratitude for my interference on his behalf. Hat in hand and features expressive of the deepest thankfulness, he addressed me as follows:

"Señor Americano, you are a good man, you are a first class caballero, a valiente. You are a very brave man. Last night you saved my life. But for you those malditos Californios, brutes that they are, would have assassinated me. I am a stranger, a Mexican. A Mexican is a man of immense gratitude. But for your Christianity and bravery I would now be a bloody corpse, dead and without absolution. Just like yourself, señor, I am a Christian. I, too, am a very brave man, a first class fighter, but what can one man do against a half dozen barbarians like these Californians? I am an honest man, señor, of a very honorable family. The distinguished trait of all Mexicans, especially of my family, is gratitude. I am a poor man, señor, but I wish to do something for you. If you have an enemy you wish to get rid of just point him out to me and I will kill him for you before the sun rises to-morrow."

I informed the grateful caballero that for the present I would permit all my enemies to live.

"Then, señor caballero," said he, "would you accept from me the gift of a very fine, well-broken saddle horse?"

I answered that I certainly would accept such a princely gift.

"Bien, señor, you know that el viejo Don Juan Rowland [1] has the finest horses in all California, delightful horses, señor?"

I responded in the affirmative.

"Then, señor, I will this very night go over to the Rancho Puente and steal the best head in Don Juan's bands. You will accept it from me as a token of my gratitude."

By this time I had become thoroughly convinced of the predominant trait of Mexican character—I mean gratitude, of course; and I decided to let it go at that. So I dismissed a very puzzled cholo with an admonition to leave Don Juan Rowland's horse pastures undisturbed, and that's the last I ever saw of him.

One day news was brought into San Gabriél that a large party of emigrants from Arkansas known as "Rubottom's Company" had just emerged from the desert and was in camp at Temescal. Believing that Rubottom must be the Uncle Bill of Trinity County memory, I rode out to visit the camp, sixty miles distant.

I first met Uncle Bill in the deepest and darkest fastnesses of the Trinity Mountains in March, 1851. He was the purest specimen of the rough diamond that it has ever been this author's pleasure to know. An Arkansas man born and bred, wholly illiterate, honest, generous and just, a lover of right and hater of wrong. He was about forty years of age at the time.

Among the pioneers of the Trinity were several other Arkansas men—the Logan boys—Boone, Jonathan and Dick—and others, all kinsfolk and all men of energy and frontier consequence. But the most eminent of all that Arkansas colony was a little negro boy, Harry, as black as a polished boot, born a slave and brought to California as a slave, until Uncle Bill took a hand and made Harry free.

This is told here because blood hangs on the manumission of Harry, an aftermath that had issue in mid-continent, on the plains of the Indian Territory.

On the Trinity during the summer of '51 little Harry changed owners about every Saturday night, that is to say, he would be played off at freeze-out poker. On each Saturday night he would be put up for six ounces, an ounce an entry, and the fortunate winner would have Harry's services at picking, shoveling or running a rocker for the week.

At the last freeze-out game played for the ownership of the human chattel, old McGullion won the pot. It being late at night, "Mac" immediately started for his cabin, saying, "Come along home, Harry."

"No, you don't!" said Uncle Bill, who had just dropped in on the game. "This infernal game has played out!"

"What do you mean?" demanded Mac.

"Just this," replied Uncle Bill. "We are in a free country and by law Harry is just as free as any of us. I've stood this nonsense so long I'm ashamed of it."

Had the Prince of Darkness entered the room and declared himself for everlasting light there could have been no greater manifestation of dumb surprise. The idea of a free nigger never entered those other Arkansas minds, they never heard of such a thing, it was preposterous.

Uncle Bill's word, however, had always been law in that camp and McGullion and the rest watched in sullen silence as Uncle Bill said to the little negro boy: "Harry, will you come home with me? I'll give you four dollars a day for the work you do for me and no one shall molest you."

Harry timorously assented. Liberator and liberated walked out into the night, leaving the Arkansas crowd dumbfounded.

Until the fall of '52 Harry remained with Uncle Bill helping him work his claim. Then the dictator of the Arkansas colony on the Trinity left the little negro in the care of the judge and the sheriff of Trinity County and made a trip to his home state.

One more instance of Uncle Bill's manhood and sense of justice while in the mining country before we ride into the camp of Rubottom's Company at Temescal:

A party of eight or ten miners, of which Uncle Bill was one, were working some bank diggings in the great cañon of the Trinity. Employed by Uncle Billy was a certain fellow named Mexican Joe.

One Sunday Mexican Joe was left in charge of the camp while the rest went to the trading post at North Fork.

PUBLIC NOTICE

All citizens of Hornitas are respectfully invited to attend the HANGING of CHEROKEE BILL, HORSE THIEF. Meeting at Rattlesnake Ikes Saloon. MINERS COURT. May 12th., 1851 7 O'CLOCK - NIGHT.

Thomas Early - Sheriff

Hornitas Times - Printer

Courtesy W. Parker Lyon, Pasadena
When the verdict preceded the trial. A "broadside" of the California gold days

Uncle Bill's companions returned to camp early, but the big fellow himself did not come back until about sundown. Then, to his amazement, he saw his man, Joe, dangling by the neck from the limb of a great oak tree. The rest of the miners had just strung him up—he was still "kickin'."

The Arkansan leaped forward and cut Joe down and began to get the breath of life back into him, ignoring the protests of his companions. Then he turned on them and demanded to know what it was all about. He learned that during the absence of the company the camp purse, containing six or eight ounces of gold dust, had been stolen. Joe had protested that he knew nothing of its whereabouts; said he had never left camp but had slept for about an hour.

Only Joe could be guilty, decided the miners, and as hanging was the common law of the mines for stealing, the poor Mexican was forthwith hanged.

Well, how Uncle Bill did vituperate that crowd! He was the most eminent swearer that ever came to California, and that is claiming a lot. He was sublime in the art. It is solemnly attested that on this occasion he cursed so scathingly that the bark peeled off the big oak tree. He swore so thunderously that the mountains shivered and great fragments came crashing down into the river. The wrath of Roland over the treason of Gan at the battle of Roncesvalles was infantile in comparison to Uncle Bill's. One of the listeners' hair turned gray and three others were stricken baldheaded.

The next day Mexican Joe was under the armed protection of Uncle Bill and seemed all right except for a stiff neck. The miners were still dissatisfied and came to Uncle Bill with a demand that Joe should be expelled from camp.

Uncle Bill forcefully reiterated his faith in Joe's innocence.

While the situation hung in the balance a coyote was seen trotting along the mountainside carrying something in its mouth. One of the men shot at the animal. It dropped the object it was carrying and ran away. The man went over to see what the coyote had dropped. Lo, it was the stolen purse!

Then Uncle Bill cut loose on that crowd again and what a lecture he gave them on lynch law! He said that he had never known in his life any lynch court—and Arkansas had been full of them as well as California—that ever came any nearer to justice than had happened in the present instance; that lynch law never was any good and never would be, and he painted a merciless picture to his audience of how near they had been to murdering the best boy on the river.

When I finally rode into the camp of Rubottom's Company at Temescal, sixty miles, as I have said, from San Gabriél, I found that sure enough it was Uncle Bill's outfit, but he was not there. From his large family I met a cold reception, which I could not understand. I sought out Lige Bettis, a son-in-law of the leader, a shrewd and intelligent man, and at last learned that Uncle Bill was hiding out in the hills, apprehensive of being arrested. When their scouts had seen me approaching in semi-military garb and equipment they had decided that I bore a U. S. warrant for his apprehension.

When Lige was satisfied of my identity and my friendly intentions he sent a man to the top of a hill. This man gave three long-drawn coyote howls, and in a few minutes Uncle Bill appeared, armed with rifle, revolvers and knife. On recognizing me he was utterly delighted.

"But what's the matter, Uncle Bill?" I asked. "Why do you apprehend arrest?"

Uncle Bill was laboring under emotional excitement and

it took a moment for him to control himself. Then he answered: "Wait until after supper and I'll tell you."

The whole camp now surrounded me with every demonstration of welcome. The train consisted of ten or twelve families from Arkansas. They were almost completely exhausted after their struggle across the desert. The camp was at the upper end of the Temescal Valley under the umbrageous canopy of some great live oaks, on the margin of a beautiful green meadow from which burst springs of cool, purling water, forming labyrinths of meandering rivulets which, finally uniting, made Temescal Creek. No lovelier camping ground could be found on the face of this beautiful green earth. What a haven for these emigrants, at the end of the "Journey of Death," as the old Spaniards called the worst section of the struggle across the burning sands from Yuma.

The author crossed the Colorado Desert three times before the railroad was built, and ever since he has felt an utter contempt for a prospective Hell!

It was the month of October that the Rubottom train was encamped here in this elysium and their empty flesh pots were supplied with fresh fat beef gratuitously from the herds of the great Serrano family, then the baronial proprietors of an eight league ranch in that region, also luscious grapes from the family vineyard and green vegetables from the garden. And the starving horses and mules were up to their eyes in green grass.

The company had sent messengers twenty miles to the Mormon colony of San Bernardino to procure flour, sugar and coffee and other things they needed for they were not beggars by any means and only accepted gifts of food when pressed upon them by the rules of Californian hospitality.

After supper Uncle Bill said: "Well, my boy, let's go

over to that big oak and take a smoke while I tell you about some of the things that have happened since I left the Trinity."

Settled on the live oak, the big Arkansas man said: "You remember Black Harry, don't you, the boy they used to play off at freeze-out? Well, you know old McGullion got very mad at me the time I enforced the laws of a free state and set the little slave at liberty. He went home to Arkansas and told everybody I had turned Abolitionist and taken his nigger away from him. After I got home he shut up about it and I never suspected any treachery, but he was planning.

"About the middle of May I made up this party of my kinspeople and friends and we pulled out from Arkansas headed for Los Angeles. One morning just beyond the settlements of the Indian Territory I lingered behind with my wife and one of the girls when the rest moved ahead toward the next night's camp. I had just finished hitching up our spring wagon to follow when McGullion and two of his friends overtook us. They had papers for my arrest. 'For what?' I inquired. 'McGullion has sued you for two thousand dollars,' replied one of the deputies, 'the value of the slave Harry you stole from him in California, and your arrest is warranted because you are running away from the state of Arkansas with intent to defraud your creditors.'

"My weapons were in the wagon, except a knife at my belt, and the three men stood between me and the wagon. 'We are officers—resist at your peril,' said the spokesman, and commanded the others to seize me. A struggle ensued.

"When I came to after the struggle I found I was lying in our spring wagon, my daughter was holding my head and my wife was lashing the horses forward at a rapid pace. My clothes were covered with blood, but I didn't feel as if

I had been cut or shot. Pretty soon we met Lige coming back to see what had detained us. My wife told Lige she thought I had killed all three men, so he got up a party and went back to see. The legal papers they were armed with I have here in my ambulance. I'll show them to you later on."

"Yes, but what about McGullion and the officers?"

"Oh, we buried them all right. May God be merciful to their poor souls. But put handcuffs on me? No, *sir!*" Uncle Bill paused to pull himself together, then added: "You just go to town, will you, and make sure they aren't trying to head me off there with a United States warrant, and I'll stay here on the lookout. I don't fear standing trial but to be taken back to Arkansas now would just break us all financially."

"Nothing else happened on your way out?" I inquired.

"Oh, nothing serious, except that we all would have been wiped out by a gang of Joaquín Murrieta's cut-throats except for Mexican Joe."

"Great goodness, you mean Mexican Joe of the Trinity?"

"That's him—as white a man as ever lived, is Joe. You know Joe was born and raised in Tucson, and somehow he had found his way back there. Well, one day about ten miles from La Ciénega,* which is a famous camping place thirty miles east of Tucson, we spied on the road ahead a solitary horseman. This seemed strange for La Ciénega was a famous lurking place for Apaches and people only traveled through there in large parties.

"As the horseman drew nearer, Great Grizzly! I saw he was my old Trinity boy Joe! The fellow was wild with joy—laughed and cried, could hardly speak.

* Properly spelled *ciénaga,* a marsh or swampy place. But in California and the southwest it is universally spelled *ciénega.*

" 'Where are you going, Joe?'

" 'I come here warn you. I come tell you robbers, bandits catch you at Ciénega and kill you all. They will take horse, mule, wagon, all to Sonora and sell 'em.' " He went on to explain that about two weeks back there came from California a gang of robbers of the Joaquín Murrieta confederacy. There were about twenty of them and their object was to lie in wait for American emigrant trains, murder the people and run the spoil off to Sonora.

"Three days before our appearance some Yaqui Indians who had passed us on the road way back by the Río Grande had reported our train when they got to Tucson, and by the number of watering places on the Journey of Death it was easy to figure out just when we ought to arrive at La Ciénega.

"Joe had got news through underground Mexican sources that it was the intention of Vulvia and Senati, leaders of the robbers, to lie in wait for our train at La Ciénega. He found that they would hide out where the road leaves Ciénega Creek about five miles below the great camping ground. 'To-morrow morning,' said Joe, 'Senati, Vulvia and three or four others will come to your camp and tell you they are officers from Tucson who have come out to greet you and escort you safely into town, where the people are planning a great reception for you. Then they will lead you into the ambuscade on the road leading up from the creek to the mesa.'

"While the sun was yet high we settled down at the famous camping place as if we knew nothing of the intentions of the reception committee.

"During breakfast the next morning sure enough a party of horsemen appeared coming from the direction of Tucson. We received them with marked politeness and asked them where from and where to. They were five, a rough bandit-looking crowd except the spokesman. He was rather white, handsome and dignified, neatly dressed and spoke English fluently. He replied to us as follows:

" 'Gentlemen, I am the alcalde of Tucson and these men are my servants. Being informed of your coming I am here to welcome you to the hospitalities of Tucson. When it suits your convenience to break camp I will solicit the honor of conducting you thither.'

"Breakfast was immediately offered the distinguished visitor and his servants, who seated themselves at a respectful distance from their master and manifested toward him the utmost deference. Joe was concealed in a wagon where he could view the outfit and I made my way over to him and spoke unnoticed. He said the pretended alcalde was the notorious Luís Vulvia, second in command of Joaquín Murrieta's California bandits, and that he had been sent by Joaquín from California on this particular mission. Another black, sinister-looking fellow with an Indian cast of countenance was Senati, said Joe; a most notorious assassin in Mexico and bandit in California. The three others were villains of distinguished eminence in the business of blood and rapine.

"The bandits were quietly eating, chatting and smoking when I gave the agreed signal, whereupon the men of my party covered them with rifles and ordered them to lie *boca a la tierra*—that is, flat upon their faces. In a minute we had them all disarmed, their hands tied behind their backs and horse-hobbles on their ankles.

"Vulvia was then questioned, under penalty of instant death if we found that he was not telling the truth. He made a full confession and proposed that if we would spare the lives of himself and companions and liberate one man to send to the band in ambush he would have every weapon piled in the road and guarantee that every bandit should retire across the line to Sonora. As for himself and those who remained in our hands with him, they would submit to being turned over to the authorities in Tucson.

"The plan was carried out; we pushed on westward from Tucson across Hell's Home Stretch, and here we are, along with Mexican Joe who has joined up with me again. He's out looking after the horses—you'll see him soon."

The next day I set out from Rubottom's Company to ride to Los Angeles, to do some scouting for Uncle Bill. There I found that no warrant had been forwarded for his arrest, that he was apparently free to come and go as he pleased in California. Riding back again to the camp at Temescal I conveyed this news, and the train drove on into El Monte.[2]

Uncle Bill bought land at El Monte and settled down to a period of rural contentment.

Vulvia and Senati escaped jail at Tucson, got some of their band together, came to Los Angeles, joined Atanácio Moreno and raided the Angel City. The end met by these bandits is told in a chapter of my "Reminiscences of a Ranger," with the details of how in the winter of '54 they were laid out in the jail yard at Los Angeles stark and strangled; how they had been betrayed by Moreno, and what, in turn, happened to Moreno.

CHAPTER 4

Bandits, Duelists and Filibusters

It has been published and republished that the noted bandit, Joaquín Murrieta, was killed on the border of Tulare Valley in 1853. Capt. Harry Love of the Rangers, with a half dozen of his men, surprised the bandit, killed him and one of his lieutenants notoriously known as "Three-Fingered-Jack." Joaquín's head and Three-Fingered-Jack's hand were preserved in alcohol and for a number of years were on exhibition at Natchez's Arms Store and Pistol Gallery on Clay Street, opposite the old Plaza in San Francisco.*

Natchez was a character. He came from Natchez, Mississippi, and that is how he got his sobriquet. Natchez furnished and loaded all of the pistols used in early-time duels and in this respect his fame became as wide as the state itself. A great pistol expert was Natchez. He was accused of contributing to the killing of Senator Broderick by Judge David S. Terry in 1859.[1] That is, he was accused of setting the triggers of the pistols used so delicately that the sudden raising of one would cause it to go off; that Terry was made aware of this fact, but Broderick was not. Broderick was said to have brought his pistol up with a jerk and it was discharged, the bullet entering the ground, whereupon Terry took deliberate aim and Broderick fell dead. This is the old story, but from my knowledge of Natchez and of all the persons concerned in that duel I am willing to say that it is all an arrant fiction.

* Head and hand said to have been destroyed in the great San Francisco fire of 1906.

Joaquín Murrieta.
From a painting by a padre of Carmel Mission in 1853, a few months before the famous bandit's death at the hands of the Rangers.

Joaquín Murrieta as pictured by an early-day artist.

BANDITS, DUELISTS, ETC.   33

In the first place Natchez was an honorable man and could not have been used for such a purpose. In the second place Judge David S. Terry was the very soul of honorable chivalry and was as incapable of taking any advantage in an encounter of that sort, as he would have been incapable of doing any other cowardly act.

Speaking of these incidents reminds me that I possess several tokens of those times. I have an oil painting of Joaquín Murrieta made by a priest of the old Mission Carmel,[2] near Monterey, only a month or two before the bandit's death. It is a fine painting, and is as natural as life. Or as natural as death, because Joaquín's head was so perfectly preserved that years after his death it looked life-like.

Along in 1853, after Joaquín's bands had been broken up in Los Angeles County, he went to Monterey County and raided up to the very portals of San José. It was claimed that he several times made forays into San Francisco itself, though his personal identity was always hard to establish on any given occasion through the widely scattered character of his organization and the fact that there were several other Joaquíns among his lieutenants.

During that summer of '53 news came to the sheriff at San José that Murrieta was camped in a cañon down towards the Mission. A posse was at once organized of which Col. S. O. Houghton, formerly a member of Stevenson's Pioneer Regiment[3] and, as I write, a leading member of the Los Angeles bar, was one. They surprised the bandits, captured Murrieta's horse and equipment, including even his hat; but he himself escaped up the mountainside. It was his last escape. In his next encounter with the law he was killed.

This time he took refuge at the Mission Carmel and was cared for by the priest there for a time—just how long is not known; but during this time the young padre painted a portrait of the famous bandido just as he appeared when he sought sanctuary in the ancient edifice of the Franciscans. A red sash is wound turban-like around his head and a *manga* of the same color does duty as a cloak. The *manga,* in South America called a *poncho,* is a mantle with edges embroidered and a hole in the center through which the head is thrust. It makes a comfortable and serviceable horseman's cloak.

A year or two after the death of Joaquín this priest sent the picture to a very Christian old Catholic lady, wife of a wealthy American at Los Angeles, accompanied by a letter explaining the circumstances under which the portrait was painted and giving information he had to the effect that a sister of Joaquín's resided in Los Angeles. He requested that the letter and picture be delivered to her. However, the sister had disappeared from the pueblo, no one knew whither, so the portrait and the epistle remained in the possession of the American woman.

Thirty years rolled around and this good old lady died. It became my duty, in a professional capacity, to take out letters of administration on her estate, on behalf of a kinswoman. In rummaging over some of the old boxes and trunks left by the deceased we found, among all sorts of rubbish, the portrait of Joaquín and the letter from the reverend artist who painted it. The edges of the oil painting had been eaten off by mice and it was in bad condition. I took it to an artist in Los Angeles to have it restored and framed. This man had seen the preserved head of Joaquín Murrieta in a museum in New York and immediately recognized the subject of the portrait I set before him. After Natchez's death the head of the bandit in some way or other got into a museum in New York, but was afterward returned to San Francisco.

There was a Billy Henderson who was a member of the party that killed Murrieta. Billy was the man who cut his head off. He was for several years my neighbor and a more genial and generous fellow I never met—a man of strict integrity, moral, sober, gentlemanly and urbane.

But Billy Henderson was haunted by Joaquín Murrieta. No question about that. He used to tell me that there was not a day, or more usually a night, that Joaquín did not come to him personally, headless, and speak—for his voice was recognizable even though his head was missing. He was always demanding his head. Billy said that the first time the apparition made this demand he, Billy, was riding from Los Angeles down to his ranch. It was just daylight when a horseman appeared at his side.

"Who are you and what do you want?" demanded Billy, hardly yet aware of the gruesome nature of the rider in the faint light.

"I am Joaquín Murrieta," replied the strange horseman, in a voice so uncanny and yet so natural that its effect was absolutely startling. "You cut my head off, and I want you to restore it to me. No rest can ever come to me until I get my head back."

Billy stared at the rider close beside him and saw that he was, indeed, headless and that he was dressed and mounted in every detail exactly as at the time of his death. Overcoming his feeling of horror, Henderson, who was a brave and rational person, replied honestly, as man to man: "Joaquín, it is true that it was I who cut off your head, but I am powerless to restore it. All I can say is that I have always been sorry that I did cut it off."

Joaquín replied: "I hold you responsible for my head and

you shall never rest until you restore it to me." Then he disappeared.

"Then for years," continued Billy, "I would wake up in the middle of the night hearing my name called, and when I responded I would hear that voice say: 'I am Joaquín and I want my head.' At such times I can not see him; it is only when he rides up beside me on lonely roads—and this has happened many times—that he is visible."

"Why, Billy!" I exclaimed, "I should think it would set you crazy to be thus haunted."

"No," he replied, "I'm not afraid of Joaquín's ghost any more than I was afraid of Joaquín in the flesh. It's not the actual apparitions that disturb me, not at all. The only thing about it is I am really sorry that I can't get that head for him. Natchez got possession of it and wouldn't give it up and since then I can't get any track of it. I never would have cut Joaquín's head off except under the excitement of the chase and the orders of Harry Love."

While Natchez is still being mentioned, it might be a matter of interest, in view of the part he was accused of having played in the Broderick-Terry duel, to mention the manner of his death. He was killed with the pistol that killed Broderick. One day he was examining that pistol with its delicate hair-trigger. It went off and Natchez fell dead.

There used to be a man named Price in San Francisco, a great pioneer knife-maker. He worked at his trade in a corner of Natchez's store. He never made a knife for less than fifty dollars. A bowie knife, you know. Some he sold for as high as two hundred and fifty dollars. None of the California chivalry of that day was of the élite unless possessed of one of Price's knives. All of these knives were bound in silver, encased in silver scabbards and the handles

Meiggs' Wharf, a favorite resort in the early days of San Francisco. Alcatraz Island on extreme right

A proclamation of June 9th, 1856.

BANDITS, DUELISTS, ETC.

were inlaid with various designs in silver, gold and mother of pearl. Some hilts were ornamented with diamonds. And the tempering of the steel was just as great an art with Price as the ornamentation. The stamp of his knives, one of which I own, was always simply "M. Price, San Francisco," without date.

I have had my knife for fifty-two years, and it came to me in this wise:

During the reign of the second great San Francisco Vigilance Committee in 1856 I was superintendent of the recruiting service in that city for the Walker-Rivas army in Nicaragua.[4] On the 5th of August I went aboard the steamer *Cortéz* with nearly a hundred men, arms, ammunition, drum corps and all that pertains to a well organized military command. Strange as it may seem old Jimmie Dowes, a leading member of the Vigilance Committee and one of San Francisco's wealthy men, proposed to turn over to me all of the arms and equipment of the City Guards, an organization that had disbanded and joined the Vigilance forces. Why they sold their equipment to Dowes I never knew, but Dowes disposed of it all to me. With the assistance of a deputy United States Marshal, Lewis D. Watkins, afterward a general in the U. S. Army during the great rebellion, we conveyed the arms and equipment down to the wharf and, with United States Marshal James Duffy looking on, stored them aboard the *Cortéz*. The reader may infer from this that the administration in Washington gave at least a tacit recognition to the privately organized seizure of territory in Central America.

Well, as to my famous Price knife: at the time of which I speak David S. Terry was locked up in Fort Gunnybags, the prison and stronghold of the Vigilance Committee. During the evening preceding the sailing date of the *Cortéz*

I was resting in my room at the old St. Nicholas Hotel, when there came a knock on the door, and then several gentlemen entered, headed by Maj. Richard Roman, who had been Treasurer of California at one time and was Appraiser General of Customs under the Buchanan administration. The others were Bob Hayes, brother of Col. Jack Hayes of Texas Ranger fame; Bill Ross, afterward killed by Charles P. Duane; Richard P. Ashe, U. S. Naval agent at San Francisco, and one or two others.

These men were all good friends of mine, although I was just twenty-five years old at the time and they were all at least middle-aged. Nevertheless I was much surprised at their generosity when they began making presents to me, including a pair of Natchez's best revolvers, one of Price's best knives and a sword. Soon I was made to realize that there was something in the wind as my visitors seated themselves very seriously and Major Roman said:

"We have positive information that Judge Terry [5] is to be shipped off to Nicaragua to-morrow on board the *Cortéz*. He is being forcibly deported by the party in power. You are going on that steamer with your arms and recruits for William Walker. Now this is what we want you to promise us, and it will make you the most important young man in California if you do: we want you to compel the captain of the *Cortéz* to put in at San Pedro and land Judge Terry. You will land your men and escort Judge Terry safely to Los Angeles, where he will raise the nucleus of an army to come to San Francisco and drive all these pork merchants into the bay."

What wild schemes, what adventurous plans were concocted overnight in those early years of the Golden State! I was as ripe for adventure as any one else, and I promised those plotters that I would force the *Cortéz* into San Pedro,

BANDITS, DUELISTS, ETC.

march on Los Angeles with Judge Terry and see him started on the recruiting campaign that was to raise an army to march against the Vigilance Committee in San Francisco! But fortunately, probably, for all concerned,

ESCORTING JUDGE TERRY, OF THE SUPREME COURT, AND OTHER PRISONERS, TO THE VIGILANCE ROOMS.

SATURDAY, June 21st, about 3 o'clock, three or four members of the Vigilance Committee called at a room in Palmer, Cook & Co's building, corner of Washington and Kearny Sts., in which were Reuben Maloney, Judge Terry, Dr. Ashe, and several others, and requested Maloney to accompany them to the Committee Rooms. He refused, and was sustained by those with him, who drew their pistols in his defence. The deputation withdrew for reinforcements, when Maloney and his companions, arming themselves with rifles, started for the Armory of the Blues, on Jackson St., but before reaching it were met by Hopkins and one or two others. The attempt was made to disarm Judge Terry and arrest Maloney, when the Judge drew a knife and inflicted a severe, if not fatal wound on the left side of the head and neck of Hopkins, and then, in company with Ashe and Maloney, made his escape into the armory. The news spread rapidly, and in a few minutes a guard of the Vigilance Committee had surrounded the Armory and Palmer, Cook & Co's building, and shortly after had possession of two other law and order armories, in all of which were a number of the Governor's men. At half past 5 o'clock the Armory of the Blues surrendered, and Judge Terry, Dr. Ashe and Reuben Maloney were escorted to the Rooms of the Committee, where they remain. At 6 o'clock the Armory on the corner of Clay and Kearny Sts. capitulated, and the arms were given up to the Committee. All the law and order depots of arms and munitions have been taken possession of, and several pieces of cannon and above 1500 muskets and rifles transferred from them to the Committee Rooms.

Courtesy California State Library

From the contemporary press of San Francisco

though I regret to disappoint my readers by ending the story so abruptly, Judge Terry was not shipped out of the country on the *Cortéz* as had been anticipated, but in the course of a month or so was released and the Vigilance Committee disbanded. I sailed on with my little army to adventures in Nicaragua, possessed of one of Price's priceless knives.

While on the subject of the San Francisco of those days I am tempted to mention the official activities of one of the most important politicians of the city—Jim Cunningham, coroner. Jim was a great coroner, no mistake about it, very active officially. So active that it caused his arrest and deportation when the Vigilance Committee was deporting right and left. This is how it happened:

The river steamboats used to land at Long Wharf at ten or eleven o'clock at night on their trips down from Marysville, Sacramento and Stockton. Long Wharf was full of holes and unlighted. Occasionally some carpetbagger would drop through and his body would be fished out in the morning and sent to Mr. Cunningham's headquarters for an inquest. This was a very lucrative business for the coroner, especially when the subject arrived at the coroner's office before his pockets were picked.

But after a time the municipal authorities stopped up the holes on the wharf and supplied oil lamps along its length. Then Jim didn't average more than one inquest a day. But Jim arranged it so that when he did possess himself of a healthy corpse he would hold his inquest and charge up his fees; then during the night Mr. Corpse would be taken down to Long Wharf, dumped over and fished up next morning. The coroner would thus make it possible to hold six or seven inquests on the same subject. If Jim's enterprise was known to other officials they said little about it, for in municipal corporations when one official is made aware of the delinquency of another official he doesn't care to interfere, for reasons of his own, with the rounding up of perquisites and emoluments and fees.

But finally the Vigilance Committee yanked Jim the Coroner up and came very near hanging him, though his case ended in deportation.

A Hanging.

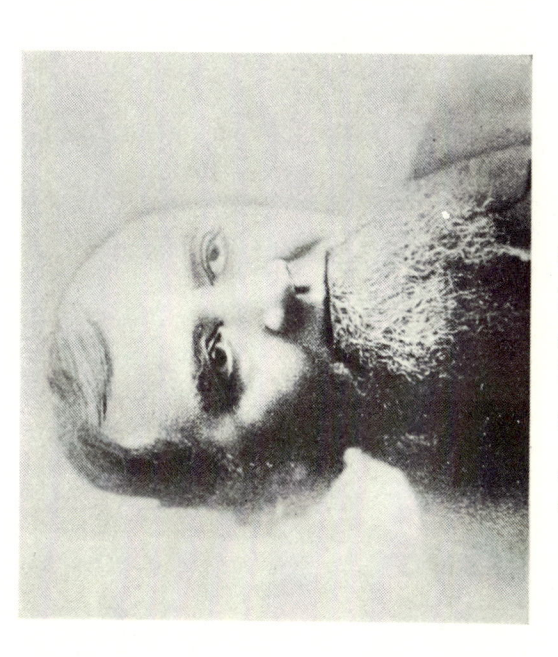

Judge David Smith Terry.
Justice of the Supreme Court of California, victor in the celebrated duel with United States Senator Broderick in 1859.

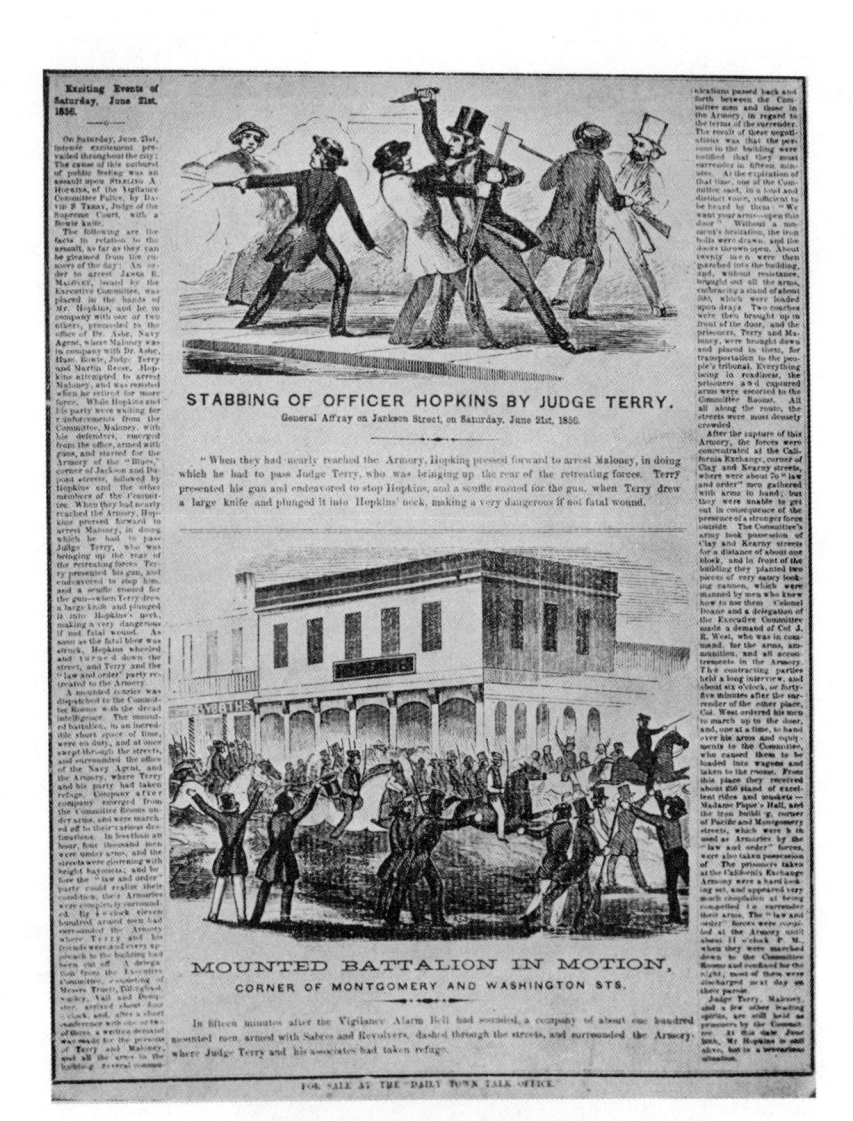

From the contemporary press of San Francisco.

CHAPTER 5

Holy Mass and Three Card Monte

EARLY in 1856 I joined General William Walker in Nicaragua and did not return to California until late in '57. In January, 1859, I went to Mexico and took service under the immortal Benito Juárez in his conflict with the reactionary party under Miramon. In the latter part of this year I found myself in Tehuantepec; and at this point I would like to commemorate a weird adventure that befell me in that strange land.

I drifted down to the City of Tehuantepec after the Miramon affair was over and became a writer for the local press. I was one of the *sábios*,* and was rated by the populace as second only to my good friend Fraile Romero in education and wisdom. This friar was a rollicking young soldier of the cross who dealt out religion in the church of Tehuantepec when not engaged in dealing monte to the light-hearted female portion of his not overly pious congregation. In parenthesis I will add that it is not, neither should it be, a libel on the Mexican padre to accuse him of dealing monte or betting on that most interesting game of which all old Californians are so fond. Fraile Romero would play monte, quaff his wine, comb the girls' hair with his delicate fingers, pat them on the cheeks with his soft palm, push them under the arms with his thumb and all that sort of Christian-like fun and made himself most popular and influential with his charges—a more popular person, I am

* Wise ones, learned ones.

forced to acknowledge, than even I imagined myself to be with the belles of Tehuantepec. Fraile Romero was a Christian, every inch of him, so the ladies proclaimed, and so I believe and will ever asseverate. I loved him dearly and after the lapse of forty years consider it no detriment to my present dignity to confess that I also loved more than one of the select women friends of the roistering Reverend Romero. "No one of flesh and blood can help it," was the way the pious padre would absolve us both, and to this doctrine I was ever ready to pledge my soul with a devotional *amen.*

El Fraile and I frequently became involved in theological discussions—the abstract variety, I mean, not the more easily settled moral questions on which we seemed pretty nearly agreed. Being the reverse of reverend in my arguments the good father gave me the nickname *El Bárbaro,* and the ladies, to pique the padre's vanity, added to my appellation the word *Hermoso.* Thus I became known as *El Bárbaro Hermoso,* or The Handsome Heathen.

For half a year I shared quarters with this jovial priest who presided over such a happy, carefree circle. Then one day he came to me looking very downcast.

"What's the matter, amigo?" I asked. "One of the favorite girls going to get married?"

"*Valgame Dios!* I wish it were nothing worse," he groaned.

"Have you been promoted away from here?"

"Promoted! That's just what it is, but, *Santa María,* what a promotion! I am ordered by the bishop to shoulder my cross and go forth to convert the *bárbaros* of the Coatzacoalcos, and worse still, of Chinameca."* The padre then began to tell me the story of Chinameca, an ancient

* In the southeastern part of the state of Vera Cruz.

Mayan town near the Coatzacoalcos River about thirty miles from the Bay of Campeche. It is noted for having been the birthplace of Malinche, the celebrated Doña Marina of the Spanish conquest of Mexico, mistress and interpreter to Cortéz. The Indians there still hold to a tradition that when Cortéz was at their capital preparing to set forth on his march to Honduras the priests of Chinameca reproached Malinche for having been the cause of all the blood and misery visited upon her people by the Spaniards, because of her devotion to the Spanish cause. To appease her accusers she entered the heathen temple, which stands to-day as it stood then, and made a solemn vow that some day she would return to Chinameca and bring four-fold blessings to her people.

Three hundred and eighty-two years have been registered on the cycle of time since then and, day and night, year in and year out, an Indian has stood on the summit of that ancient tower, ready to apprise the people of the return of Malinche in order that she may be received in a manner befitting the importance of the occasion.

Thus have these peculiar people remained true to their religion, their traditionary faith in the coming of their promised Redeemer, through these ages of woe which have crushed out the religion, liberty and manhood of millions of less fortunate tribes of Mexico. The Indians of Chinameca are about the same now in dress and customs as they were when in 1519 Cortéz fought his first battle in front of their capital and secured the person of the beautiful Malinche (Marina) who, it is claimed, did more toward the conquest of Mexico than any other one person except Cortéz himself.

The people of Chinameca had always resisted the efforts of the Catholic priests to convert them and had persisted in their dogged adherence to the faith of their fathers. Missionaries sent there had always been glad to escape to more sympathetic fields.

Such was the place to which duty had called my society-loving friend Fraile Romero. Great was the lamentation of the ladies of his flock when the news was made known. But the men of the congregation somehow seemed pleased.

"I will confess the whole town at a stiff price before leaving and make hard times for these fellows who remain in possession here," he declared acridly. "You, amigo, will go with me and at least see me settled down in heathendom. We will have a goodly supply of coin after the town is confessed and can supply ourselves with every available comfort."

The fraile filled his goblet and pushed the bottle toward me. I followed suit and pledged him my company on the dreaded journey that was to wrest him from the voluptuous beauties of Tehuantepec.

In ten days we set forth, and will the reader believe me, it took fifteen mules to carry the missionary outfit of the churchman. Our journey was to be through the mountains to Suchiltepec, where we would strike the head of navigation on the Coatzacoalcos River.

"And then," growled Fraile Romero, "I am doomed to stop a week at San Juan Guichicova and minister to those infernal mule-worshipers. Then another week with the Africans. May the wrath of heaven fall upon them!"

At the place first named there is a tribe of Indians possessed of a great number of mules, fat and fine, which they pamper and regard with as much religious veneration as the Hindoos regard their sacred bulls.

The second stopping place referred to by the reluctant missionary was inhabited by a vigorous colony of Africans descended from a cargo of slaves that mutinied, murdered the crew of the slaver, ascended the Coatzacoalcos River, planted themselves in the mountains of Tehuantepec and are flourishing to-day with the language and customs of their African ancestors little altered.

Such were the two places where Fraile Romero and myself were doomed to do penance for two weeks on our way to Suchil. We did not do much business at San Juan Guichicova in the way of confessing the populace, and absolutely none at all among the Africans; but we took in quite a quantity of small coin at monte. The padre in the meantime instructed me in the mysteries of the mass and the confessional. I learned to chant *Dominus Vobiscum et cum spiritu tuo* with great unction. But the heathenish Guichicovans refused to take any stock in me in a religious rôle, so I finally turned my entire attention to corralling their *reales* and *medios* at monte and did a better business than Fraile Romero did at confessing them. As a matter of fact their spiritual natures were considerably upset and rebellious at the time of our visit because of horror and indignation aroused by agents of the Louisiana-Tehuantepec Company who had just been through there offering to purchase the sacred mules for use in their scheme of transportation across the Isthmus of Tehuantepec.

Arriving finally at Suchil our *arrieros* returned to Tehuantepec and we engaged a large bongo to transport us down the river. By the middle of the afternoon we were gliding along the somber shades of the river bank and at sunset we landed on an open space at the foot of a high mountain. Said the captain of the bongo: "Myself and the peones will stop here for the night but your worships can ascend the mountain and stay at Doña Margarita's." In answer to our inquiries concerning Doña Margarita the man replied merely: "Doña Margarita is very rich and hospitable."

Curious that such a female personage as the river native described should reign here in the tropical wilderness, we climbed to the plateau above and found a large plantation of oranges, plantains, bananas and pineapples in the highest state of cultivation. And who do you imagine Doña Margarita to have been? None other than Mrs. Margaret Brewer, who lived here with her two daughters and one son, full-blooded Americans, surrounded entirely by natives. Here in the very heart of this jungle dwelt these four Americans, their own brave hearts and strong wills their only security.

My astonishment knew no limit as I learned what a power in the land was Doña Margarita, and with what fearless activity she managed her estate. The girls would remain in charge of the plantation while the mother, accompanied by her young son, would load a bongo with fruit and with a crew of her native employees float down to Minatitlán, sell her produce, purchase necessary goods and, always steering the big canoe herself, voyage back to the plantation and to her really magnificent home.

Mrs. Brewer was the widow of a Maine sea captain who had been in the mahogany trade to this coast. He had died at Minatitlán, leaving a cargo and other interests in the country. His widow came out to settle up his affairs and the business took her so long that she became attached to the region and settled down.

Early the following morning we left this hospitable Yankee abode in the tropical wilderness and floated down to Minatitlán, then proceeded to Chinameca, several leagues distant. A part of the way we passed over a most beautiful prairie where Cortéz fought his first battle on Mexican soil.

Chinameca we found to be a large town built for the most part in the style of the country, the habitations consisting of posts set in the ground, canes lashed horizontally thereto and then plastered with mud. The better ones were whitewashed and all were thatched. The old tower-like temple, however, was of solid construction and although it was only about fifty feet high and thirty feet square at the base it stood out prominently. It was made of a kind of concrete with a sort of sentry box on its summit, palm-thatched, where sat the perpetual watcher for the return of Malinche. Because of certain events that happened to us here later in this ancient edifice I am led to describe it rather in detail. On the ground floor was a large room with several smaller ones opening out of it, while a stairway at the opposite side ascended to a room above, and so on up, with a zigzag turn through two more superimposed rooms to the summit. On the stairway on the ground floor was a rude closet-like place which, on our first inspection, we did not notice at all. In the middle of the groundfloor apartment was a pile of rude masonry about four feet high, six feet square at the base and four feet square at the top. The place was without light or ventilation and when we were shown *el edificio anciano* by the governor of the town we inspected it by candlelight.

There were few even nominal Christians in Chinameca and I greatly deplored the misfortune of Fraile Romero, doomed to remain here until recalled by the bishop. The governor, or Indian alcalde, with whom the padre and I were quartered, was a soft, benevolent kind of an elderly person who declared himself to be a Christian but said his people were *muy cabesudo*—very stubborn. There had been trouble recently between Chinameca and a neighboring town called Cosaleacaca and blood had been freely spilled on both sides. It seemed that the Chinamecans had taken the initiative and invaded the territory of their neighbors, where they committed outrages which the governor feared would be followed by bloody retaliation any day. The only Mexican official in the country was a customs official at Minatitlán, so the Indians had everything to themselves.

We were not sufficiently familiar with the situation to realize the danger until one morning about ten days after our arrival the storm burst in demoniac fury when there erupted into Chinameca about two hundred infuriated Cosaleacacans.

Machetes and clubs were their only weapons. The Chinamecans were surprised, in spite of the governor's forebodings, and were slaughtered mercilessly. Houses were burned, women and children horribly mutilated, men and boys cut into pieces. From the governor's house we witnessed these horrid scenes, expecting every moment that the attack would be turned against our establishment and that we would be served in like manner. Along toward noon the Chinamecans made a desperate rally and drove the enemy from the town, but they returned reënforced and the fighting continued with varying success until a night of pitchy darkness drew a mantle over the scene of diabolical cruelty. Victory seemed to rest with our Chinamecans, for the enemy retired. We had witnessed enough fighting to have killed half the Indians of Mexico if they had fought as our northern Indians fight, but as a truthful historian I am forced to state that I saw a greater amount of cruelty and cowardice, and less of bravery, on that day than I thought possible of the human race.

We thought the danger over with, but our relief was brief for it developed that we were now in for it from the Chinamecans themselves. About nine o'clock at night the alcalde came and warned us that our lives were in danger, that his house and authority would no longer protect us, because of an incident in which the padre and I had figured during the afternoon. The padre's compassion had been aroused at sight of one poor devil of the enemy forces being pursued to his death right outside our door by a band of Chinamecans. Fraile Romero had opened the door and given the wretch sanctuary. When his pursuers tried to break down our door I threatened them with my revolver, so we were both now marked for massacre.

"No time is to be lost," urged the alcalde. But where were we to go? In the pitchy darkness we could never follow the jungle trail back to Minatitlán. The alcalde said our only hope was to let him conceal us in the old temple until the moon rose at 2 A.M. when, if possible, he would guide us into the jungle and set us on the proper trail.

So after several times barely avoiding detection we reached the temple with the governor, who stuffed us into the small aperture under the stairway and hurried away saying he would return if he could when the moon rose. The watcher under the thatch high up on the tower had not detected us.

I suggested to my fellow prisoner, the padre, that he should have brought some holy water with which to sanctify the infernal place. He replied by passing me an earthen flask from beneath his priestly garment. I raised it and swallowed a most exhilarating drought therefrom. Returning it to the friar I heard it gurgling at his lips, whereby I was informed that he knew as well as I the best way to use "holy water."

We now heard a great clamor growing ever louder and nearer. Stuffing rubbish into the small opening whereby we had entered our cubbyhole we extinguished our stub of a candle and remained in Stygian darkness. But not for long, for soon shafts of light broke through the crevices in our barricade as about twenty Indians, some bearing torches, entered the main room of the temple, dragging two bound prisoners, which they laid on the floor in front of the pyramid or altar before described. The Indians ranged themselves in two parallel lines facing the pyramid, while two of them raised to the summit of the pyramid a dark convex block apparently of mahogany. Two others with an instrument called a *macana* proceeded to remove some adobe bricks from the wall directly in front of us. All this we watched breathlessly through the crannies of our barricade, wondering to ourselves, what next?

In a few moments a recess in the opposite wall was exposed, revealing, in the light of torches planted each side of it, a horrid image—the most infernal looking object that devils in hell could conceive. One of the two who had assisted in arranging the altar, now arrayed in a scarlet robe, took from the hand of the image a knife. While he mumbled something in a sepulchral voice others seized one of the prisoners and spread him on the dark block, face upward. Five others held him fast, one at his head, one at each hand and one at each foot. Then the demon in the red robe deliberately cut the victim's heart out and with a guttural chanting deposited it in a boiling cauldron which had been arranged in front of the image in the recess.

The body of the first victim was then thrown onto the floor and the second victim seized and served in the same manner.

A stifled moan escaped Fraile Romero and a dizzy, sickening feeling overcame me. I suppose I lost consciousness from the combination of emotional shock and the stifling atmosphere of our cell, because the next I knew all was dark and silent again in the temple.

Soon I heard a muffled footstep; the gleam of a candle

invaded the outer room and the governor began to pull away our barricade of rubbish, expressing surprise that we had walled ourselves up so suffocatingly. When the candle-light revealed the interior of our cell we found the priest senseless. I applied the "holy water" to his lips; he revived and we emerged into the main room which now bore the same appearance as when we first entered it.

Apparently the governor was profoundly ignorant of all that had transpired in the ghastly place that night for he seemed uninterested and unemotional, except that he was provoked at our lingering to glance about in awed amazement at the silent old temple so recently aglow with torches, spurting human blood and savage figures performing the horrific ancient mysteries.

"Come on, hurry!" he demanded, and soon we were in the fresh air, breathing deeply and half inclined to believe that it had all been a nightmare. As we followed our guide the padre and I sprinkled our throats once more with "holy water" to restore our power of speech and conferred together in whispers. No, it was indeed real what I had witnessed, for the padre had seen the same, detail by detail.

The governor had ponies waiting at the edge of the jungle and he himself rode with us to Minatitlán. Safely there he promised to send our baggage after us when the excitement should have subsided sufficiently for him to smuggle it out. Then, with a sigh of genuine relief at getting us safely off his hands, the loyal representative of the majesty and might of the Mexican Republic bid us a hasty adiós.

Sure enough, after some days our baggage arrived in Minatitlán under guidance of the good alcalde. Whereupon Fraile Romero announced that he was going straight back to Tehuantepec even at the risk of excommunication; and back he went. But first he begged me that what we had witnessed in the temple of Chinameca should not be told in Mexico, for, said he, "It would be a great scandal on the Church and also on the government of Mexico."

How the priest came out with the bishop I never knew, for immediately on my return to Tehuantepec with him I took passage for San Francisco and saw no more of the genial companion with whom I had gone adventuring to the birthplace of beautiful Doña Marina, beloved of the great Cortéz.

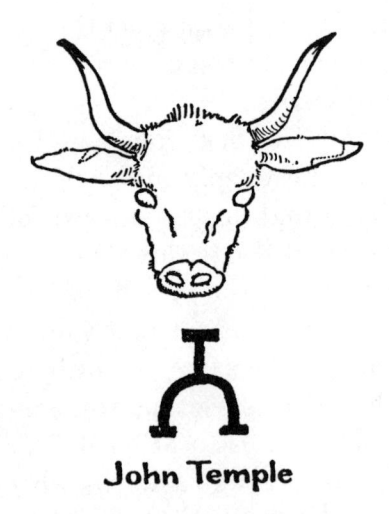

John Temple

CHAPTER 6

How Ran Runnels Decorated the Ramparts of Panamá

It seemed that all of the great thieves, highwaymen, gamblers and general desperados, or at least the ablest of them, were congregated at Panamá from 1849 to 1854, when those who had not been shot or hanged came to California. Along the Chagres River and the road across the Isthmus were stationed at so-called roadside inns these cut-throats, and the number of returning miners robbed and murdered could never be estimated.

Finally the steamship and railroad companies (the railroad was under course of construction) proposed a plan to the Panamá state government, which was to authorize the appointment of a man to be paid by the American companies but to have absolute and arbitrary power from the government to inflict the death penalty summarily without the usual court processes. This, argued the companies, is the only way to rid the Isthmus of this intolerable banditti.

The local government agreed, with the result that a slight-built, diminutive, beardless American boy was invested with this frightful power of life and death without accountability. He was Ran Runnels, of whom we spoke in a former book of reminiscences where we told of the part he took with the author in the great Panamá riot and massacre of 1856.

At the time of his appointment to the head of the Isthmus patrol and secret service Ran may have been twenty-two or twenty-three years old, but he did not look over eighteen, smooth-shaven and weighing only one hundred and thirty-five pounds. He organized his force secretly, picking some Americans, some black negroes and some Spanish mestizos, and for months, until he had perfected his plan, the public did not know what was going on.

He sent his men out as secret agents, the negroes to work among the blacks who were suspected of alliance with the robbers, the Americans associating with the English-speaking riffraff and the mestizos with the native element. Then lo! one morning, to the astonishment of the city, thirty-seven corpses of all colors were found hanging from the ramparts of Panamá. Acting on information gathered by his agents Ran had swept the gold road from the Chagres to the Pacific, and the first fruits of his campaign were displayed along the seawall. How the dead men came there, who hanged them, was left to the speculation of the populace. No information was given out; the secret operators were well enough paid to induce loyalty to the cause in which they were enlisted, and they couldn't afford to talk, anyway, or their own lives would have been forfeit.

What struck the populace with most consternation and awe was the fact that in this first exhibit of dead robbers were the bodies of several prominent citizens of Panamá City!

The criminal fraternity lay low for two or three months, trying to figure out what had happened; then conditions became dangerous again, and once more Panamá experienced the thrill of awakening one morning to find an even larger assortment of bodies suspended by the necks from the timbers jutting out of the masonry along the waterfront.

It was not long before Ran Runnels' campaign had made travel across the Isthmus as safe from bandits and sharpers, for the time being at least, as a journey from Boston to Salem. Some of the crooks escaped, disconcerted by the weird secrecy and ruthlessness of the forces operating against them; others were banished from the country instead of being hanged. The majority of these lucky ones made their several ways to California.

Among the most eminent of these gentry that complimented California with a visit were two whom I particularly remember, Jim Holmes and Jim McLean, both big, handsome, athletic, educated and apparently well-mannered Americans—but cut-throat robbers, nevertheless. The author had the distinguished honor of personal acquaintance with these two celebrities. They honored San Francisco by their arrival in 1854. Holmes was gathered into the fold at San Quentin * in short order, but the authorities did not lay claim to Jim McLean until January, '55, when he took up his quarters at the state's boarding house under a ten year sentence for a Wells, Fargo robbery.

I forget what it was that caused Mr. Holmes to reside temporarily at San Quentin; but it was apparent that he was too great a man, too useful to certain classes of the outside world, to be kept inside prison walls for any considerable period of time. So in March, '56, our then great, beer-drinking governor of California, John Bigler, pardoned him.

It was like this. By some means or other Jim Holmes entered into negotiations with John Bigler for his freedom. He represented to the governor that he had $200,000 worth of gold dust buried on the Isthmus of Panamá, and that if His Excellency would only let him out he would make an equal divvy.

Jim Holmes went free. He immediately sailed for Panamá, accompanied by an agent of the governor. The author was a passenger on the same steamer.

* Principal State Prison of California,

Oh, what a swell Mr. James Holmes did cut on that boat! Many thought he was a statesman on his way to Washington, others that he was a confidential agent for Cornelius Vanderbilt, on whose steamer we were traveling, which appeared probable because he certainly seemed to own the vessel. Some contended he was Sir Harry Huntley, an eminent English traveler who was then doing the Pacific Coast incog. But a few of us on board knew who the fellow was and somebody let the secret out. But that the gentleman was an eminent cut-throat and Isthmus robber only increased the awe with which he was regarded by the majority of his fellow passengers, because Jim, when the cat got out of the bag, told an appealing story of how the fair treatment he had received from the authorities in California had made a new man of him, had reformed him; that now he was going down to claim a fortune which awaited him so that henceforth he could live a good and charitable life. After this sentimental outburst most of the passengers seemed to deem it an honor to touch the hem of the convert's garment, and Mr. James Holmes stalked around the steamer with all the dignity of a mastiff in the presence of poodles.

Having once set foot in Panamá Mr. Holmes gave the governor's confidential agent the cold shake. He advised the gent to go back to Governor Bigler with his compliments and tell him that he would lay for him the next time His Excellency crossed the Isthmus going east.

But like most men of his type his boastful self-confidence was his undoing. Holmes had been banished from the Isthmus by Ran Runnels and he was now rashly counting without his host. Jim had scarcely imbibed his third cocktail at "The Shades," a popular Panamá resort, when gendarmes encircled him with bayonets on the ends of old flintlocks and marched him off to the calaboose. In less than a month he was sentenced to penal servitude in the mines of Colombia for life. That was what his $200,000 myth did for him. It got him out of jail and in again for keeps.

It is not to be inferred that only men eminent in a criminal way distinguished the Pacific Coast in those days, though one is tempted to pick these out as the most entertaining to write about. Some of the most remarkable characters that have illumined the world's history within the past fifty years were somehow or other identified with California in her golden age, 1849 and the early '50's. The Californian connections of some of the great writers and artists of various kinds in that period are familiar to the public, but there is also a list of military and naval names that afterward became eminent. For instance: Grant, Sherman, Stoneman, Hooker, Halleck, Mansfield, Steadman, all of whom later won fame on the field of carnage. Even grand old Farragut was a familiar figure at the Oriental Hotel in San Francisco when he was in command of the Mare Island Navy Yard.

Speaking of General Mansfield, who was killed in one of McClellan's battles on the Potomac, reminds me of two other California Mansfields, one killed in a brawl in Stockton in 1853, the other elected lieutenant-governor in 1879. This Mansfield, the lieutenant-governor, during his popularity in California was thought to be *the* General Mansfield who won such enviable fame in the Army of the Potomac; and to Shakespeare's question, "What's in a name?" our Mansfield could have answered: "Everything! The name made me lieutenant-governor of a great state when without it—"

The other Mansfield, who was shot down by John Tabor, a rival newspaper editor, left two little daughters, very beautiful, very smart. They went on the stage. What became of one I never knew, but the other grew to fame. This was Josie Mansfield, that famous, and some say infamous, star of her day. She was made one of the glittering constellation by the notorious Jim Fisk.

Josie was ten years old when her father was killed. She was just sixteen, possessed of a strange, dark beauty, when the actor Lawler married her in San Francisco in 1859. Her husband did his meager best to reform her, but this modern Nana, after Lawler went broke over her extravagance, disappeared from his life at the end of one year. From 1860 to 1867 her location was a mystery. Ignorant and unpolished as Lawler's wife, she reappeared seven years later in the polished company of Annie Woods, an actress who knew high livers and men who "went the pace." Among the latter was Col. Jim Fisk, Jr.

Josie Mansfield—she had dropped the Lawler through the medium of divorce—soon had Fisk under her Circe-like enchantment. The beautiful, but uncut, unpolished gem of 1859 was now a brilliant, flashing woman of the world. But when she met Fisk her last dollar was gone and she was arrayed in her last gown. By 1868 she occupied a splendid mansion with servants, jewels and equipages.

Those who basked under her smiles at this time describe her as of fair skin, lustrous as a lily, with broad white brow covered with masses of silky black hair, like clusters of rich grapes—fruit of the vine from the garden of Bacchus. Long gold hoops, gypsy-like, hung from her tiny pink-tinted ears. Small, plump hands with faultless nails and a figure of ravishing curves finished off by tiny feet, completed her ensemble with the exception of her eyes. Gray eyes they were, full of sorcery, fitful as a tropical sea with phosphorescent gleams.

This was the queen who now reigned in the brownstone

front No. 329 West Twenty-third St., New York City, where Jim Fisk and his friends enjoyed feasts fit for Lucullus, and poker games filled in the nights.

It was at one of these feasts that Fisk, boasting of his power, declared: "I have this city and state in the hollow of my hand. I think I'll have an act of legislature passed changing its name to Fiskville."

With carmine lips close to his ear and in her softly sweet voice Josie Mansfield said, "Why not name New York after me?"

"By God," exclaimed Fisk, "you're beautiful enough to have this town named after you! Now let's see—Josie is hardly dignified enough, is it? Ah, I have it! You're as fair as Helen of Troy. Henceforth I'll call you Helen and name New York Helena!"

This was our little Stockton girl of the '50's.

Juan Ábila

CHAPTER 7

Historic Treasure Buried in Cahuenga Pass

IN 1866 Don Jesús Martínez, a native of Sonora but long a respected citizen of Los Angeles, resided on the south side of Washington Street near Georgia Bell Street.* He befriended another Sonorense named Diego Moreno, who fell ill and was taken by Martínez to his (Martínez's) comfortable home to be cared for. This Diego Moreno was apparently in very humble circumstances, and others of his countrymen gave him scant attention.

One day while convalescing Moreno called his host to his side and said: "My good friend, you have been very kind to me. You succored me when as you thought I was destitute, you nourished me back to bodily strength. But I am not poor, Don Jesús, I am rich, and I propose to reward you."

The two friends were sitting under a grape arbor enjoying their siesta when Moreno began to speak, and great was the astonishment of Don Jesús at what he heard as he moved over closer to the sick man, who continued:

"Don Jesús, you marvel at what I say, but if you will hear my story patiently the whole mystery of my being a rich man will be made clear to you."

"Don Diego, I am all attention. Proceed before I die of curiosity."

"Your gracious interest compliments me greatly, Don Jesús. Thus unfolds the tale: A year or more ago I was engaged as a herder and general helper on a rancho near

* Named for the author's first wife. Now called simply Georgia Street.

Fancy Ball, California Exchange, San Francisco.

Lodging Room in San Francisco.

Suffering Immigrants.

French Shoeblacks.

San Francisco. It was not far from San Bruno. I had the full confidence of my *patron*. Late one afternoon I was seated in a copse watching my herd on the adjoining slopes when three mounted men appeared about a quarter of a mile from me, riding in a leisurely manner and apparently spying out the land. I was surprised, for they were a long way off any traveled road. They finally halted in a clump of liveoaks, dismounted and after a careful survey of their surroundings removed some packages from their horses and began excavating. They were now within three hundred yards of me and I watched their every movement with a growing sense of mystery.

"Finally satisfied with their excavation they placed the packages therein, filled the hole and smoothed off the loose earth. Then they gathered fuel and built a fire over the spot; then sat down, ate some refreshments, smoked and chatted, remounted and disappeared over the ridge.

"That evening, after corralling my little herd and performing my ranch duties I took a spade and returned secretly to the place of mystery among the liveoaks.

"I dug up the packages. I am telling you, Don Jesús, that although they were not of such great size, each package was so heavy that I could barely carry one under each arm and had to make three trips that night conveying them to my cabin. After covering over every opening in my cabin through which I might be spied on I dared open one of the packages. It contained gold doubloons, gold watches and fine jewelry. Of the value I had no idea. Such was my alarm and so confusing were my emotions that I made no attempt to make an inventory, but quickly covered up the treasure, concealed it and put out the candle. All night I lay on my blankets, gun and knife beside me, unable to sleep, turning over in my brain the mystery of the three horsemen and trying to decide what the consequences might be should I not report the matter to the authorities, and afterward be detected with the treasure.

"For a month this great treasure lay concealed in my cabin without my touching it again, and I tell you, *amigo mío,* that the battle between fear and avarice was almost bursting my brain. But I knew which way the battle was going; I knew I must soon feast my eyes upon it *all;* and after that it must be mine.

"At last one night by a flickering taper I opened the second package and spread its contents upon my blanket. There I beheld one hundred gold doubloons, a good many fine watches with their chains and three or four pint cups full of diamonds, emeralds, rubies and pearls, some still set in necklaces, pins, ear-rings and finger-rings.

"It all seemed to be typical Mexican jewelry, which puzzled me very much, for here we were now living in an American state and the Mexican population very poor. The doubloons were Spanish and Mexican money. The watches were of an ancient character and some bore dates of absolute antiquity. I was convinced that all this treasure had been brought up from below the border. But by whom? Why?

"Opening the remaining packages I found the contents all about the same and each package wrapped exactly alike, in buckskin, with the coins separately arranged. I bound them up exactly as I had found them, hid them away and continued with the losing battle in my mind.

"After three months I went to my *patron* and told him I wished to draw my wages and return to my old home in Mexico. He expressed his regret and balanced my account, paying me a month's extra wages which enabled me to buy a good riding mule and two pack animals. At daybreak one morning I started southward, bearing the mysterious treasure deep in my camping pack.

"Finally my journeying brought me close to the Pueblo de los Angeles and, night overtaking me on the southern slope of the Cahuenga Pass, I stopped at a roadside *jacal* at a spot near where the road crosses the *arroyo*. This mean tavern was kept by a countryman of ours with whom I struck up an acquaintance. It was my intention to proceed the next day by the brea pits road [1] to the Pueblo, but that night I was warned in a dream that if I went to Los Angeles with the treasure I should never leave the town alive. Accordingly I decided to tarry where I was until I found an opportunity secretly to bury the precious packages there in the Paso de Cahuenga.

"One night, everything being quiet in the tavern, I slipped out with the treasure to a previously selected spot on the side of the pass about half way from the *jacal* to the summit on the hillside opposite the main road, and buried it. I buried it in six different holes, taking measurements from a fresno tree east, west, north and south.* It's the only fresno tree in that locality. But there is no use going into further details, dear friend; I am getting well and in three or four days we shall go out there together, dig it up, and you shall have half of it. With my part I shall go home to Sonora.

"So you see, my good Don Jesús, your condescending patience in hearing my long story will have been exerted not in vain—not in va—"

At this very moment Diego Moreno was seized with a vio-

---

* The tavern stood near the present junction of Cahuenga and Highland avenues. The treasure was apparently buried about opposite the famous Hollywood Bowl. A fresno is a Western ash tree.

lent recurrence of his illness and died before either physician or priest could reach him.

Soon thereafter Jesús Martínez with his stepson, Gumisindo Correa, then fourteen or fifteen years old, went to Cahuenga Pass and searched for the deceased Moreno's treasure. They pretended to be wood choppers. Just as the fresno tree was located Señor Martínez fell down in a fit and died. The boy, Gumisindo, filled with superstitious terror, fled and did not resume the quest.

Along about 1885 or '86 a Basque sheepherder was grazing a flock in the pass when he noticed that his dog paid particular attention to a certain spot. Every day that the flock grazed up through the pass the dog would go to this same spot and sniff and dig. Examination showed no indication of an animal's burrow to excite the dog, yet he would dig and dig.

So the Basque decided to dig. He dug up a package rolled in buckskin. It contained exactly one hundred doubloons of gold and a large amount of jewelry. In great excitement he took it to his friend Etchepare, the tavernkeeper in the pass. He gave him some part of the treasure and pledged him to secrecy; with the remainder of the swag he left for the land of his ancestors in the Pyrenees.

The tavernkeeper later let the secret out, but it was taken for granted that the sheepherder had made a cleanup of whatever loot there was and treasure hunting in that vicinity was dropped.

Now, let us go back a little in a hunt for the origin of this loot and introduce Captain Henry Malcolm, who came to Los Angeles about 1874. The captain was a Maine man, a soldier of fortune. He had been my messmate and friend in the Walker "Filibuster" War in Nicaragua, commanding a battery of howitzers. A Maine man is generally

From the Ingersoll Historical Collection, Los Angeles Public Library
General William Walker of Nicaraguan fame with whom the author campaigned

a true man, a good, strong, brave and honest man. Such was Captain Malcolm. And a good story teller, too, with a remarkable memory for detail.

Of course I was overjoyed to see him in Los Angeles and he spent most of his time at my office, where we fought over the battles in Nicaragua and rehearsed the remarkable adventures we had shared during those memorable months. One day we were discussing the subject of Granada after it was sacked by General Heningsen under orders of General Walker. At the time of the sack of Granada I was on the transit route, guarding it from invasion from Costa Rica. The transit route was a big, broad smoothly graded turnpike built by Cornelius Vanderbilt for the transfer of his passengers from his Atlantic to his Pacific steamers during the California gold excitement and extended from Virgin Bay on Lake Nicaragua to San Juan del Sur on the Pacific.

This day in my office in Los Angeles Captain Malcolm was telling me the details of how the loot taken from the old churches by Walker was handled; of how he, Malcolm, had been chosen by Walker one of ten men to convey it to a secret burial place and how day after day from the moment of the hiding of this loot one or the other of the ten men would die a violent death, some immediately that an action with the enemy began, others from mysterious bullets fired by snipers or by seeming accident, until only he was left of the group that had held the secret of the hiding place of the two tons of silver and gold plate, holy images and symbols.

Malcolm said that he had begun to be suspicious that there was human design behind the quick deaths of nine of that group of ten, and when he was singled out by Walker for a mission that apparently meant sure death, he decided that he was warranted in looking to his own safety. So while apparently carrying out the desperate orders given him by Walker he surrendered to the enemy and finally escaped to Panamá.

"There it is, worth at least $200,000, still buried down there, for General Walker's end came before he could reap the benefits of it. I—and now you and I—hold the secret, Major. But I have no luck with buried treasure. I buried treasure in California once—how it happened and how it disappeared was the strangest thing that ever happened to me."

Naturally I pressed him for the details, and this is the amazing story he told:

During the Maximilian [2] War in Mexico, Captain Malcolm was a trusted aide to Gen. Placido Vega, the great patriot fighter of Sinaloa. Vega had held Mazatlán manfully against the Maximilian forces, but in 1865 the siege was reducing the Mexican cause to desperate straits. It became absolutely imperative to raise funds with which to purchase arms, ammunition and supplies from outside sources. The general made a fervid appeal to the whole state to contribute toward a fund to be sent to San Francisco for supplies. A wealthy woman of Mazatlán set the example by contributing her whole family fortune in jewels. Contributing jewelry became a patriotic craze and all the wealthy families turned over their heirlooms.

"Why," said Malcolm, "talk about patriotism, you never saw anything like it. Women with rings on their fingers not worth a dollar would rush in and contribute them, while aristocrats with diamonds and pearls that had been heirlooms for generations threw them into the common heap until it was estimated that $200,000 had been acquired in this way, without counting the cash contributions."

A friend of General Vega, a man of great character and

prudence, was selected as the special agent to convey this treasure to San Francisco. Captain Malcolm, an Englishman and a Mexican captain named Dávila went along as escorts.

On the voyage up the special agent, who alone had authority to spend the treasure, died suddenly and mysteriously.

"We had to be extremely careful of our treasure," said Malcolm, "for we knew that not only had Mazatlán been infested with Maximilian spies but that San Francisco was full of them; and we suspected now, of course, that there were enemy agents aboard our ship. We finally landed with it safely in San Francisco and went to the Russ House, where we held a consultation. I suggested that we deposit it with some business house in San Francisco until we could communicate with General Vega, but Captain Dávila insisted that it should be buried somewhere so that the secret of its presence in California should rest with us alone. The Englishman seconded him, so we took it out into the hills, first making our own inventory of it, taking out enough to defray additional expenses which would now face us, and wrapping it up in six separate packages covered with buckskin.

"We buried the packages in the hills beyond San Bruno, smoothed over the ground and built a fire over the spot. Of course we took bearings in detail so that we could return to the location without difficulty.

"In response to our urgent message sent by return steamer, Gen. Placido Vega himself came to San Francisco to expend the treasure.

"Captain Dávila, the Englishman and myself rode out to our secret spot in the hills and dug for our six precious packages. They had been removed! They were gone!

"Our consternation was beyond words. The Mexican turned on the Englishman and accused him of stealing the

TREASURE IN CAHUENGA PASS 69

treasure. The Englishman answered him with a blow. The Mexican drew his knife and the Englishman his revolver. Before I could realize what was taking place these two were on the ground weltering in their blood. The Englishman gasped out, 'I die an innocent man.' But the Mexican did not hear him. He was already dead. In three minutes the Englishman also was stone dead.

"Well," continued Captain Malcolm, "I have experienced a great many surprises, mortifications, terrors, but I was never in a situation like this before. In a daze I mounted and rode back to San Francisco. I laid the whole matter before General Vega. Crushed as he was by the terrible news, he exonerated me from blame and held me above suspicion."

Now, to continue further with the accounting of our large cast of characters in this tragedy of treasure trove: When the Tombstone gold strike was made in Arizona in the '80's, Captain Malcolm went there. I presented him with a fine shot gun before he left. He settled on a waterhole and laid claim to it. One day a man came along who claimed prior right to the water, and during the ensuing argument the stranger picked up the shot gun which I had presented to Malcolm and shot him dead.

Young Correa, who had accompanied Martínez on the hunt for the fresno tree in Cahuenga Pass, overcame his superstitious dread after he reached manhood and renewed the search for the tree. But he could find none; the inference was that some woodchopper had felled it.

About 1891 or '92 I happened to meet Correa and related to him the circumstance of the Basque sheepherder having actually found treasure in the pass and also told him Captain Malcolm's story. His interest was at once revived and he solicited my aid in a plan to find the treasure. He proposed that we rent the land for farming purposes, that we clear it and plow with an immensely deep plow and then subwork it with smaller plows so that we would cover every foot of the ground deep enough to root out the buried wealth.

We entered into an agreement to do this. While I was negotiating with the owners of the land poor Gumisindo Correa was shot down in the streets of Los Angeles by an assassin. The murderer or his motive was never known.

Some time later I was conversing with Etchepare, the tavernkeeper, about the startling chain of events connected with the treasure hunt in Cahuenga Pass and he said: "Oh, I forgot to tell you about my friend the Basque sheepherder. He never reached home with his treasure. He was so fearful of losing it that he made himself a buckskin garment extending the length of his body from his arm pits to his hips, with straps from the shoulders. He quilted it and stowed the treasure under the quilting. Arriving at Barcelona he stood on the rail of the steamer in high glee waving to supposed friends on the distant dock. He lost his balance, fell into the sea and sank like a lead brick."

I abandoned my plan to unearth the Mazatlán treasure, and I do not know that any one else has ever taken up the hunt. There it lies along the road that leads down through La Nopalera * to the brea pits and the City of the Angels, waiting to be mined out. Who will be next to take a chance against the mysterious unseen forces that seem to haunt this reminder of the Emperor Maximilian and his Empress Carlota?

Mind you, the characters named in the above account are not imaginary people. José Gumisindo Correa, for instance, was an honorable and substantial citizen of Los Angeles, held several offices of trust, was at one time on the police

* "The Cactus Patch" as the location of modern Hollywood was once called.

force, was water overseer, horticultural inspector and a man with a record for honest efficiency. He was born in Los Angeles, the son of a Mexican army officer. His mother was a sister of Leonardo Cota, a citizen of great influence in the early history of the city.

Ygnácio Del Valle

CHAPTER 8

Los Angeles During the Civil War

LOS ANGELES was ardently Southern in its sentiments at the outbreak of the great War of Secession. The leading men of the county were for the Jeff Davis government first, last and all the time. Men loyal to the United States Government were in a hopeless minority. The whole mob was composed of Secessionists. All the office-seekers, the foragers at the public crib, the thieves, gamblers and general vagrants were of that persuasion. And I may truthfully say that vagrants were a power in this land. By vagrants I mean men who were living in illicit intercourse with the low class Mexican and Indian women. These men were not only powerful as a voting influence, they were also petty politicians and office holders.

To illustrate the influence of this class let me go back of the war two or three years, that is, to 1858, and speak again of the uprising which has been dignified in history as the Juan Flores Revolution, and which I detailed in one of the chapters of an earlier book.

One ought to write true history or not write history at all; and with this in mind I state that a lewd Indian woman was the cause of the murder of Sheriff Barton, as a result of which a great many lives were sacrificed on the altar of public vengeance.*

James R. Barton had been sheriff for two or three suc-

* See Newmark's *Sixty Years in Southern California* for a different account of the Barton affair.

Panorama of Los Angeles in the '50's looking north along Main Street (left) and Los Angeles Street (right). *From an old lithograph.*

Major Horace Bell about the time of the Civil War.
From a painting.

cessive terms. He was an uncouth, illiterate man, a carpenter by trade. He had lived for years prior to his death in illicit intercourse with a Capistrano Indian woman. She had a brother named Andrés Fontes, a loafer around Los Angeles and a desperate sort of fellow given to the use of his knife on slight provocation.

Barton's woman left him and went to live with the Indians in a rancheria * east of the Los Angeles River. The high sheriff of Los Angeles County, who, by the way, had an income of $10,000 a year from his office, went to the Indian settlement to recover his woman. She refused to return to him. After long argument he seized her by her scalp lock and started to lead her away. It happened that her brother Andrés put in an appearance at this moment and interposed. There was a fight with the result that the sheriff retreated without his woman.

Two days later the sheriff arrested Andrés on a charge of horse stealing, had him indicted, tried, convicted and sent to San Quentin for two years. When Fontes was placed on the stagecoach on his way to San Quentin he leaned out just as the driver was letting go the brakes and said to Sheriff Barton: "I am innocent. You put up this job on me. In two years I will return and kill you."

Andrés Fontes served his term and returned, his existence probably quite forgotten by those who had most to fear from him. Soon unrest was manifested among the natives of San Juan Capistrano and vicinity. It resulted in an uprising against American authority led by Juan Flores, an ardent Californian malcontent. Andrés Fontes was not in evidence at the seat of disturbance; he let Flores have the limelight while he himself was taking note of Sheriff Barton's movements at the county seat.

* Indian village.

The sheriff mustered a posse of ten men to go down and suppress the disorder.

As the sheriff and his force prepared to start southward Andrés Fontes slipped out ahead of them and rode straight for San Juan Capistrano.[1] There he enlisted several trusted companions from among the malcontents, returned with them to a chosen ambush on the highway eight or nine miles out of the mission town, waylaid and killed the sheriff and all but two of his posse.

When the two survivors struggled back into Los Angeles with the news the American population and the better class of all the elements rose in arms. Indignation at the massacre boiled over and before it cooled again many lives were sacrificed to appease public clamor.

I repeat that I relate the above to verify the declaration heretofore made that the vagrant and the squawman was a power among us. And this is the class and manner of men with a few highly honorable exceptions, that made up the Los Angeles County Secessionist mobs.

Los Angeles furnished three generals to the Confederates: Gen. Albert Sidney Johnston, killed at Shiloh; J. L. Brent, a lawyer, who won distinction in the service, and a man named Pearson, a surveyor who became a Texas brigadier. There were colonels, majors and captains without end, besides about two hundred and fifty of the rank and file who were fitted out in Los Angeles County and sent over the desert to the Confederate forces in Texas. These I do not class with the mob left behind; the generals above named were forthright men who had the strength of their convictions and sought the field of honor according to their lights.

There were two Los Angeles men and no more who actually fought in the Union army, I mean on the actual battlefields in the East. One of them is the author of this

San Francisco in April 1850, showing Clay Street, opposite Portsmouth Square.

The Post Office, Corner of Pike and Clay Streets.

Emigrant Train.

Scene in the gold mines.

THE CIVIL WAR

book who went east and joined up in time to participate in the first land skirmish, and who was present at the headquarters of Gen. E. R. S. Canby in New Orleans when the last unit of the Confederate army was surrendered by the commissioners of the Trans-Mississippi Department, Generals Sterling Price, Simon Bolívar Buckner and J. Lancaster Brent (whilom Los Angeles lawyer).

The other Union soldier from Los Angeles who actually participated on the battlefields of the Civil War was Charles N. Jenkins.[2] He went east December, 1862.

Times were hot in Los Angeles during this historical period and the Secessionists had it all about their own way. A small garrison of California Volunteers was maintained by the United States Army at Drum Barracks,[3] also a detachment at Ballona.* But they scarcely dared appear in town on account of the wrath of the populace. The few Union men of the county had a hard time of it; the mob insulted them and the upper crust execrated them. When the news of Abraham Lincoln's assassination reached the Pueblo the Southern "patriots" got on a bust; they howled themselves hoarse—they howled and they hurrahed until they fell in the streets, dead drunk.

On this occasion the garrisons at Wilmington and Ballona mustered their courage and their men and made a dash into Los Angeles, loaded the "patriots" into army ambulances and escaping successfully from the town with them, put the prisoners in camp chain gangs. Among these unfortunates was Nigger Pete the barber, hero of some of the lighter incidents of early life in the Pueblo de los Angeles related in a former volume. Pete won the cognomen during Secession

* Known as Fort Latham, just back of the present Playa Del Rey, where the Ballona estuary was a possible shipping and landing place for Southern sympathizers.

times of the Black Democrat on account of his political adherence to the local majority.

Los Angeles at the close of the Rebellion was the most vindictive, uncompromising community in the United States. It had not been chastened by the hand of war; it was eager to go on vociferating its bitterness long after regions which the conflict had laid waste were willing to quit.

Having served his country's flag for four years and eight months and having won a certain amount of distinction in that service, the extent of which may be discovered in the records of the War Department, the author returned to Los Angeles July 31, 1866, bought a ranch and settled down to peaceful agriculture. I now had a wife, whom I had married in the East, and two little children. My reception in the Pueblo was cold. Old friends, with a few honorable exceptions such as Judge A. J. King and Col. E. J. C. Kewen, turned their backs on me. "The idea," said they, "of a Los Angeles man of your stamp fighting on the side of the blacks!"

A short time after my return I narrowly escaped assassination on the road between Los Angeles and El Monte. Failing to get me this time the El Monte "patriots" put up their greatest fighting man to chastise me, and here is what followed:

One afternoon I rode into town from my ranch, hitched my horse on Ducommun's corner * and went into Kraemer's store on Commercial Street to make a purchase for my wife. While in there Polaski, an adjoining storekeeper, entered and whispered to me that a great big man was waiting outside with a whip, intending to chastise me. Such a proposition seemed to me so absurd that I paid no attention; as a matter of fact I was quite proud of my war record and I

* Main and Commercial streets.

was not in the frame of mind to accept discipline from any individual, especially from a stay-at-home scoundrel. So, finishing my business I started out, but Polaski again claimed my attention and pointed to a huge man now standing outside the front door. He held a big blacksnake in his hand, butt foremost, and was backed up by a dozen El Monte men who had come in to see the fun.

I saw that it meant a fight so I said, "My dear sir, are you looking for me?" He bristled up and drew back to strike with the blacksnake. I threw the strength of a lifetime into one blow with my fist and caught the fellow on the ear. Down he went his full length, tripping over a boot-box as he fell. I stepped up onto that boot-box and then came down onto that fellow with both feet with sufficient force to break three ribs from his backbone. Then I seized the whip and lit into him. Good old José Mascarel, then mayor of Los Angeles, who was himself a giant, caught me from behind with a great grizzly grip and commanded me to keep the peace. By this time the street was crowded and the sentiment turned in my favor so that the El Monte party was jostled and hooted when its members tried to take up the battle. The downfallen blacksnaker tried to get to his feet and come after me as I walked toward my horse. I turned on him and said with apparent ferocity: "Now, sir, you lie right down there again and don't attempt to get up until I am out of sight." The bully flopped, jeered at by the crowd who could not extend their sympathies to such an ignominious champion, and I rode home. It seems that a few minutes before encountering me the El Monte "patriot" had taken by surprise and blacksnaked another man of my build and general appearance whom he mistook for me; and, as I walked away it was amusing to hear this aggrieved victim of mistaken identity say, after he had pushed his way through the crowd to the side of the prostrate form in the street: "Well, you found the right man, did you?"

Now what was this all about?

Simply this: I was the first man to reappear in Los Angeles who had fought on the Union side in the war, and as I had gone from this town to do this nefarious thing, I was simply a red rag to the Secessionist bulls of the vicinity. So in that neighboring hotbed, El Monte, Wiley McNear had been selected as their champion to "put me in my place." To them the war was still going on. McNear was six feet six inches high, weighed two hundred and forty pounds and claimed to be a quarter-breed Cherokee. This claim may or may not have been true, for the ugliest fighting men of the Southwest, to make themselves seem very terrible, always claimed kinship to the Cherokees. This fellow had long been a terror to the few Union sympathizers around the classic Monte. Doctor Whistler and Little Potts were the particular objects of his persecutions.

When Wiley McNear got out of bed six or eight weeks after his misshap with me he found his popularity gone. Whipped by an Abolitionist Yankee—that left him a fallen idol. So great was the disgust of all Montedom that they turned on him cruelly; they put up a rascally job on him, a nefarious, shameless job. They accused him of an infamous crime of which, in my judgment, he was innocent; got him convicted and sent to San Quentin for fourteen years. The poor fellow died there, all because he did not know how to properly "size up" a Yankee.

I got into at least forty other fights after my affair with Wiley McNear, all over the same subject. The Civil War continued to rage here, largely around my person. I was

THE CIVIL WAR

determined to remain here where I wanted to live, and without bragging I will simply state that I held my own in every one of these battles and finally fought my way to respect and peace. How peace was finally achieved was rather amusing.

Not long after my fight with the Monte badman I was passing along Main Street in front of the Downey Block.* There were a lot of gamblers and loafers sitting on some boxes whittling and as I went by "Stock," one of the gamblers, remarked, apparently intending that I should hear: "There goes that —— that got away with Wiley McNear. I'm going to lay for him."

I pretended not to hear but went straight over to Billy Workman's saddlery store and got a big, loaded rawhide whip and went out to lay for "Stock."

I didn't have long to wait. Los Angeles in those days, 1866-67, was a very sleepy old town. Along about noon time you could ride your horse from Temple Block down Main to the last building, usually, without seeing a person. But to-day I rode past "Stock" as he sauntered by the Courthouse. I continued until I was in front of Rowan's place, where the Natick House † now stands, dismounted and pretended to be adjusting my saddle. As "Stock" walked past I emerged from behind my horse, grabbed the gambler by his long hair, jerked his revolver from its holster and proceeded to give him such a walloping with that whip —oh, such a walloping! Rowan came out and saw me at work. When I let "Stock" go I turned to Rowan and explained my motive.

* An early landmark built by Gov. John G. Downey at Main and Temple streets, present site of Federal Building.
† Still operated as a hotel at Main and First streets. Long a well-known gathering place for old prospectors in from the desert.

"I didn't see a thing, Major," he answered and turned away.

I then went to O. H. Allen, Justice of the Peace, told him what I had done and was fined $5. Judge Allen was a strong Secessionist but an honorable, noble gentleman. He was a member of that great Allen family of Kentucky. I then had a heart to heart talk with the Judge—told him how these fellows were trying to get rid of me and how I proposed to stop it. I told him that I proposed to whip every one of them with a loaded rawhide until they stopped even looking cross-eyed at me.

"Now, Judge," I said, "will you let me off with $5 for each future affair of this kind?"

"Yes," he answered, "if you don't use anything worse than a whip."

Before I was through I had paid in a large sum in five dollar fines to Judge Allen, but had won an absolute and perfect peace. Somehow I always managed to "get there first" with my enemies, before they could draw on me, and after their chastisements, which always called down on them the ridicule of the onlookers no matter where their sympathy originally lay, they seemed too humiliated to follow the matter up with a gun.

Jenkins, the other townsman who actually reached the battlefields as a Union soldier, returned from his long imprisonment in Andersonville in the midst of all this guerrilla warfare. This he did in spite of a warning his brother sent him that he would be hanged if he reappeared. But after getting here he went over to San Clemente Island where he stayed until the local Grim Visage had smoothed out somewhat.

The year 1866 went out and '67 dragged itself through. Union war veterans from the East and other parts of the

Georgia Herrick Bell.

A Massachusetts girl whom Major Bell married in the East during the Civil War and brought across the plains to California. *From a daguerreotype.*

Famous winery of Jean Louis Vignes built in 1831.

It stood on Aliso Street, Los Angeles. From here in 1854 was made the first commercial shipment of California wines to New York by the Sainsevain Brothers, nephews of the original proprietor. *From an old lithograph.*

West began to find their way to Los Angeles and times waxed better. In 1868 we formed a Grand Army post of which I became the commander. We determined to get into politics and make things hum; we raked in all of the old California Home Guard as veterans and we operated secretly in elections until we began to feel that we had some power, as well as some rights.

With the aid of the Spanish-speaking population the Republicans elected Billy Warren city marshal. Billy Warren wanted one more policeman to add to the force, then numbering six. He came to me about it and I named Jack Rhodes, who had been a gallant member of the Second Illinois Cavalry, and with whom I had served.

Did this produce a sensation? You can imagine! Joe Dye, a noted man-killer, was a member of the police force, and he began to brow-beat and insult Warren because of this appointment, and two years later the feud thus engendered ended in Dye killing Warren. Shortly after killing the marshal Dye killed a couple of other men, and then fell out with his foster son, who barricaded himself in a window on the south side of Commercial Street and sat there with a double-barreled shotgun loaded with buckshot until Joe came along and then riddled him.

Having won such distinction in the Jack Rhodes appointment our Grand Army post went after other game. There was a deputy water overseer to be appointed and we petitioned the Council to name Jenkins, the soldier who had returned from Andersonville.

It happened that Don Félix Gallardo, one of the natives who had associated himself with the Southern party, was sent to the penitentiary for horse stealing about the time Jenkins went East with the California Hundred to fight for the flag of the United States. The Secessionists nominated this now-released convict against our candidate and the Council actually appointed the ex-convict in place of the ex-soldier. The councilmen did this out of their love of Jefferson Davis and hatred for Abraham Lincoln.

There was a printer here named Creighton who published a little weekly paper and I went to him to see if he wouldn't haul the Council over the coals for its disloyal partizanship. Creighton said: "Major, I'm afraid to do it. Some of those fellows might catch me and beat me to death."

"Well," said I to Creighton, "just let me edit your paper for a few weeks."

"All right," said he; and if I didn't give that Council hot shot, grape and cannister, shell and shrapnel for the next few issues! Some of them live here yet, and if they should be charged now with preferring a convict to an honorable Union soldier for a place of preferment and profit, they would deny it flatly, for they have been taught better.

Hard times fell upon the southern counties of California about '58 and continued for fully ten years, during which we had one year of smallpox and two years of absolute drought. The region became terribly poor and very much demoralized. The bad population that had drifted down from the mines lived a lazy, gambling, vagabond life; in fact, conditions deteriorated until absolute barbarism ruled. It was thus I found it when I returned to Los Angeles in 1866.

After looking the situation over I was inclined to weep tears of regret over having decided to return to a country now so forlorn. California had been my home since I was nineteen and my memories of Los Angeles were glowing. But now, returned with the serious responsibility of a family and a living to make, I found it the most God-forsaken country I had ever seen. The revolution-smitten towns of

Nicaragua and Mexico, with which I was familiar, were prosperous in comparison, as were the war-stricken towns of Mississippi, Louisiana and western Texas through which I had ridden on my way back to the Pacific Coast. The wealth of the Californians was gone, the cattle had all died, the Spanish grandees who in '56 had adorned themselves in rich velvets, broadcloth and gold embroidery, were now in '66 wearing old soldiers' cast off clothes.

I startled the whole countryside by buying farm land at twenty dollars an acre. I secured a place for a home at Figueroa and Pico streets and began to build a house. Jean Louis Vignes, an early French settler, came over to see me, excited over the fact that somebody was actually buying land, and offered me his adjoining thirteen acre tract for three hundred dollars. It later became the three city blocks bounded on the north by Twelfth Street, on the east by Grand Avenue, on the south by Pico Street and on the west by Figueroa Street. I promised him I would think it over, and went on building my home.

In the meantime a man named Jesús L. Cruz, a native who got real estate ambitions from hearing that things were looking up, purchased the Vignes thirteen acres for two hundred and fifty dollars, to be paid in installments of twenty dollars a month. Don Jesús then held a position with the city government which yielded him a salary of thirty-five dollars a month, leaving him fifteen dollars a month for the support of his numerous family when his land installments were paid. This, however, was considered quite a liberal income at the time.

The former Mexican governor, Don Pío Pico, also got wind of me as a man that had money, and he came over to borrow three hundred dollars. All of this old grandee's hundreds of thousands of acres of land were mortgaged and about to slip from him except the one hundred acres of his home place called El Ranchito.[4] The way he happened to have this one hundred acres free was this:

In 1856 we had in Los Angeles a talented Scotch journalist named Brodie and Pío Pico, a friend of his, gave him this piece of land. Just made him a present of it as a friendly gesture between comrades. About the time of my return from the East Mr. Brodie, who had returned to Scotland, hearing of the financial distress of his old friend the ex-governor, sent the latter a deed reconveying the land to him.

"Now," said Don Pío to me, dismounting at my new doorstep, "for three hundred dollars I will convey to you this hundred acres, El Ranchito, or I will mortgage it to you." To such a point as this were the old land barons reduced!

It is only proper to add that the little boom I started by my modest investments in '66 grew so rapidly that in four or five years Don Pío was enabled to sell enough land to save him from the loss of much of the rest and he became fairly rich again before his death.

In March '69 I paid $3,600 for a thirty-five acre piece adjoining the vineyard land I had purchased for twenty dollars an acre in '66. This land I cut up into lots and blocks and made about $8,000 out of it in a few weeks. On the city maps this is called "Bell's Addition," and was the first subdivision of land ever made in Los Angeles. It is the parent tract of all our real estate booms.

CHAPTER 9

The Feliz Curse

ANTONIO FELIZ was a rich old don who owned eight thousand acres of valuable ranch and farm land adjoining the city of Los Angeles on the northwest.[1] This good old hidalgo had cattle upon a hundred hills; horses, mules, oxen, asses, goats and sheep. His lands were the most fertile, his parks of great oak trees the grandest, his springs of water the coolest and most limpid. His vineyards, orchards and cornfields were the most productive, his meadows the greenest, his cattle the fattest. The rippling Los Angeles River meandered along the northern, eastern and western boundaries of this terrestrial paradise, enfolding it, as it were, in a life-giving embrace; and beautiful verdure-clad mountain slopes defined its southern border. This rancho was the loveliest and most romantic property in Southern California, unexcelled, I verily believe, anywhere in the universe.

Besides all these agricultural riches Don Antonio Feliz had money in good hard silver and gold coin. When he died in 1863 he, unlike most of his compatriots of the period, owed only one man in the wide world and that man was Jew Solomon to whom he had somehow become indebted in the sum of sixteen dollars.

In the year named the smallpox raged and the master of all the Feliz acres fell sick of it.

At 1 P.M., so it was reported, he was speechless. At 3 o'clock, it was further reported, one of our then well-known citizens, Don Antonio Coronel,[2] came to the Feliz rancho, sat in the corridor of the great house some twenty feet from the room where the proprietor lay, and proceeded to write. The writing finished, Don Inocente, one of the witnesses, stole into the sick chamber and, notwithstanding that Don Inocente later admitted in testimony in court that the master of the rancho was speechless several hours before the document was written, he read the same to him and he, Antonio Feliz, answered that it was "all right." Then some one signed the name of Antonio Feliz to the instrument. It was never actually proven who did actually write the signature, but written it was, nevertheless.

It is said that Don Inocente did read the will to the stricken ranchero and that the latter assented to all its provisions by affirmative nods of the head; but it was also further stated by those "in the know" that the dying don had been propped up in bed with a stick fastened to the back of his head wherewith he was made to nod correctly. This, however, would seem open to reasonable doubt as the good man had smallpox and no one would have wanted to handle his person under such circumstances.

Be that as it may, the filing of his last will and testament disclosed that he had bequeathed to his godson, Juan Sánchez, twelve gentle mares with the pinto stallion, and a colt to each mare. The household furniture, movables and bedclothes were to be divided equally between "my sister, Soledad Feliz, and my sister-in-law, Juana Valenzuela." Then followed the disposition of the grand estate—the real riches —as follows: "All the rest of my goods and property I order and direct to be administered, governed and directed by my friend Don Antonio Coronel; that when he shall deem convenient and that the price shall appear to him good he shall sell all my said property and employ the proceeds in the suffrages of my soul; and I further direct that no bond shall be required of my said executor."

"Suffrages of my soul" as interpreted by the learned court that passed upon the validity of the will meant that the executor might employ the proceeds of this great estate in such good works as to him might seem best for the benefit of the soul of the dear departed.

Like his illustrious predecessor, Don Quixote de la Mancha, Don Antonio Feliz had been a bachelor and his household had consisted of a housekeeper (his own sister) and a niece, Petranilla.

It will be seen that in the last will and testament a sop had been thrown to the sister-housekeeper but nothing at all to Petranilla. The old retainers and servants, too, had been utterly ignored.

Now this Petranilla had been very close in the affections of the deceased; indeed, she had been his favorite relative, almost like a daughter. When she had been persuaded to stay with friends of the family in the Pueblo while the mansion was under the terrible influence of contagion she had gone weeping bitterly, her only solace the thought of returning eventually to the old home which she felt sure was to be her very own should her protector die.

But what did Doña Petranilla find when, after a decent interval of beguiling her grief, she approached the old homestead again? She found a new owner in full occupancy with a new set of furnishings in the house and he himself engaged in disposing of horses, cattle and crops for cash.

The terms of the will had not been understood by the young niece; but now suddenly to her shocked brain came the realization that she had been denied any part in the inheritance of a princely domain. Soledad Feliz apparently submitted philosophically to the sad situation; but not Doña

Petranilla. She was a girl only seventeen, a fairy-like creature, tall, slim, graceful, beautiful and educated; but in her slight frame burned a fiery spirit. Her dark deep eyes blazed, she stiffened, drew a deep breath, turned on her heel and walked out to the *corredor* or veranda where she stood gazing across the river and the lush bottomlands to the blue mountains on the north.

The new master of the house, uneasy, approached the girl and with Mexican suavity sought to explain the terms of the will. Struggling for self-control Petranilla turned her burning gaze upon him and gave tongue to wrath. "Señor, at the expense of the Feliz family you have become a rich man. Now you turn us from the house, the house that has sheltered me from the day I was born. The judge has approved my uncle's will, you say. *I* say my uncle's wishes have been ignored and that a corrupt judge has confirmed the infamy! Now all these scenes of my childhood, these springs, these brooks, these green meadows, these parks of lordly oaks—"

The man tried to interrupt her, to offer explanations, but the girl drew herself up and menacing him with a long, slim forefinger she seemed suddenly imbued with supernatural fervor as she denounced him and all his works in these words:

"Señor, do not dare to speak until I have finished! This is what I hurl upon your head: Your falsity shall be your ruin! The substance of the Feliz family shall be your curse! The lawyer that assisted you in your infamy, and the judge, shall fall beneath the same curse! The one shall die an untimely death, the other in blood and violence! You, señor, shall know misery in your age and though you die rich your substance shall go to vile persons! A blight shall fall upon the face of this terrestrial paradise, the cattle shall no longer fatten but sicken on its pastures, the fields shall not longer respond to the toil of the tiller, the grand oaks shall wither and die! The wrath of heaven and the vengeance of hell shall fall upon this place and the floods—!"

Here the inspired Petranilla swung round and stepped to the end of the veranda until she could see the sun sinking in the west beyond the Tejungas.

"See!" she cried with a far-flung gesture. "Behold! Cast your glance toward the dark entrance of the great Cañon of the Tejunga, and what do you see? Ha! ha! a myriad demons floating in air like so many vultures! They ride the storm clouds, and ay! they are lashing the clouds as the vaqueros lash the cattle to bring them together! Now the air darkens, the thunder rolls, the lightning flashes, the rain falls—ha! ha! the rain falls in torrents! Do you hear the roar of the descending flood? Bowlders grind and crash, the demons ride the crest of the storm, they lash it into fury, it is coming—coming—coming! Ay, see! It has struck our willow dale, my old playground—it crumbles away into the great seething torrent! Now the royal oak is gone! See what the lightning flashes reveal at the base of the mountains—they reveal the oaks withering in the tongues of flame—their bright green leaves are scorched to cinders—because they were above the reach of the waters it is the fire from the clouds that has destroyed them. Woe, woe, woe to you and yours, señor! The meadows are gone, only the hills remain, the mere bones of the rancho, and no man shall ever enjoy peace or profit from what is left of this once beautiful spot! Misfortune, crime and death shall follow those who covet these remains!"

The frail maiden had reached a high degree of emotion, her cheek was flushed, her eyes seemed to emit flames, her arms were outstretched as though to welcome the storm king. Suddenly in a piercing, agonized tone she cried out, "Woe,

woe, woe unto the Despoilers!" and fell prone upon the tiled floor of the cloister-like veranda.

The man and the girl's aunt bore the limp little body into the house and laid it on a couch.

"Ay, woe, woe in very truth, for she is lifeless!" sobbed Soledad Feliz.

"She is merely distracted," declared the man. "She got too excited over what couldn't be helped. Bah, the girl is loca, call a priest."

The priest arrived, the maiden partially revived and the good padre told her in soothing tones that she had suffered a delusion, that the devil was tempting her to evil thoughts, that the sun had set in glorious serenity and there was no sign of storm.

Here Petranilla raised herself on her elbows and stared out at the towering Tejungas, her face a mirror once more of all the cataclysm she sought to evoke from their dark cañons.

"Fools, I can see what you cannot see," she said in a low, firm voice and fell back on the couch. "Father, give me absolution for I am dying," she gasped. The padre bent over her, chanting as her young spirit winged its flight to a paradise safe above the storms.

For reasons best known to himself Don Antonio Coronel conveyed the entire property to his lawyer. Finally, after the rights to a group of springs had been passed to the Los Angeles City Water Company for a consideration of eight thousand dollars, the ranch was sold to a rich and elegant American family.

Leon Baldwin was the purchaser. He improved the ranch regardless of expense, stocked it with imported breeds of cattle, established a model dairy, fenced and cross-fenced the hitherto open land, remodeled the old Feliz house until it was the perfection of elegant comfort. A new mansion was erected on a hill for the home of a brother, Gen. John M. Baldwin.

The Baldwin family settled down to enjoy rural pleasure and profit on a grand scale.

But everything went wrong. The cattle sickened and died in the fields. The dairy business was a disastrous failure. Fire destroyed the ripening grain and a myriad grasshoppers devoured the green crops. The vineyard was stricken with a strange blight and perished. Baldwin was forced to put a mortgage on the property, and finally the ranch went for the mortgage. In a few years the family had moved away from the accursed place.

Then the Prince of Wales succeeded to the property. Not really the Prince of Wales, though at the time many of our credulous citizenry actually believed this personage to be 'Is Royal 'Ighness. He was really a Welch nobleman by the name of Col. Griffith J. Griffith,* with lots of money. And the princely air he had! The majestic mien! When this grand personage was seen on our streets with his long coat buttoned from top to bottom, head erect and eyes disdaining to look upon the earth, the humble Angeleños could hardly be blamed for mistaking him for royalty. Shoulders thrown back, abdomen thrust more than correspondingly forward, knob-headed cane carried under the right arm and an immense chrysanthemum or dahlia in his buttonhole—a conqueror surely, we thought—a Highness in our midst incognito.

This Welch prince, or whatever he thought himself to be, bought the Feliz rancho. Soon bad luck overtook him. In March, 1884, great storm clouds gathered in the dark re-

* For years a prominent figure in Los Angeles. His death occurred July 6, 1919.

cesses of the Grand Tejunga. They crashed together and in one mighty, angry, roaring advance swept down on Rancho Feliz. The waters raged and seethed, the thunders caused the earth to quake and the mountains to rattle in their sockets like teeth in an ancient skull. The electrical display was unprecedented in the country. Thunderbolts struck trees and blazingly exhausted their fury in the water-soaked earth. Great sheets of lightning scorched and seared the oaks. On this one night the famed Potrero de los Feliz, the vast meadow and pastures, suffered wreck and desolation, the best part swept away to the sea and the remains left like a disfigured corpse on a battlefield.

Weird stories were told by the Mexican retainers on the ranch of what they saw the night of the great *crescenta*. One old man declared that the ghost of Antonio Feliz, followed by hosts of demons, was plainly seen riding the waves, lashing them to fury and directing the torrents against the dissolving margins of the land. The ghost reappeared, the old man testified, and he was borne out by the testimony of others, after the water had subsided and danced *El Jarabe* over the ruin that had been wrought. The natives fled the place, and it was claimed that Baron Griffith escaped to town at midnight the night of the storm and never again reappeared on the property except for brief intervals in bright midday.

Woodchoppers were hired from town to convert the blasted oaks into revenue for the unlucky ranch owner, but after one night on the place they would always desert, bringing back with them this one unvarying tale: "Those lands are haunted. A spirit declaring itself to be Antonio Feliz stalks up and down the river and sometimes stands on a projecting crag of the hills denouncing with wild gesticulations all before and behind him, to right and to left of him.

Among the trees angry demons make the marrow quiver in one's bones."

Finally the Baron induced some newcomer to rent a corner of the ranch where least damage had been wrought, for the establishment of an ostrich farm. All was well with the birds during the daytime, but reports from out there were that when night fell there was the devil to pay. Stricken with inexplicable panic the ostriches would break their folds and stampede wildly, and the keepers, becoming superstitious, left their jobs.

The Baron was in a terrible quandary. I can imagine the decision for the eventual disposition of the accursed land being arrived at something after this fashion in a consultation between the owner and his business secretary:

"What, oh, what can I do with the terrible property?" groans the Baron.

"You can't sell it," muses the secretary.

"No."

"You won't live on it."

"I wouldn't spend a night on it for a million."

"You have to pay taxes on it right along."

"Horrors, yes, taxes—taxes."

"I'll tell you what I would do," announces the secretary, coming to life. "I'd give the bedeviled place away."

"Who in hell would take it—a place that is all taxes, no income and stocked with demons?"

"Donate it to the City of Los Angeles!" cries the secretary, an inspired look in his eyes. "Give it to the city as a park and the municipal council will rise up and call you blessed. With resolutions and what-not they will immortalize you! You can never be President of these United States but you might be ambassador to the Court of St.

James. Give the infernal place to the city and you are made!"

The Baron grasps his secretary's hand and cries: "Old fellow, you are indeed a bird of happy omen! Prepare the deed at once, present it to the City of Los Angeles on a silver platter with a gold embossed announcement to each councilman personally. Ambassador to the Court of St. James! Oh, you have raised me from the slough of despond to the pinnacle of happy anticipation!"

The deed was tendered, the offer was welcomed and the council appointed a time to accompany the Baron and his secretary to the ranch, the owner to deliver and the councilmen to accept *seizin of the fee,* as they used to do in Wales. There was a great ceremony in the giving and receiving of that three thousand acres of mountainside, all that was left by the flood of the original eight thousand. Refreshments were served at the old ranch house, which had been long deserted but which the "bird of good omen" had attended to putting into order and stocking with goodies for this glad day.

The dignitaries tarried over the liquids and perhaps dallied with the solids until lo! the night crept upon them unawares. The Baron and his "bird" had crept away in the early gloaming, 'tis said, but the rest lingered on, heedless not only of the arrival of night but of the approach of that hour of night when ghosts do walk abroad.

With the actual striking of that hour there was the devil to pay and, according to reliable reports, the whole scene may be re-created by the brief statement that the stampede of the ostriches was tame in comparison to the stampede of the city fathers. When they reached home in the dawning they were already men turned old and gray.

What had wrought this terrible change in these debonair fellows overnight?

In time some of them told, and what they told tradition has retained as follows:

At midnight there appeared among the celebrants in the Feliz *sala* a gaunt, sepulchral figure with fleshless face. The eye-sockets emitted sulphurous flashes; over the left arm trailed a portion of the rotting funeral vestment; the right hand was raised as if to command silence. Thus the skeleton figure shuffled with bony sound over the concrete floor. Then the ghost seated himself—it was distinctly a male ghost, or more properly, perhaps, the ghost of a former male —in the very chair which Baron Griffith had occupied at the inception of the festivities, at the head of the noble oaken table, and in the traditional voice of the tomb announced:

"Señores, I am Antonio Feliz, come to invite you to dine with me in hell. In your great honor I have brought an escort of sub-demons."

An awful din at once broke loose—lights went out, gongs and cymbals clashed and with demoniac screechings the demons came dancing into the hall.

At this moment a wild rush was made for the exits by the guests from the city, so there is no available record of the further pranks that night in the ancient halls of Feliz.

From the time of the curse pronounced by Antonio Feliz's niece bad luck came to the Coronel family in general, though it strangely seemed to spare Antonio Coronel himself. Disastrous litigation fell on some and death came in a violent manner to others. There were family quarrels and lawsuits. Those who did not die became impoverished. By various means—wills, deeds and agreements—all of the wealth of the various sections of this rich family became vested in Don Antonio Coronel.

How strange that he alone should prosper when the rest of the family should suffer and die.

However the mills of the gods grind slowly but they grind exceeding small.

About the time of Antonio Feliz's death Antonio Coronel had taken unto himself a young American girl as wife, though he was then far beyond the meridian of life. At the age of eighty he died childless, bequeathing nothing to his only brother, who was poverty-stricken, nothing to his daughter by a former marriage nor to a nephew whose inheritance he had earlier absorbed, and so leaving his American widow very rich in money, lands and a sumptuous home.

The widow not long afterward married a young adventurer. Attempting to obtain possession of the concentrated wealth of the Coronels the husband got into difficulties with his wife. They separated and began to fight each other in the courts with the result that the fortune became the spoil of contending lawyers that came swarming to the legal feast.

What were the words of little Doña Petranilla that day on the veranda of the Feliz manor? *"And you, señor, though you die rich, your substance shall go to vile persons!"*

The reader may draw his own conclusions, make what he will, out of this chain of circumstances; but all will doubtless agree that it's a hard reflection on lawyers!

In concluding this narrative I must add that the lawyer chum of Coronel's who deeded over the water rights to the Feliz springs to the City of Los Angeles celebrated so violently after receiving his portion of the $8,000 that a citizen whom he assaulted shot him dead in self-defense. The judge that probated the Feliz will came to an untimely end and is forgotten except for his licentious judicial ways.

Leon Baldwin, the first American owner of the property, was eventually murdered by Mexican bandits.

THE FELIZ CURSE

(NOTE: At the end of this chapter in his manuscript Major Bell added this observation in longhand: "All of the above narrative was written years ago at the time Baron Griffith gave the three thousand acre rock pile, all that was

dents, it can be truthfully said that disaster, disgrace, grief and shame came to all who in any manner had to do with El Rancho de los Feliz, and the post mortem will.

The lawyer who sold the springs for $8,000, felt so grand that he immediately went on a war path, assaulted a citizen and was shot dead in self defense.

The judge that probated the will came to an untimely end, and is for‑ gotten except for his licentious life and evil judicial ways, and FINIS.

Reproduction of a page from Major Bell's manuscript, with notes in his handwriting

left of the Feliz paradise, to the city to be cultivated into a park.

"In this year 1903 a sequel ensued which conclusively shows that the curse of Los Feliz is still vindictively in pursuit of all that have profited by the 'ruin of Los Feliz.'

"It makes another story."

The author undoubtedly refers to the marital tragedy at the Arcadia Hotel, Santa Monica, involving Colonel and

Mrs. Griffith. A singular chain of events certainly, upon which hangs the tradition of the Feliz Curse. It is rendered still more weird by the fact that the translation of *feliz* is "happy." The public was reminded of old tales as recently as Christmas week, 1929, when a disastrous fire of sudden and undetermined origin swept a considerable part of Griffith Park bare, took one human life, threatened to destroy some of the palatial mansions of East Hollywood and necessitated rapid work on the part of the municipality to avert possible flooding of portions of the city during the expected winter rains on account of the thus suddenly denuded watersheds.—Editor.)

José Sepúlveda

CHAPTER 10

Tragic Fate of Mexican Joe

On returning from the war the first friend I met was Uncle Bill Rubottom. We drove into Spadra at nightfall and found Bill, his son Jim and his ten-year-old grandson in an improvised camp hard at work rearing the first permanent home in this settlement. The place is situated two or more miles from Pomona, toward Los Angeles, on the Southern Pacific Railroad. There was then, of course, no railroad. Uncle Bill founded Spadra, naming it for his old home on the Arkansas River. It is a Cherokee word signifying a bluff or bank, and a well-known bluff on the Arkansas bears the same name.

Uncle Bill was delighted to see me. I was nineteen years old when I first met him; now I was thirty-five, but Uncle Bill treated me as if I were still a boy. With a warm embrace he said, "God bless you, my boy, what a lot we're going to have to talk about." After supper, when the rest of the camp was in dreamland, we drank strong coffee and talked for hours—or rather he talked and I listened.

He got started on the subject of the Juan Flores uprising in '58, the murder of Sheriff Barton and posse and the blood and slaughter that followed. I had occasion to interrupt him with an inquiry concerning his former protégé, Mexican Joe. Uncle Bill lapsed into silence and his jaw set. Then he shoved back his stool and paced the room, after which he sat down again, folded his arms on the table and buried his face in them. He actually sobbed. I looked at him in astonishment. Soon a tempest of anger swept him; he jumped up again and began to curse terribly. This seemed to quiet him, for he drank some more coffee and spoke as follows:

"It is eight years now since brave, honest Joe left me and I have tried in vain to forget the wicked, hellish manner of his taking off.

"It has been estimated that one hundred and fifty-eight persons were killed to avenge the death of Sheriff Barton and his posse, and not one of his murderers was of this number. No, not one! They escaped and innocent men were slaughtered. It makes my blood run cold to think of it.

"During all this Barton excitement I remained quietly at home. I then lived at El Monte. I had cribs full of corn and hearing that Don Benito Wilson [1] wanted to purchase corn I sent Joe to his place, about seven miles over, near San Gabriél.

"Joe should have returned by noon, but as the sun went down he was still absent. About dark a fellow rode past our house and called out that they had killed one of Barton's murderers over at the Mission. 'Yes,' said he, 'there's no mistake about it for he had Barton's saddle, bridle and spurs.'

"My wife observed: 'Is it possible, William, that they could have killed Joe?' I rejected the idea and yet uneasiness seized me. In a few minutes I was mounted and riding the Mission road. Arriving at San Gabriél I found quite a crowd around the Mission doggery. A blear-eyed gambler, Bill Bayley by name, came over to me and said, 'Well, we got him!'

"'Got who?' I demanded.

"'One of them greasers that killed Barton and the boys.'

" 'Where is he?'

"The scoundrel showed me to a dirty dark room in a tumble-down adobe, lighted a candle and exhibited a headless, bloody corpse on the floor. So horribly was the body mutilated with knives that it was unrecognizable, nor could identity be established by clothes for most of them were gone.

" 'Where's the head?' I demanded.

" 'Oh, it's gone to Los Angeles. Doctor Osborne, Barton's friend, did all the cutting—kept on cutting till Bill Jenkins made him quit.'

" 'Where are this man's saddle, bridle and spurs?' I asked. These things were hunted up and shown to me. They were his own, the same that Joe had left my house with in the morning. They'd never been Barton's, though they may have resembled his a little. For a moment I felt paralyzed, the world seemed to have slid from under my feet, I gasped for breath. There was a great roaring in my head. The next thing I knew I was in the bar-room draining a pitcher of water, for my emotions seemed to be burning me up. My impulse was to turn on the roomful, find out who had participated in this murder and shoot them down like dogs. But fortunately I was unarmed. I had left home so hurriedly, so upset by my fears for Joe that I had forgotten both my revolver and knife. I've thanked God ever since that this was so because I've always been a law-abiding man.

"How I got home I don't know but I woke up in bed the next morning with a raging fever. Some friends of mine got together, found the doctor who was accused of cutting Joe's head off, recovered the head and the body and gave our friend Mexican Joe a Christian burial."

"What became of this doctor?" I asked.

"The hand of retribution hit him hard," replied Uncle

Bill. "His body died some years ago, but his head still lives. He is paralyzed from his neck to his toes."

Uncle Bill abruptly changed the subject. "You will be disappointed in this glorious country. It's not what it was. The Californians have all gone broke and the Shylocks have everything tied up. We are overrun by a horde of low-down blacklegs, squawmen and such cattle. They feast off the country but do no work. They vote taxes upon us, yet pay none themselves, for the big bugs among them fill the offices. Taxes and interest are eating the country up."

Here my informant switched to the subject of the renowned Register of the U. S. Land Office in Los Angeles, whose personal encounters have been referred to in a previous chapter. It will be remembered that I there inferred that it was none other than Uncle Bill Rubottom who had finally put a quietus on the giant.

"You know the Register married one of my daughters," resumed Uncle Bill. "He was a good man in some respects, but an over-bearing bully. Unlike most bullies, though, he was brave. He was the bravest man I ever faced and he came within an ace of getting me. He wasn't so bad but he didn't know how to treat a woman. My daughter was high-spirited and she left him and claimed my protection for herself and child. The day after she left him the Register sent word to my house that I might keep the wife but that on the morrow he was coming to get the boy. He warned me that he would arrive at a certain hour, fully armed.

"At the appointed time I was sitting on my front porch with a double-barreled shotgun across my knees. The Register arrived promptly, hitched his horse to the fence and started for the gate about twenty feet from where I sat. 'Enter that gate at the peril of your life,' I called out. He didn't hesitate one instant but walked right in, revolver in hand. I hated to shoot him. I begged him to stop, but on he came. At the foot of the steps he raised his revolver and fired. Instantly I had dropped on one knee and the bullet just missed the top of my head, lodging in the side of the house. The next moment the Register was dead in his tracks and that was the end of that marriage."

"That was my daddy, wasn't it?" asked a small voice, and the head of a blue-eyed boy peered from one of the bunks in the room in which we were talking.

"I thought you were sound asleep or I wouldn't have talked about it, boy," replied Uncle Bill, regretfully, going over and caressing the child. "But, remember, boy, I'm your father now." The youngster cuddled down to sleep again contentedly and the man returned to his seat shaking his head and passing his rough hand over his hairy face as if to wipe off the evidences of emotion that showed there.

"Yes, I killed the boy's father," he mused, "but I'm going to be more to him than his father ever could have been. I'm going to give the best of my life to him."

There was silence for a while, then Uncle Bill, realizing that I was consulting my watch, shook himself together and sought to entertain me longer. "By the way," he said, right cheerfully, "there's been a lot of killing here while you were away. A rich ranchero at Cucamonga was killed last year and his wife was accused of complicity in the murder. Excitement ran high and blood flowed among the various factions.

"I was keeping a roadside tavern over there then. The suspected wife was still living in the Cucamonga home and there were a good many threats made against her so that the air was buzzing with things that might happen any time. One afternoon Eli Smith dropped into my place; in a little while George Dyches came in, then another and another, all of whom I recognized as personal friends of the dead ranchero. About a dozen of them all armed to the teeth. They ordered supper. I listened around until I gathered that they had assembled for the purpose of hanging the suspected widow.

"I made up my mind that it wouldn't happen. I'd seen enough of lynching in my time, and when it came to stringing up a woman without a trial, I wouldn't stand it in my neighborhood. So I set to planning. Lige and Jim were at the tavern with me. I told Lige what was up and for him and Jim to arm and conceal themselves in a room adjoining the dining room and await orders.

"I served the men at the long supper table myself, then when they all had their heads well down into their plates I returned, stood at the head of the table and said: 'Now, gentlemen, don't make a move or I'll shoot.' They all looked up with their mouths full of food and saw me standing there with a double-barreled shotgun at ready. 'I know what you're here for,' I continued, 'and permit me to say that no man nor set of men can murder a woman while I'm around. Ho! Lige,' I called, 'come on in.' Lige entered and stood at the foot of the table with his shotgun at ready. Then I called Jim in and ordered him to go round and disarm each rascal. Those fellows were too astonished and ashamed to offer any resistance. The victory was ours and we sent 'em away without their guns.

"Afterward I sent out word that they could call at my place, one at a time, and get their weapons back. They did and none of 'em held it against me, I guess. After thinking it over they were glad they'd had their minds changed."

I was looking at my watch again.

"What time is it?" asked Uncle Bill, disappointedly.

"Half-past-two," I answered.

"Let's have another cup of coffee and I'll tell you how I got this land here from Chino Phillips. You know he was a Jew shopkeeper in Los Angeles who went broke—hard to believe, isn't it, that a Jew trader let the *mañana* habit get the better of him and went completely Mexican? Dressed like a Mexican, rode like a Mexican, smoked like a Mexican, assumed a Mexican name, rode with them, danced with them, slept with them—"

"But, Uncle Bill, how about a little rest?" I interposed, and my host reluctantly let me go to bed while he refilled his coffee cup and mused over it alone.

Tomás Sánchez

CHAPTER 11

That Grand Californian, the Grizzly Bear

THE grizzly bear is a lordly animal. An ordinary-sized one will weigh from nine hundred to twelve hundred pounds, a large one a ton. The grizzly is the king of beasts. When, a few years ago, a Los Angeles County grizzly was sent to Monterrey, Mexico, to be pitted against the man-killing African lion "Parnell" the great Californian handled the African king as a cat would a rat. He killed him so quickly that the big audience hardly knew how it was done.

These grizzlies stand on their hind legs and spar, fence, parry and strike like a skilled fencing master or prizefighter. This reminds me of Ramón Carrillo, who overtook a huge grizzly in the Encino Valley, challenged him and fought him single-handed with a light sword.

This Ramón was a desperado, a man who fought for the love of it and who was never defeated until finally riddled with American buckshot. General Covarrúbias with a party which included Ramón Carrillo [1] was journeying from Santa Bárbara to Los Angeles when they sighted the bear, out on the San Fernando plain. They surrounded the Old Man of the Mountains, who promptly stood up like a man and offered defiance.

"Stand back, please, señores," requested Carrillo, dismounting and drawing his sword. "Allow me to fight a personal duel with this grand old gladiator."

"The boy is crazy," the rest muttered, but nevertheless they formed a wide circle and leaned forward breathlessly in their saddles to watch the contest. Their mounts reared and snorted but with consummate horsemanship the Californians maintained the circle.

Ramón advanced like a dancing master flourishing a rapier-like blade which he always carried. Bruin stood on the defensive, staring with angry astonishment. Deftly and with a smile and a banter always on his lips the young Californian, with all the skill and grace of a trained bullfighter, danced around the grizzled giant and got in his stinging, maddening thrusts here and there. The grizzly rushed him time and again with terrific roars, but the man waited only long enough to sting the huge menacing paws with the rapier point and then sidestepped to safety.

The excitement of the picturesque mounted audience grew almost beyond control, and the "vivas!" first for the caballero and then for the bear, drove the animal duelist almost frantic. With utmost coolness and always laughing Ramón Carrillo fenced with that grizzly for one hour. When all concerned seemed to be tiring of the sport he stepped in and with a quick thrust to the heart laid the splendid brute low.

No doubt it will surprise the reader to be informed that the burro, the ordinary Mexican donkey, can give the grizzly a good fight. I know of several fiestas where burros were put into a ring with a bear and fought to the death. If the bear was a real grizzly he always won, so far as I know, but the burro would worry him desperately for a long time. The bear would suffer terrific jolts on the jaw from the burro's heels, that would send him staggering back time and again. When the grizzly would finally get hold of his lowly but far from humble antagonist the burro would bite and hang on to the death like a bulldog. I must add that I always considered a match like this unfair, brutal and barbarous.

In the great fiestas of times past at the Missions and Presidios there was always a bull and bear fight for the entertainment of the crowd. The last one on record that I know of took place at Pala, a branch or *asistencia* of the once great Mission San Luís Rey, in the mountains of San Diego County, nearly fifty years ago. One of the American newspapers in California published an account of it written by a correspondent who was present. I have the clipping of that and as it is a better-written description than I could produce myself, I give it herewith:

The bear was an ugly grizzly that for years had roamed the pine-clad region of Palomar Mountain, rising six thousand feet above the little Mission. Tied to a huge post in the center of the old adobe-walled quadrangle he stood almost as high as a horse, a picture of fury such as painter never conceived. His hind feet were tethered with several turns of a strong rawhide reata, but were left about a yard apart to give full play. To the center of this rawhide, between the two feet, was fastened another heavy reata, doubled and secured to a big loop made of doubled reatas thrown over the center post. The services of a man on horseback with a long pole were constantly needed to keep the raging monster from chewing through the rawhide ropes.

By the time the bear had stormed around long enough to get well limbered up after being tied all night the signal was given, the horseman effected his disappearance and in dashed a bull through an open gate. He was of the old long-horn breed but of great weight and power. He had been roaming the hills all summer, living like a deer in the chaparral of the rough mountains and was as quick and wild as any deer. He, too, like old bruin, had been captured with the noosed lazo in a sudden dash of horsemen on a little flat he had to cross to go to a spring at daylight and felt no more in love with mankind than did the bear. As he dashed across the arena it looked as if the fight was going to be an unequal one, but the bear gave a glance that intimated that no one need waste sympathy on *him*.

No creature is so ready for immediate business as is the bull turned loose in an amphitheater of human faces. He seems to know they are there to see him fight and he wants them to get their money's worth. So, as soon as the gate admits him, he goes for everything in sight with the dash of a cyclone. Things that outside he would fly from or not notice he darts at as eagerly as a terrier for a rat the instant he sees them in the ring.

This bull came from the same mountains as the bear and they were old acquaintances, though the acquaintance had been cultivated on the run as the bull tore with thundering hoofs through the tough manzanita or went plunging down the steep hillside as the evening breeze wafted the strong scent of the bear to his keen nose. But now, in the arena, he spent no time looking for a way of escape but at a pace that seemed impossible for even the great weight of the bear to resist he rushed across the ring directly at the enemy as if he had been looking for him all his life.

With wonderful quickness for so large an animal the bear rose on his hind legs and coolly waited until the long sharp horns were within a yard of his breast. Then up went the great paws, one on each side of the bull's head, and the sharp points of the horns whirled up from horizontal to perpendicular, then almost to horizontal again as bull and bear went rolling over together. In a twinkling the bear was on his feet again, but the bull lay limp as a rag, his neck broken.

In rode four horsemen and threw reatas around the feet of the dead bull, while the grizzly did his ferocious best to get at them. As they dragged the body of the vanquished victim out one gate, the runway to the bullpen was opened once more and a second bull, a big black one with tail up as if to switch the moon, charged into the arena. On his head glistened horns so long and sharp that it seemed impossible for the bear ever to reach the head with his death-dealing paws before being impaled.

But this problem did not seem to worry the grizzly. He had not been living on cattle for so many years without knowing a lot about their movements. When this new antagonist came at him he dodged as easily as a trained human bullfighter, and as the bull shot past him down came one big paw on the bovine's neck with a whack that sounded all over the adobe corral. A chorus of shouts went up from the rows of swarthy faces, with here and there a white face, as the victim, turning partly over, went down with a plunge that made one of his horns plow up the dirt, then break sharp off under the terrific pressure of his weight and momentum.

The bull was not done for; he tried to rise and bruin made a dash for him, but his tethers held him short of his goal. In a second the bull got to his feet and wheeled around with one of those short twists that makes him so dangerous an antagonist. But once he is wheeled around his course is generally straight ahead and a quick dodger can avoid him; however, he is lightning-like in his charge and something or somebody is likely to be overhauled in short order. So it was this time and before the bear could recover from the confusion into which he had been thrown by being brought up short by his tether, the bull caught him on the shoulder with his remaining horn.

Few things in nature are tougher than the shoulder of a grizzly bear and a mere side swing without the full weight of a running bull behind it was insufficient to make even this sharp horn penetrate. The bear staggered, but the horn glanced from the ponderous bone, leaving a long gash in the shaggy hide. This only angered bruin the more. He made a grab for the head of the bull but again was frustrated by the reatas which allowed him only a limited scope of action.

The bull returned to the charge as soon as he could turn himself around and aimed the long horn full at his enemy's breast. But just as the horn seemed reaching its mark the grizzly grabbed the bull's head with both paws and twisted it half round, with the nose inward. The nose he seized in his great white teeth and over both went in a swirl of dust while the crowd roared and cheered.

Now one could see exactly why cattle found killed by bears always have their necks broken. Bears do not go through the slow process of strangling or bleeding their victims, but do business on scientific principles.

This time the grizzly rose more slowly than before, nevertheless he rose, while the bull lay still in death.

The owners of the bear now wanted to stop the show but from all sides rose a roar of *"Otro! Otro! Otro! Otro toro!"* "Another! Another! Another! Another bull!"

The owners protested that the bear was disabled and was too valuable to sacrifice needlessly; that a dead bull was worth as much as a live one, and more, but that the same arithmetic did not hold good for a bear. The clamor of the crowd grew minute by minute, for the sight of blood gushing from the bear's shoulder was too much for the equilibrium of an audience like this one.

Soon another bull shot toward the center of the arena. Larger than the rest but thinner, more rangy, he opened negotiations with even more vigor, more speed. With thundering thump of great hoofs, his head wagging from side to side, eyes flashing green fire, he drove full at the bear with all his force. The grizzly was a trifle clumsy this time and as he rose to his hind feet the bull gave a twist of his head that upset the calculations of the bear. Right into the base of the latter's neck went a long sharp horn, at the same time that the two powerful paws closed down on the bull's neck from above. A distinct crack was heard. The bull sank forward carrying the bear over backward with a heavy thump against the big post to which he was tied.

Again the horsemen rode in to drag out a dead bull. But the grizzly now looked weary and pained. Another powwow with his owners ensued while the crowd yelled more loudly than ever for another bull. The owners protested that it was unfair, but the racket rose louder and louder for the audience knew that there was one bull left, the biggest and wildest of the lot.

The crowd won, but bruin was given a little more room in which to fight. Vaqueros rode in and while two lassoed his forepaws and spread him out in front, the other two loosened his ropes behind so as to give him more play. He now had about half the length of a reata. Allowing him a breathing spell, which he spent trying to bite off the reatas, the gate of the bullpen was again thrown open.

Out dashed an old Red Rover of the hills and the way he went for the bear seemed to prove him another old acquaintance. He seemed anxious to make up for the many times he had flown from the distant scent that had warned him that the bear was in the same mountains. With lowered head turned to one side so as to aim one horn at the enemy's breast he cleared the distance in half a dozen leaps.

The bear was still slower than before in getting to his hind feet and his right paw slipped as he grabbed the bull's head. He failed to twist it over. The horn struck him near the base of the neck and bull and bear went rolling over together.

Loud cheers for the bull rose as the bear, scrambling to his feet, showed blood coming from a hole in his neck almost beside the first wound. Still louder roared the applause as the bull regained his feet. Lashing his sides with his tail and bounding high in fury he wheeled and returned to the fray. The bear rolled himself over like a ball and would have been on his feet again safely had not one foot caught in the reata which tied him to the post. Unable to meet the bull's charge with both hind feet solid on the ground he fell forward against his antagonist and received one horn full in the breast, up to the hilt.

But a great grizzly keeps on fighting even after a thrust to the heart. Again he struggled to his feet, the blood gushing from the new wound. With stunning quickness in so large an animal the bull had withdrawn his horn, gathered himself together and returned to the charge. The bear could not turn in time to meet him and with a heavy smash the horn struck him squarely in the shoulder forward of the protecting bone. Those who have seen the longest horns driven full to the hilt through the shoulder of a horse—a common sight in the bullfights of Mexico—can understand why the bear rolled over backward to rise no more.

CHAPTER 12

The Last Words of Ramón Carrillo

It was a memory of Ramón Carrillo that started this bear chat, I believe. Ramón was a dashing Hotspur, a member of that famous Carrillo family that had its stronghold in Santa Bárbara. It is hardly necessary to say that he was a handsome fellow because all of the Carrillos are of that type.

In 1865, in Los Angeles County, Ramón got into trouble that landed him in a bloody grave. He was accused of the murder of John Rains, whose wife was the owner of the Cucamonga Rancho.[1] John was foully murdered on his way to Los Angeles, lassoed, dragged from his horse and killed without having the chance to defend himself, apparently. The suspicion of Rain's friends settled on the dashing young Carrillo. There was never sufficient proof brought forward to warrant his arrest, yet the Rains faction settled into an abiding conviction that he was the murderer.

Uncle Bill told me the manner of Ramón's end. Said he:

"I was keeping the station at Cucamonga and Ramón was a guest at the ranch house. He was paying court to a fair lady in the vicinity and she used to drive out with him in the cool of the evening.

"One day there came to my station a man with a double-barreled shotgun, revolver and knife. He said he had made an engagement to wait here for a party that was coming through from the upper country and go on into Arizona with them. I took him in and he seemed to be killing time around the place, going out rabbit hunting a great deal as a pastime.

"Ramón had been called away from his courting for a spell but there came an afternoon when he returned and drove out with his lady love past the station as usual. I noticed that a few minutes after they passed my guest picked up his shotgun, buckled on his revolver and knife and said, 'Well, Uncle Bill, guess I'll go out and get a few more rabbits.' I remarked to myself that this was the first time he had ever buckled on revolver and knife since he had arrived.

"In about an hour I heard two shots. A few minutes later the team hitched to the buggy came tearing down the road with Ramón's lady managing the reins. I ran out and helped her to stop the horses. Ramón lay in the bottom of the buggy, all bloody and frothing at the mouth. I'll tell you that little lady was as cool as a cucumber, she was game, and insisted that we carry him to her house. I proposed sending to San Bernardino for a doctor, but Ramón, overhearing me, shook himself together and in his commanding way forbade it, saying, 'No, don't bother. I am done for.' I then proposed to send for a priest. There came over his face a smile of scorn; it was that way he faced the approach of death, with bitter gayety. Game—he was game! 'No priest for me, I want to go to Hell!' he said. 'I've fought everything I've met on this earth and was never vanquished in a fair fight. I never did a cowardly act nor fought a man except face to face, but for all this I am murdered from behind! I know why; it is because they accuse me of killing John Rains. I am as innocent of that as you are. If I had been the enemy of John Rains I would have challenged him face to face.'

"Ramón Carrillo was dying," concluded Uncle Bill, "and I believed every word he said. He was innocent, for a man who could talk like that in the presence of death could not be lying. Later he roused himself again and said: 'I'm going to die and I'm going to Hell. There I'm going to meet the Devil and fight him, and may the best man win!' These were the last words of Ramón Carrillo."

A great family were these Carrillos. Some of them were mighty men and the women were all beautiful to look upon. The most noted of the men was General José Antonio.[2] He commanded the Californians at the battle of Los Cuerbos, commonly called the Battle of Domínguez, when the American marines under Captain Mervine of the frigate *Savannah* were marching on Los Angeles from San Pedro during the Mexican War. It occurred near where Compton now stands. He had previously represented California in the Mexican Congress. A remarkable fellow he was, standing six feet four inches tall, weighing about two hundred and forty pounds and bearing a perfect resemblance to the statues of some of the old Roman senators.

General Carrillo was full of humor and boiling over with sarcasm. He came very near getting into a duel with a captain in the Mormon Battalion in Los Angeles in 1847. Doña Luisa Ávila was married to a Mexican officer, Lieut. Col. Manuel Gárfias, who was a nephew of Porfírio Díaz, later ruler of Mexico for so many years. Gárfias had been a member of the famous Micheltorena Battalion which had been expelled by the revolting Californians. He had resigned his commission in the army and returned to Los Angeles to marry the daughter of Doña Concepción de Avila. Doña Concepción was owner of the San Pascual grant where Pasadena now stands and which later passed into the possession of Colonel Gárfias.

A great fiesta followed the nuptials and the party developed into an occasion of reconciliation between the American army officers and those of the late Californian army. The generals were all there and the captains and lieutenants. General Carrillo was there, grim and sarcastic. He was far from being reconciled. There was a certain Mormon captain there, too, who thought himself a great dancer. Carrillo stared with pointed disapproval at his awkward performances and finally remarked to some dignitary of the American faction: "That officer of yours dances like a bear."

The Mormon captain was informed of the remark and on the following day sent a challenge to General Carrillo to meet him in mortal combat. The Californian at once accepted the challenge and appointed his seconds and excitement ran high on both sides. General Kearny, the commander-in-chief of the American forces of occupation, decided there must be no bloodshed and offered his services as mediator.

In the course of these peace negotiations the whole crowd, principals and all, brought up at the hospitable home of Nathaniel Pryor. The Pryor house was famous for good cheer; it was a fine house backed up by a fine vineyard that supplied a fine cellar with fine wines. The vineyard was bounded on the east by Alameda Street and extended from Aliso Street south to Wolfskill's line.[3] The place had a high whitewashed adobe wall around it and was altogether quite grand.

Going into conference again here, in the midst of these congenial surroundings, General Kearny, aided by Major Emory,[4] brought such diplomacy to bear on General Carrillo as to persuade him that he owed an apology to the Mormon. But the friends of the Mormon stubbornly insisted that the apology must be in writing. To the pleased surprise of the sticklers for the written word Carrillo immediately agreed; whereupon it is to be presumed that the cheery stock in Nathaniel Pryor's famed cellar suffered further depletion.

General Carrillo's only stipulation was that he was to be given until the next day to write and deliver the apology, delivery to be made here at this same pleasant gathering place.

At the appointed time the principals, mediators, seconds and friends were present; indeed, the crowd was considerably larger than it had been the day before. The Americans were on tip-toe to see what sort of an apology a haughty Californian ex-general and high dignitary would make to an American volunteer captain.

After the wine had circulated a translator was selected to read aloud the apology, which was as follows:

> "I am a native of California; I love my country and stick up for it, the bear is my countryman so I love the bear. I now apologize to the bear for suggesting that the red-headed captain danced like a bear. The injury is to the bear, because the captain could not dance half so well.
> "JOSE ANTONIO CARRILLO."

The Mormon captain was more wroth than ever and insisted on a fight then and there. But the droll apology had struck everybody's funny-bone. Both factions turned on the aggrieved redhead with so much ridicule that he was laughed off the place and the crisis was averted for good and all.

There was another Carrillo—we will call him the Judge. The Judge was a highly educated gentleman, in fact he was educated in Boston. A hide drogher carried him from Santa Bárbara around the Horn to Boston to college when he was about twelve years old, and brought him home again some four years later. That was, of course, when California was a province of Mexico.

The home coming was somewhat startling. The young graduate presented himself at the parental mansion, a delightful old adobe in the town that was the seat of old Spanish aristocracy in California, dressed in high Boston style and feeling himself to be a very important Yankee-wise cosmopolitan. The Señora, his mother, was overjoyed to see her boy and after tears, laughter and caresses she sat him down in the *sala* to have a talk with him in dignified Castilian. But the boy seemed to have forgotten his mother tongue; his replies were couched in the Yankee idiom.

With amazement which grew to indignation the Señora de Carrillo rebuked her son, but he continued to show off his superior education. Whereupon the Señora stalked out of doors, armed herself with a length of rawhide rope, swept into the *sala* again like an avenging goddess and sailed into the embryo judge with such expletives as: "Thou canst no longer speak Spanish, hey? Well, *I'll* teach thee Spanish!" Rap! Whack! Slap!

"*Por Dios, mama—mamacita—por Dios, no, no!*" yelled the previously arrogant cosmopolite. Swish! Snap! continued the rawhide until the youth poured forth a torrent of Spanish, imploring and promising without the least trace of Boston accent. At that moment he reverted to his racial heritage and remained thenceforth quite typical, as some of the incidents of his distinguished career may suggest; although the fact that he had enjoyed a Boston education he stressed with great success in advancing himself under the American régime. He was a member of the first State Constitutional Convention that framed the Constitution of the State of California in 1849, became a state senator and a member of the judiciary.

The Judge's lordly appearance and superior education gave him prestige among all classes and he became almost everything that a leading citizen could become except a capitalist. This distinction seemed beyond his talents. He was always "broke." He sought to remedy this failing by laying claim to one hundred leagues of land in and surrounding Soledad Pass, Los Angeles County, at the time land titles were under examination by the United States Land Commission, but the government refused to recognize the validity of the Judge's claim and he continued to remain chronically in need of money.

Nevertheless, the leading people always esteemed it a pleasure, indeed an honor, to drink with this lordly and impressive representative of the high Spanish past. The Judge was never compelled to go thirsty; it was a privilege to stand treat to him, so he kept pretty well filled up all the time.

At one time the weight of debt became so crushing that this distinguished person sent for an American lawyer whom he believed to be more versed than himself in certain legal technicalities and asked him to put him through insolvency. The lawyer sat down with him and said:

"Now, Judge, whom do you owe and what are the amounts?"

The Judge pondered for a moment and replied: *"Es todo el mundo."* ("It is the whole world.")

Taken aback for a moment, the lawyer continued:

"Well, Judge, who owes you and how much?"

"Ninguno," replied the Judge. "Nobody, señor. It has always been entirely one-sided."

A building once projected into Main Street, beyond the usual property line, just north of the St. Elmo Hotel * in

* Still standing on west side of Main Street a little north of the Federal Building.

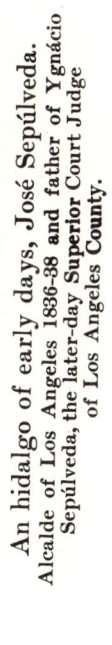

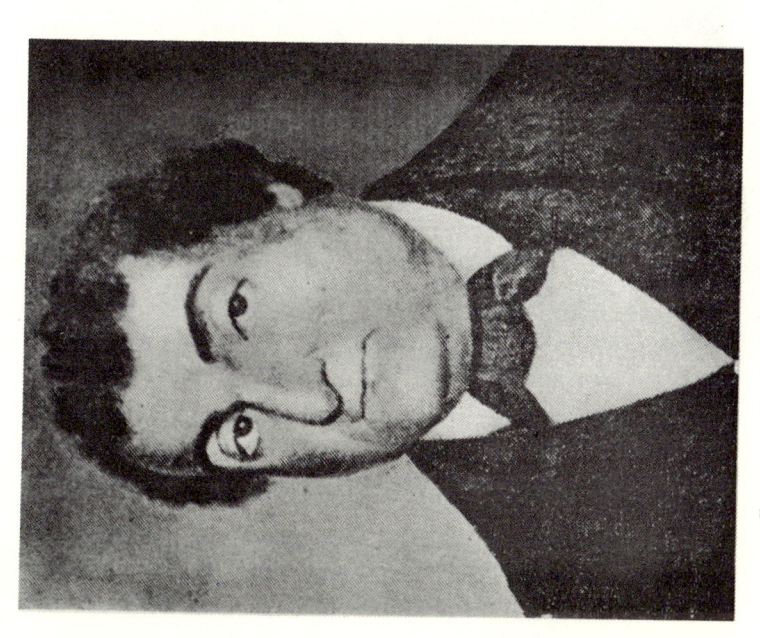

General José Antonio Carrillo.

An hidalgo of early days, José Sepúlveda. Alcalde of Los Angeles 1836-38 and father of Ygnácio Sepúlveda, the later-day **Superior Court Judge** of Los Angeles **County.**

Young native dandies of 1850.

Pictured just before leaving for Boston to enter college. Left to right Ygnácio Sepúlveda, Antonio Yorba, Andronico Sepúlveda. Ygnácio served for years as a Superior Court Judge of Los Angeles County. *From a daguerreotype.*

Los Angeles. A pair of stairs led up on the outside of this abutment to the second story. The head of the stairway rested on a platform built out from a doorway which admitted to Judge Carrillo's courtroom.

In those days the courtroom rent was paid by the judge himself from the fees and emoluments of office.

Our Judge got way behind in his rent and the landlord, growing tired of constantly climbing the stairway to dun the tenant, resolved upon a high pressure plan. Each time he called without getting results he removed a step from the stairway, beginning at the bottom, until the stairway was all but wrecked. Then the landlord laid low and awaited results. The situation was embarrassing to the tenant, for he had business of his own beside the court grind and clients found it increasingly difficult to reach him. However, it also discouraged visits from his creditors, so this state of affairs remained in *status quo* for some time, despite the strain on the Judge's dignity occasioned by the daily struggle to reach and to leave his place of business.

One day, on a professional call, I entered the courtroom after a difficult crawl up the great notched plank that had formed the outer support of the missing steps, a feat accomplished by reaching over and balancing myself against the wall of the building at critical moments.

Upon entering and regaining my breath I addressed the Court as follows: "Your Honor, what in the world is the matter with your stairway?"

The Judge answered in great indignation. "Why, it's those damn Mexicans up in Sonoratown! It's been a long time since we've had an election and those fellows have got to live somehow. So they're stealing my steps to cook their *frijoles.*"

Of course the Judge wasn't telling the truth, and the

reason was that he was planning. In furtherance of his plan he one day said to his constable: "Cachete, I want you to watch for that damn Frenchman and next time he approaches just let me know."

Sure enough not long thereafter the Frenchman who owned the building began to struggle up the notched plank, for he had become tired of laying siege without any visible results. The constable warned His Honor; His Honor took his seat on the judicial rostrum, lined up his constable and instructed his clerk to call the court to order. Several loafers in the courtroom, hoping for something to happen, sat up in anticipation. The landlord entered, rent bill in hand. He hesitated as he found himself intruding on the dignity of a court in session, but with Gallic determination, where money matters are concerned, sidled over to the bench and laid the bill in front of His Honor.

"What is this?" thundered the Judge.

"My bill for rent on this courtroom, that's what it is," replied the intruder doggedly, determined to press his point.

"An outrage!" announced the Judge. "Do you not know, sir, that this court is in session, and that your conduct, sir, is in contempt? Mr. Clerk, enter this order: The Court imposes a fine upon Mr. Parlezvous of fifty dollars for contempt of court, in lieu of payment thereof he to be confined in the County Jail at the rate of a day for each two dollars until the fine is satisfied, and in addition thereto that he be confined in the County Jail for five days *anyhow*. Make out a commitment, Mr. Clerk. Mr. Constable, take charge of the prisoner."

Over his sputtering protests the Frenchman was led out by the constable; but in a few minutes the two returned and the officer spoke privately to the Judge. The prisoner, said the constable, had weakened; he had pressing business affairs to attend to and would compromise by receipting the rent bill, amounting to about eighty dollars, in payment of the fine.

The Judge accepted, the bill was receipted and the fine was marked paid on the docket.

Mr. Parlezvous started out.

"No, you don't," called the Judge. "Mr. Constable, take this man to jail. The sentence carried five days of imprisonment *anyhow.*"

The landlord was a diplomat and sounded a parley. He had business to attend to, he simply couldn't afford those days in jail. The Judge finally agreed to suspend execution of the sentence until the stairway was placed in order, and added: "If the work is done to my entire satisfaction I will pardon you, sir; but first write me a receipt for a month's rent paid in advance."

The Judge's terms were met by the landlord; but following the restoration of the stairway the Frenchman returned with a lawyer and served his tenant with a month's notice to vacate, which the Judge had to obey.

This our Judge was as wise as Solomon. A Jew lost a purse that he said contained a twenty dollar gold piece and three silver dollars. A Mexican found a purse that he said contained when he picked it up a twenty dollar gold piece and no more.

The Jew claimed the purse and the Mexican handed it over with the twenty dollar piece in it. The Jew insisted that the Mexican hand over the three silver dollars that he claimed should have been in it. The Mexican said he never saw them, and the Jew in high dudgeon hied himself to the Judge. The Mexican was arrested and brought before the court. After the Jew had testified, exhibiting the wallet and the gold piece, the Court demanded possession of the evidence. Then the Mexican was put on the stand. He admitted finding the purse, swore that it contained only the twenty dollars and that he had honestly handed over what he had found to the supposed owner.

When all testimony was in the Judge summed up as follows: "To the Court this seems a very plain case. The complaining witness lost a purse containing twenty-three dollars. The defendant found a purse containing twenty dollars. Evidently, then, this was not the purse lost by complainant. Defendant honestly but mistakenly handed the purse he had found over to the man who had lost a purse containing a different sum of money. The Court finds the defendant not guilty of the offense charged and the case is herewith dismissed."

The Jew reached out for the purse on the Judge's bench. The Judge raised his eyebrows and said: "Why, the purse is not *yours!*"

The Mexican, taking hope at these words, turned back and reached for it himself.

"Why, *hombre,* you merely found it, it isn't *yours!*" admonished the Judicial Presence.

"Den in de name of Holy Moses who dos it belong to?" burst out the Jew.

With great solemnity the Judge declared: "The purse and money are confiscate to the government and appropriate to the Court as costs in the case."

On one occasion a Mexican had a negro woman arrested and haled before this same court on a charge of stealing his chickens. She was tried and found guilty. The Judge pronounced as follows: "Under the Mexican Law of Restitution [5] I order the defendant to return the chickens to the complaining witness before sunrise to-morrow morning."

Accordingly at daybreak the negress returned certain

chickens to the Mexican and they were shut up in his corral. So far so good, but lo, when court opened later in the day three other Mexicans appeared and demanded the arrest of the first Mexican on the charge of robbing their henroosts during the night.

He was haled into court, pleaded not guilty and demanded immediate trial. Before proceeding the Judge ordered the fellow to bring the chickens into court. This being done Don Jesús, one of the complaining witnesses, pointed out three of the birds as his, and Juan de Dios pointed out others that he said belonged to him. They could prove it, they said, by the fact that they had parts of the same brood at their respective chicken corrals. Whereupon the Judge ordered them to bring samples into court, and further ordered the first Mexican to fetch *all* the chickens at his place to see how they compared in breed with the disputed fowls. Still further, he commanded the negress to bring all *her* chickens before the tribunal so that there might be a general comparison; and before the day was over the courtroom was swarming with chickens.

When court adjourned that afternoon the Judge ordered his constable to place all the chickens in the yard in the rear of the courtroom and guard them until morning.

On the morrow the wrangle was resumed. By the time of adjournment that day the fowls had become so mixed that the Court declared he couldn't tell them head from tail and abruptly closed the case with this decision:

"It is scandalous, it is outrageous, it is an insult to justice that a court of the great State of California should be brought into such contempt by such a set of people. You," turning to the negro woman, "are fined five dollars for contempt of court in not returning the same chickens that you were supposed to have stolen from the first complainant.

And you," addressing himself to the original Mexican, "I fine you five dollars for contempt of court in receiving from this woman chickens you knew were not yours. And you," he said to the other complaining Mexicans,—"The Court fines each of you five dollars for contempt of court on the ground of general molestation and impertinence. Mr. Constable, how many chickens have you in your custody?"

"Sixty, may it please Your Honor."

"Case dismissed. I suppose the chickens will just about pay the fines; the clerk will see that the matter is squared up on this basis. Court is adjourned."

Juan Villa

CHAPTER 13

A Tale from Nicaragua About Tails in Kentucky

TOM was a Kentuckian, and a typical one; he was also a '49er and a typical pioneer. At this writing he is a resident of Los Angeles County, still hail and hearty and full of rich old tales of adventure. Something of a philosopher he is, too, who has tried to search out the possible inner meaning of certain weird happenings in his life. Tom and I were schoolmates in Kentucky a long while ago, though he was six or seven years my senior. After some ups and downs we went to Nicaragua together with the Walker forces and after the war there he remained several years in Central America before returning to California.

In 1866, after his return to the Golden State, I met him out on his Temescal Ranch. He insisted on my remaining several days as his guest and we spent practically the whole time exchanging experiences since last we were together. I asked Tom for a detailed history of his adventures in Central America after the expulsion of the Americans and some of the tales he told seem worth recording here. For instance, the story that was brought up by Tom's answer to my inquiries, when he said: "Well, it wasn't so bad down there; I got into business, was making good money and I doubt not would have become rich but for my misfortune in shooting old Rafe Rezer."

"Old Rafe Rezer of Kentucky?" exclaimed I. "Why, I remember old Rafe and all the other Rezers big and little."

"Sure you do," continued Tom, "but do you remember

it was always claimed that the Rezers were part monkey? That they mixed with the Whimps since which both the Rezers and the Whimps have had tails? And you remember the feud between the Whimps and the Shackletts and what it was about? They were game fellows, those Whimps, even if they were mixed with monkey, and the Shackletts were mighty men of valor. Full of fight all the time. Remember Gen. Blant Shacklett? And Big Ben, Little Ben and Devil Ben?"

"Oh, yes," I answered. "And there were a lot of other Ben Shackletts."

"Yes," went on Tom. "And there was Dan Shacklett, that is Old Dan, and Redheaded Dan and Dan the Horse Racer, Black Dan and Dan White-Eye."

"Yes, yes," I exclaimed, impatient with the slow progress of the story, "I remember all those and several other Dans, but what about them?"

"Well, I was about to explain how the feud came about between the Whimps and the Shackletts so you'll understand it all better. You know the Shackletts were rather high-toned, proud fellows. Did you ever see any of the fights between the Whimps and the Shackletts?"

"Oh, yes, I've seen fights between the Whimps and the Shackletts. What about it?"

"As I said before, and as you know, the Rezers were part monkey," continued Tom, unperturbed by my impatience.

"Oh, I've heard all that," I answered, "but I guess it was only a slander on the family."

"Why," said Tom in slow surprise, "you know as well as I do that they were part monkey. Don't you remember how their men, women and children used to climb trees and shake down hickory nuts, how they used to swing from limb to limb just like the monkeys do down in Central America, except that they didn't use their tails?"

"How do you know they really had tails?"

"Well, I'll tell you. Remember big Redheaded Jim that used to go to our school when Norman J. Coleman was schoolmaster? Remember the slide we used to have down into Lick Run? The slide was down the steep blue-mud bank into deep water. We used to carry buckets of water up the bank to make it smooth and slick—and Great Grizzly wasn't it fun! Well, that's all over with for us now. But you ought to remember just as well as I do that our slide had worn itself into such a deep groove that it exposed a root that ran at right angles across its course. This Redheaded Jim Rezer was about fifteen years old and I remember it just as well as if it happened yesterday, that Jim in sliding down the chute caught his tail under the root and, oh, didn't he howl! I tell you, Bell, he howled just exactly like some of those Central American monkeys when you make a bad shot and only break a leg.

"Jim's tail was at least two and a half inches long. The Rezers had always resented imputations of kinship with the monkeys, but this settled it. As I said before they had mixed with the Whimps, and when Long Bill Whimp proposed marriage to the daughter of Dan White-Eye Shacklett, the only answer Dan White-Eye made was, 'I don't propose to invest in monkeys at this particular time.' Right straight there was a fight; other Whimps and other Shackletts came on the ground to see it through, and that was the origin of the feuds between the Whimps and the Shackletts."

"But in the name of common sense, Tom," I demanded, "what has this to do with your life in Central America?"

"It has everything to do with it. Changed my whole fortune. Didn't I tell you I shot old Rafe Rezer down there? But I'll come to that in a minute. Do you remember Dave Merriweather?"

"Why, yes," I answered. "A fine old Kentucky gentleman he was too. When I first saw him he was governor of Kentucky."

"Did you ever hear him talk about men turning into animals after they died?"

"Come to think of it I did," said I. "When a boy I traveled from New Orleans to Louisville on the same boat with Governor Merriweather. The boat was the *Kate Aubrey,* and the Governor was talking about something he called the transmigration of souls. We were putting out freight at Natchez-Under-the-Hill and the negro draymen were lashing their horses through the mud. The Governor remarked that it was his constant prayer that he would never be turned into a dray horse."

"Well, of course," went on Tom, "we used to think the Governor was joking about that sort of thing, but in Central America I had proof positive that his doctrine was true. After the Walker War I went down to Greytown, on the coast, and there I got acquainted with a Frenchman who was in the business of killing monkeys up on the River Chiripo."

"Killing monkeys! What for?"

"For their skins. There was a French merchant at Greytown who paid twenty cents each for monkey skins to be sent to France to be made into kid gloves. It took a good shot to work at the business because you had to use a rifle and had to hit your monkey in the head every time or the skin would be worthless. I hired out on this job, with three or four others, all Frenchmen except myself. I did all the shooting while they did the skinning and stretching. They could skin about five dollars' worth of monkeys to the man each day, and I was making good money keeping them supplied.

"I thought it was the best job I ever got into until one morning I went out shooting monkeys and saw one old fellow hanging to a limb. He made a splendid target and I blazed away. He fell. When I got to him I couldn't find where I had drawn blood. He just seemed stunned, and when I had taken out my knife ready to dispatch him after reloading my gun he just raised up on his elbow, opened his eyes and looked me square in the face. I hope I may never speak again if it wasn't old Rafe Rezer looking at me!

"He actually seemed to speak to me but I couldn't understand what he said. 'Great God, Uncle Rafe, is that you?' I cried, and he nodded his head as if to say, 'It's me!' He recovered the use of his limbs and sprang into a tree, then away through the jungle.

"I wouldn't kill a monkey now any more than I would a human. I quit my three partners and went to Greytown with a capital of a thousand dollars. There I met up with an Englishman who had mining interests in Honduras and went with him to Tegucigálpa, the capital of that country. Something entirely different happened to break up this Honduras venture.

"I'd been managing the mining property out in the mountains near the capital for a year and began to feel like a real mining magnate on my way to millions when along comes a Fourth of July and with it a feeling to celebrate. I concluded to give the natives a regular old-fashioned Kentucky barbecue. We were making lots of money and I staged the fiesta lavishly, telling the native miners to go into Tegucigálpa and bring out all their friends.

"The day arrived, and how things hummed! Unwisely I had supplied the camp with *aguardiente* and that's what worked our ruin. There were several native bands of music, enthusiasm ran high, everybody got mellow, I along with the rest. Along toward afternoon I decided to deliver an oration. I spoke Spanish pretty well then, but I couldn't seem to get them to take much interest in my speech until I began reading from a copy of our Declaration of Independence and translating it as I went along.

"The first time I used the words, *'Independencia y Libertad,'* they all began to prick up their ears and a few yelled out 'Independence and Liberty forever!' Then I began talking about tyrants, the bands began playing patriotic airs and the whole gang started to yeowling like demons. They all thought it was a *pronunciamento,* a declaration of revolution, and began calling me General and shouting, 'On to Tegucigálpa!'

"I attempted to explain. The more I talked the greater grew their enthusiasm and the first thing I knew a half dozen fellows put a great big cocked hat on my head, buckled a sword belt around my waist with a great long straight blade attached and vociferated, 'On to Tegucigálpa! Down with tyrants! Viva el General!'

"There was a mad rush toward the capital and I was borne along on the current. Such excitement I never saw in my life. We emerged from the mountain road onto the Camino Real leading to the city and rushed headlong down it, the crowd screaming all the time, 'Viva el General!' and brandishing machetes. Speak to them! Explain! Might just as well have tried to reason with a Kansas cyclone or a Dakota blizzard.

"As we rolled along we gained in numbers and when we neared the city there were at least a thousand of us. The garrison of the capital had been warned of our approach and as we reached the city gates they were ready for us. They just naturally gathered us in without firing a shot, and that night I slept in the calaboose.

"The next morning I had a drum-head court martial and was sentenced to be shot at sunrise. The American consul came to see me and when I explained how it had all happened he interposed on my behalf and got the sentence changed to immediate expulsion from the country. All of my property was confiscated and all I had to get to San Francisco on was a purse that my American friends made up for me. I got back to California with just four-bits in my pocket, after an absence of four years and experiences that cost me several little fortunes.

"The first thing I did was to write back to Kentucky to inquire about old friends and among them Rafe Rezer. What do you think? I learned that just one year before I knocked that last old monkey out of the tree down on the Río Chiripo old Rafe Rezer died in Kentucky."

Tom had another idea that was as original and radical as his faith in the transmigration of souls. This was his belief in Tansy Bitters.

Speaking of the high average of manhood produced in Kentucky, the superiority of the Kentuckians as a race, I told him the reason lay in their origin. That is, that their ancestors had all been born right of proven pioneer stock; that in conquering the country from the Red Man, subduing the forest, resisting the elements, building up a society of their own in the wilderness, always working, always combating dangers, they had developed a race of giants, physically and morally. This is what Tom replied to my line of argument:

"That's only partly true. The main cause for the superiority of those people is Tansy Bitters. When you were a boy did you ever enter a Kentucky home without encountering the demijohn or the decanter containing Tansy Bitters? Didn't they all drink it, men, women, boys and girls, three times a day? Don't you know that Tansy Bitters taken regularly will keep you in absolute physical perfection and moral equilibrium? A man who is raised on Tansy Bitters will never lie and will never steal, is always true to every trust. I just tell you, Tansy Bitters made Kentucky what she is."

About '87 or '88 Tom became jailer of the Los Angeles city jail, and what a perfection of a jailer! Besides keeping the place as clean as a Dutch dairy he lived up to his convictions concerning Tansy Bitters and supplied a great demijohn of the concoction which he dealt out three times a day as part of the regular ration to every prisoner.

What a jolly old jail that was! In that calaboose the blessed millennium had arrived, the prisoners thought. But, of course, there is always somebody to come along and point out imperfection in the heart of perfection. A member of the city Police Commission was a preacher. In nosing around he discovered this benevolent practice of Jailer Tom's and had him hauled up before the commission on the charge of dispensing liquor to prisoners.

Well, Tom just lit into that commission with a red hot defense of his beliefs; said yes, it was true he was serving Tansy Bitters to the city boarders because the stuff was not only good for their bodies but good for their souls; that it toned their livers and thereby sweetened their spirits; that he was supplying it at his own expense for the benefit of unfortunates and he didn't see how it was anybody's business but his own. He felt that a man in his position was not there merely to insure the imprisonment of men committed to his charge, but also to reform them morally, and Tansy Bitters would do it. He offered to stake his reputation that they could take the most arrant thief in the jail and could reform him inside of six months by dosing him three times a day with Tansy Bitters. Furthermore if they interfered with his dispensary they could run the jail themselves without him.

The commission tabooed Tansy Bitters and Tom quit his job.

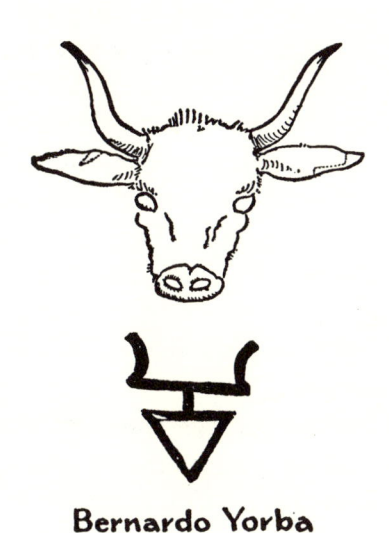

Bernardo Yorba

CHAPTER 14

Peg-Leg Smith, the Death Valley Party and John Goller's Mine

THE story of the "Death Valley Party"[1] of emigrants is only second in horror to the tale of the Donner Party, caught in the snows of the Sierras in 1846-7. Details of the Death Valley tragedy are less familiar to the public and the setting, in the below-sea-level furnace of the desert, strikingly different from the frozen dreadfulness of the high mountains in winter.

In February, 1850, a few forlorn human beings, starved to skeleton-like thinness, staggered into Los Angeles after having rested for a few days at the hospitable ranch house of Don José Salazar—the old adobe house on the hill, the remains of which may be seen to this day as one journeys from Los Angeles to Santa Bárbara by rail, near the present Newhall ranchhouse.*

Among these survivors was the Rev. J. W. Brier, mentioned by me in a former book as having been the first Protestant minister to preach a sermon in Los Angeles. Another member of the party was honest John Goller, our pioneer blacksmith. John died about fifteen years ago honored and respected by all our people who had known him for so long, for he resided here continuously from the day of his arrival.

This John Goller was a sturdy German about thirty years old when he stumbled into José Salazar's house with

* Via the old Saugus branch.

Death grabbing at his heels. When he hit town he was still loaded down with gold nuggets he had picked up in Death Valley and clung to in spite of Hell. John reported that where he found them he could have loaded a pack mule with gold had there remained with the party any such animal uneaten. There must be a mine there, he said, of fabulous richness; and during the whole of his long and prosperous life in Los Angeles John Goller spent his spare time and money fitting out expeditions to search for his lost bonanza. But he never found it. The "Goller Mine" is one of the real phantoms to-day in mining lore; real because it has an actual substantial value far exceeding that of the mythical Peg-Leg Mine. This from the fact that Goller was known as an honest, truthful man not given to spinning yarns and one who entertained an earnest conviction that the rich place existed; in addition he had produced corroborating evidence in actual gold.

The author has little faith in the actual existence of the Peg-Leg Mine because it was reported by that artistic old liar, Peg-Leg Smith, whom he had the honor of knowing in the palmy days of Peg-Leg's lawlessness. Peg-Leg was the biggest horse thief that ever ranged the country between the Missouri River and the Pacific Ocean. In 1850, away up in what is now Idaho, I saw old Peg-Leg with a herd of fifteen hundred horses which the year previously he had stolen from the Los Angeles valley—the "Spanish Country," as he called it, after the habit of the trappers and early explorers.

Indeed, Peg-Leg was a magnificent thief on the wholesale plan and the most superlative liar that ever honored California with his presence. In the latter days of the '50's, dilapidated and played-out, he found his way once more to Los Angeles and sat around the old Bella Union bar, telling big lies and drinking free whiskey, the latter especially easy to procure when he would begin on the subject of his alleged mine of fabulous richness somewhere out on the borders of the Colorado Desert.

Ever since the old man died people have been searching for the Peg-Leg Mine, but they will never find it in spite of certain ore which he procured somewhere and exhibited, because it is a myth, a Peg-Leg lie. But the Goller Mine will some day be found, and it will provide plenty of excitement.

This section of the Death Valley Party with which Goller arrived struggled for fifty-two days across a blistered volcanic desert. It makes a terrible tale, this journey of fifty-seven people through the then unknown and desolate region. They covered eight hundred miles of utter wilderness, climbed dead volcanoes never seen by white men before, traversed the hideous Death Valley, dragged along for days without water, ate the hides and very bones of their starved cattle. The party, with a train of forty wagons, started from Galesburg, Illinois, one of the thousands of expeditions made up in '49 for the trip to the gold country. Most of them were young men and they were well equipped.

They set out on April 5th and traveled across Missouri in the leisurely style of the ox trains of those days. They crossed the Missouri River at a point where Omaha stands to-day, but then there was nothing there but a few lazy Indians roosting on the river bank and staring at the long line of prairie schooners. Then across the plains to Salt Lake. Their passage did not differ materially from the experiences of the numberless others pressing westward. Indians stampeded their cattle so that they were late in arriving at Salt Lake, which they reached in the middle of August. Here the usual halt was made for rest and refitting before attempting the most difficult stretch—the final

THE DEATH VALLEY PARTY

ordeal across the desert and mountains into California.

From Salt Lake there were two trails to the Farther West, the northern one known as Sublette's Cut-off and the southern one as the Old Spanish Trail. The Galesburg party decided to take the Spanish Trail which crossed the Wasatch range near Little Salt Lake two hundred and fifty miles south of the Mormon town. This decision was made after consultation with Kit Carson, Peg-Leg Smith and John Bridger and was influenced by the tragic fate of the Donner party a few years earlier, which had attempted the northern trail and made a failure of it.

The Galesburg party combined at Salt Lake with several other wagon trains and the combined forces hired a guide in the person of Captain Hunt, who had served in the Mormon Battalion during the Mexican War. He agreed to guide the train for twelve hundred dollars. Captain Baxter of Michigan was elected to command the party, which now consisted of one hundred and five wagons and two hundred and ninety persons. Doctor McCormack of Iowa City was chosen lieutenant.

The start from Salt Lake was made December 4, 1849. Everything went smoothly to the point where the trails forked fifty miles south of the lake. Here the Spanish Trail turned to the left and Walker's Cut-off to the right. Nobody knew anything about the Walker route except that Frémont the Pathfinder had tried to get through that way and failed. But it was rumored that it was a much shorter route and many of the party insisted on trying it.

"If you do," said the positive Captain Hunt, "you'll all go to Hell."

A certain Captain Smith, however, said he could guide them over it, and one hundred wagons turned into Walker's

Cut-off. Three days later the rest of the party got the craze and came chasing after them.

It soon became evident that this Captain Smith knew nothing at all of the route. The party became hopelessly lost in a maze of untracked mountains. Scouts were sent out and a pass to the southwest was finally reported. Sixty-five of the wagons swung off to try this pass. The others had had enough and turned back for the forks.

Two days later the wagons that had continued on to the southwest encamped for Sunday on the spot made memorable afterwards by the Mountain Meadow Massacre[2] and the Rev. J. W. Brier preached a sermon from the text, "There shall be no more death." A sad mockery, that text!

In the next few days of increasingly difficult travel which seemed to lead them nowhere the weaker spirits began to drop out and attempt to struggle back. Soon there were left only thirty-seven persons who were determined to push ahead. Among them were one woman and two children, the family of the Reverend Brier.

Briefly, their sufferings from here on were almost beyond belief. Through the dismal volcanic mountains of Nevada they struggled, over ranges never crossed before, into dark cañons, across blistering waterless deserts, through regions of alkali and sulphur, and then through Death Valley itself.

For days they had no water at all. For fifty-two days they subsisted on their oxen. After six weeks of this they found that they would have to abandon their wagons, for what was left of their starving cattle could not drag them along. In Forty Mile Cañon, where there was water, they constructed two two-wheeled carts, loaded on these such water as they could carry, and the children, and struggled on. Soon the few remaining cattle became too feeble to drag the carts over the mountains and these vehicles were abandoned. On Christmas Day they set about improvising pack saddles for the oxen. While thus engaged they caught sight of another party far off. They started after these strangers but could not overtake them until the second day, traveling entirely without water. They discovered that the men were Georgians who had belonged to the main band when it set out from Salt Lake and who had decided to try to cross the mountains directly westward.

These Georgians, too, were in a pitiable condition and wild to get out of that region despite a discovery they had made which under different conditions would have brought them great happiness. These men were all skilled miners, and they reported that they had come upon a mountain fabulously rich in silver ore, specimens of which they carried. Only two of these Georgians ever reached the coast. Continuing by themselves on the route they had chosen, the rest of them were killed by Indians. One of the survivors has declared that no sum of money would tempt him to try to guide a party to seek the silver mountain. His experiences were so terrible that he cannot be tempted into that infernal region again.

The Galesburg Party continued to struggle wretchedly along in the direction which they hoped would see them through. They had no shoes now and wrapped their bleeding feet in pieces of hide which they spared from the cookpots. The remaining cattle upon which they were now subsisting were rendered unwholesome by the alkali and the sulphur that permeated everything that they consumed; such flesh as they had was yellowish with a sort of slime, a putrefaction which set in even while they were still alive, and rendered the flesh revolting even to the hunger-crazed gold hunters. Yet eat these miserable beasts they did, even to the thin blood-and-water marrow in their bones, and to their hides, which were singed and boiled into a semblance of soup. This cowhide soup, when water could be found sufficient to wet it, was the chief subsistence of the party for a long time toward the last.

Finally the dreariest region on earth, Death Valley, in California, was reached. Here their sufferings were intensified even beyond what they had already endured. Death Valley is the empty basin of an extinct lake. It is largely sand and alkali and lies below the sea level; the heat, even late in the season, in the day time, is fearful and the lack of water deadly. There is no life there. It takes its name from the discovery in later years of the bodies of nine men of this and following parties.[3]

For one stretch of one hundred miles these desperate Illinois people found no water. There were five successive days when they went without a drop. Finally they discovered one small spring, known to this day as Providence Spring. Just before the discovery one of the men, named Ishem, gave out utterly. The others were too feeble to carry him and had to leave him where he lay. Finding the spring and feeling refreshed the strongest hurried back to him with water and found him dead. But he had crawled after them for four miles on his hands and knees before he died.

Another, William Robertson, had been carried for days on the back of a surviving ox. When the animal succumbed this miserable man crawled along over the burning sand as best he could. On one of the terrible long stretches without water Robertson fell further and further to the rear while the stronger members of the party pushed on in a desperate attempt to locate moisture before all should be reduced to the same hopeless predicament.

A trickle was found. A messenger was hurried back to shout the tidings to the straggler, to keep courage alive in his brain until a water bottle could be filled at the slow seepage and rushed back to him. Madly joyous at the news Robertson struggled to his feet—then fell, utterly overcome by the tidings. The water bottle was brought to him; he drank deeply, smiled his thanks and died.

Another of the party, old Father Fisher, struggled hard with the rest to clamber out of a deep cañon in the mountains enclosing the Valley of Death; he reached the top and fell dead without a groan. The worst fate of all was that of a Frenchman of the party who went crazy one night and wandered off into the desert. Fifteen years later hunters found him a prisoner among the Digger Indians, still wildly insane and for this reason feared and respected by the superstitious tribesmen.

Mrs. Brier, the lone woman, withstood the ordeal better than any one else. When the men were too weak to put the pack saddles on the animals it was Mrs. Brier who did the work. When a traveler fell by the trail it was Mrs. Brier who encouraged him to make another effort. She was a delicate woman weighing but one hundred and fifteen pounds at the start of the trip. She brought her children, four and seven years old, through it all alive.

Reverend Brier, telling of the final experiences of the party as it approached the Newhall Ranch, then known as the San Francisquito, said:

"We crossed a little prairie into a dry waste. Here we saw grizzly bears. We struggled on down a cañon that had a little water in its bed and came to a valley three or four miles wide. There was no sight of any more water. I sat down under an oak tree concluding to die there but was cheered on by finding some acorns which we ground and ate.

"My wife begged me to try just once more and we struggled on. Getting ahead of the party I sat down on a little knoll. The wind brought me the lowing of cattle. We pressed on and getting to the top of a small divide saw a rich country and ten thousand cattle feeding. One of the boys discovered a ranch on a hill. An old Spaniard came out with his servants all armed but on seeing who we were welcomed us with great kindness. They killed a bullock and ordered us to help ourselves. We feasted. We bathed in the limpid waters of the Santa Clara and basked in the shades of the umbrageous willows. These Spaniards received and treated us more as welcome guests than as strangers in a strange land. Our sufferings were over. It was the fourth day of February, 1850."

The section of the Galesburg Party which followed the Old Spanish Trail under Captain Hunt arrived safely at the end of the Trail where San Bernardino now stands and some of our oldest Los Angeles citizens of American origin were among these arrivals, namely: John G. Nichols, one of our first American mayors of the city; our pioneer lawyers, Louis C. Granger and Jonathan R. Scott; George D. W. Robinson, Johann Graff, who had a farm at the corner of Figueroa and Jefferson streets, and several others whose names I fail to record. These are now all dead but their descendants are residents of Los Angeles. The guide, Captain Hunt, became one of the founders of San Bernardino and represented Los Angeles County in the State Legislature in 1853-4.

To conclude with Peg-Leg Smith, he was born in Missouri about the beginning of the nineteenth century and was a great character among the mountaineers of early days. He turned Indian, had Indian wives and became a Blackfoot chief. I was at his camp one year (all Indians except Peg-Leg and myself) at Soda Springs on the Bear River about two hundred miles northwest of Salt Lake and about twenty-five miles from old Fort Hall. Shortly afterward he went to the forks of the emigrant road where one led to Oregon via Fort Hall and the other to California via Sublette's Cut-off and sold the horses he had stolen from the Spanish Country (Los Angeles) to the emigrants.

Later in the season he came down to California with bags full of money and hung out around the mines, especially at Hangtown, now Placerville. He had abandoned his Indian friends and left his wives behind. He had no one with him except his son Jimmy, a twelve-year-old halfbreed. Peg-Leg considered himself quite a gambler and thought he could gamble among the sharps of Hangtown as successfully as he had among the trappers and Indians of the mountains. The result was that it didn't take long for Peg-Leg to lose all his money, and I don't think he ever made another raise.

One day I was on my way down from Hangtown to Diamond Springs with some companions and we found old Peg-Leg lying beside the trail dead drunk. Jimmy, his son, was standing over him trying to beat him into consciousness with a club. What became of Jimmy I never knew and I do not recall exactly when or where Peg-Leg died but I think his death occurred while I was absent in the army during the War of the Rebellion.

Smith was called Peg-Leg because he wore a wooden limb, and this is the way he came to lose the original member: It was on his last foray into the Spanish Country, when he made the big drive of horses heretofore mentioned. With his equine booty he fled through the Cajon Pass,[4] vigorously pursued by the Californians. In a skirmish that ensued one of his leg bones was shattered by a bullet. As soon as the pursuers were shaken off one of his Blackfoot Indians amputated the leg with his knife and Smith continued to ride his horse until he had arrived well beyond the danger zone before giving his injury further attention. At least this was the explanation given by Peg-Leg and I have corroboration of his statement from his companions of the Blackfoot tribe.

Thereafter Peg-Leg was equipped with a special stirrup.

CHAPTER 15

Really Important Events

THE author is writing history as it was made in the City of the Angels. If some of it is diabolic instead of angelic that is not his fault. Purely angelic information becomes monotonous, commonplace and untrue. Too much of this sort of thing has been written and published in the form of biographical sketches of pioneer characters of the Angel burgh. Absolutely commonplace, such as:

John Jones was the first man in Los Angeles to curry a horse American-fashion.

James Augustus baked the first loaf of American bread.

John G., shod the first horse * and Tom P., built the first wagon.

Dick Smith opened the first peanut establishment and Harry Smith drove the first dray.

And so forth. All angelic characters, no doubt, pioneering necessary tasks, but tasks of small importance historically as compared, for instance, to the opening of the initial first class American saloon and the establishment of the first Protestant church.

Thus far no historian has designated for posterity the man who opened the first American saloon or consecrated the first American church; and believing these to be characters of real historical importance because of these momentous acts of theirs, I am going to inform the present generation

* The native Californians did not shoe their horses.

REALLY IMPORTANT EVENTS

and transmit to the future their names and how it all came to pass.

John Bankhead Magruder was colonel of the First United States Artillery and commandant of the military district including Los Angeles in 1851-2-3. His headquarters were at San Diego.

Samuel R. Dummer, a captain in the United States Voltigeur Regiment in the Mexican War, had hung his hat on a Los Angeles peg when he was mustered out of the service. Dummer was a warm-blooded, convivial chap, a superlative boon companion.

Magruder sympathized with Dummer in all his genial propensities; they were both typical hail-fellows, well-met; and when the colonel of artillery came up from his lonesome post on the shores of San Diego Bay to enjoy the indulgences of a lively town these two would get together and make our Rome howl. Los Angeles was a lively little city in those rough days; San Diego was a place of historic renown but was, except for the presence of the military garrison, as dead as a door nail. Magruder liked life as it was lived in Los Angeles and whenever he honored our pueblo with a visit he certainly livened things up, even here where they were already very lively.

There was then—that is, when Magruder and Dummer first figured in town topics—no first class drinking place, and of this drawback the Colonel and the Captain complained loudly when they "got on a time." They hankered for a really respectable saloon where two gentlemen could get on a bust in the grand manner.

So the two heroes got their heads together with the startling result that they opened a saloon of their own—a respectable saloon for the gentility, according to their notions. First they bought a lot on Main Street, adjoining the present

Pico House [1] on the south. The materials for the building were imported from Maine and the edifice finally appeared as an oblong frame building consisting of one room downstairs and one room upstairs, the latter a sort of attic used as a dormitory, where the owners slept off their indulgences when their friends didn't usurp all the space. The house was weatherboarded on the outside and lined on the inside with tongue-and-groove boards. It had a shingle roof and was altogether quite an imposing curiosity in the adobe town. A pioneer improvement that was pointed to with pride.

The building finished, the proprietors placed a large sign over the entrance inscribed:

EL DORADO

But they now found to their consternation that the military chest was empty with the saloon still lacking liquors and billiard table. So the new firm had recourse to the rich man of the Pueblo, Don Abel Stearns, who loaned them five hundred dollars, taking their joint note for the same bearing interest at 5 per cent. per month, compounded monthly. The note was secured by a mortgage on the lot.

This transaction took place just fifty-two years ago and now as he writes this truthful historian is holder of that note and mortgage. Just how they came into his possession is another story but if the reader is curious to know the wealth represented in that security he can figure it out for himself. I imagine the note and mortgage, if they could be realized on, represent a sum of money larger than our national debt at the date when one of the signers, J. Bankhead Magruder, major-general in the Confederate army, disbanded his army in Texas in May, 1865, with the words,

"Boys, the jig's up, just help yourselves," and every man broke ranks and went home carrying with him all the movables he could lay his hands on. Besides what individuals took, mules, wagons, horses, general stores, cotton, powder and lead, thousands of stands of arms and parks of field artillery were sold into Mexico for a good price and helped the Mexican patriots expel the Franco-Austrian usurpers under Maximilian. Magruder did not surrender his army, he just told them to "git" and they got. The disbandment of Magruder's army is known in Texas as the "Break-up." The Mohammedans reckon time from the Hegira. The Texans count from the Break-up.

Well, to return to the beginnings of El Dorado Bar—the billiard table, liquid supplies and other necessities were duly installed and the establishment opened in grand style. An elegant and highly educated young Irishman, John H. Hughes, was installed as the high-muck-a-muck behind the bar and with a corps of underlings was busy every minute dealing out high class liquid refreshments. The proprietors did not in any wise demean themselves before their public; indeed, the elegant Colonel Magruder and Captain Dummer figured only as leaders of the practitioners at the bar.

What a jolly, high-toned place was El Dorado! What a memory—while it lasted. The run on it was awful, for a while. Suddenly supplies failed and it was discovered that there was little or no money in the locker with which to replenish the stock. The hospitality of the proprietors had been too much for the business. It seemed that every gambler who could put on the grand manner, every down-and-outer that had the art of being a boon companion in the style of a gentleman at other gentlemen's expense, had found a regular home in the dormitory over the saloon and was partaking of free liquor downstairs. Often Colonel Magruder, spending his week-ends in town enjoying his own hospitality, had to go to bed on the billiard table as dawn approached, so crowded was the roost upstairs.

Faced with a financial impasse the partnership was dissolved and Colonel Magruder fell back on his defenses at San Diego. Captain Dummer went to Tulare where he became a pioneer sheep raiser and the elegant Irishman behind the bar, nephew of Archbishop Hughes of New York, took over the proprietorship of the Dorado.

This was in 1852. There was much rejoicing at the reopening, but the Dorado, so successful socially, seemed doomed to failure financially. Gentlemen do not seem to be successful saloon keepers. The very accomplished Hughes, trained in the Magruder-Dummer school of the bar, succumbed in '53 to the situation of more outgo than income, and he was succeeded in the Dorado by the Rev. Adam Bland.

So here we have, under one roof as it were, the story of the first American saloon and the first American church in the City of the Angels; for Father Bland desecrated the premises of El Dorado by converting the building into a Methodist church. The Reverend Brier of Death Valley fame had already preached a sermon or two in the Pueblo but in a room merely loaned for these occasions.

I remember that the Dorado property was offered the missionary for fifteen hundred dollars and he started out to solicit the money. The first man he appealed to was Capt. Alexander Bell who promptly gave him five hundred dollars. Delightfully surprised, the Rev. Adam Bland was no less than joyously astonished when Captain Bell introduced him to Don Benito Wilson and that old-timer donated one thousand dollars. The purchase price of El Dorado achieved in but two calls, the Methodist pioneer caused the impish free

REALLY IMPORTANT EVENTS

lodgers upstairs to be summarily dispossessed and presto, the saloon was a church.

Alas, poor Hughes, that elegant Irishman! The like of him was seldom seen except in the days of old, the days of gold in California. Occasionally I am reminded of him by meeting a very beautiful old señora, now seventy years old but stately, lithe and sprightly, with lustrous black eyes and rose-colored complexion. She is a widow now these many years, but once Johnnie Hughes was desperately in love with her. She jilted him for a native son and it broke his heart. He became morose, desperate, and after a fling at San Francisco drifted away to Arizona. Tucson was Arizona then.

In 1857 when the filibusters under Crabb [2] were besieged at Sonoita, Hughes and Grant Oury raised a small force to go down into Sonora to their relief. The gallant rangers rode hard but were too late. Crabb and his followers had on the day before been forced to surrender and, as the Hughes-Oury relief party neared the gates, were already being treacherously slaughtered on the plaza of Sonoita.

The Mexicans attempted to decoy the relief party into a trap but failed to fool Hughes and Oury, who both had seen service, and the smaller American force withdrew, fighting as they retreated. A stubborn running fight was kept up all the way from Sonoita to Tucson, about seventy miles, Hughes covering the retreat of his comrades. About ten miles from Tucson, in a hand to hand combat with three Mexicans, the gallant Irish-American was shot dead.

Colonel, later the Confederate general, Magruder, was a great man in his way. When General Canby was commanding the Union army in Louisiana and Texas in 1864-5 Magruder was one of the Confederate generals who confronted him. A great game of strategy followed with St.

Louis as the stake. Canby afterwards designated Magruder as the "greatest strategist on American soil."

Magruder's habits of life impaired his military career. He made a mistake in being born in America. The man was a Grand Turk in all of his natural instincts and in any Christian land was out of place. What finally became of this great pioneer California military commander I never knew, but I do know that I shed tears of sorrow when some thirty years ago I read in a New York paper that the defender of Yorktown had been arrested and thrown into Tombs Prison for drunkenness.

Antonio Franco Coronel

CHAPTER 16

A Death Sentence at Monterey and a Sporting Event at Gilroy's

THERE were many queer and original characters in California during the early days and I knew a lot of them quite intimately; but none of those I remember was more strikingly original than Judge J. W. Redman, who presided over the courts of San José, Monterey and San Luís Obispo when they were first organized under American authority. He was a *nisi prius* judge, traversing his wide circuit on horseback, booted, spurred and armed like a vaquero. He was honored for his integrity and good hard sense. A man of learning and judicial wisdom, he was nevertheless very direct and practical in his modes of procedure and some of his decisions were arrived at without reference to precedent.

One morning Judge Redman saddled his horse at Monterey to ride to San Luís Obispo in pursuit of his legal duties. After mounting he recalled that a certain Mexican convicted of murder was to be brought before him in Monterey that morning for sentence. So the Judge rode over to the courthouse, threw the bridle-reins over a post, strode into court with jingling spurs, took his seat on the bench and called upon his bailiff to produce the murderer for sentence.

The bailiff conveyed the news to the sheriff at the calaboose and the prisoner was led into court. The sheriff informed the court that the Mexican could not speak English and asked if he should go out and drum up an interpreter. The Judge, recollecting the long, hard day's ride ahead of him, was disinclined to lose time while the morning air was fresh so he said he thought he knew enough Spanish to work his way through the brief business, and anyway these fellows always knew some words of English.

"Stand up!" ordered Judge Redman, addressing the Mexican.

"*No entiendo.*" (I don't understand.)

"You no speakie *Ingles?*"

"*Poquito.*" (A little bit.)

"You sabe that *hombre?*" The Judge pointed to the sheriff.

"*Sí, señor. El es jerif.*"

"That's right, he's the sheriff. He's going to do this to you, see?" The Judge took from his coat-tails pocket a big bandanna, twisted it up to look like a rope, and continued:

"You sabe lariat?"

"Oh, *sí señor—chicote,* what you call him, rope?"

"That's right—lariat, *chicote,* rope. Now, you sabe tree? What you call him?" The Judge descended from the bench, walked to the open window and pointed to a large live oak standing on the mesa near the courthouse. "What you call him, eh?"

The Mexican shaded his eyes and peered out the window. "*Es un encino, señor.*"

"All right then, that's an *encino.* We call him tree, sabe?" Remounting the bench, the Court then proceeded with the sentence. "The judgment of this court is that the sheriff put a *chicote* around your neck, that he take you to that big *encino* and that he then and there hang you, Jesús Mendoza, by said neck until dead. Now, in case you do not understand clearly, you sabe hang? How you say him in

Spanish?" The Judge twisted the bandanna around his own neck illustratively.

"*Ahorcar, señor.*"

"Yes, yes—that's it—I had forgotten that part of my Spanish. Now, what you call this?" indicating his neck.

"*Pescuezo, señor.*"

"All right, now we understand each other. Next Friday between the hours of ten A.M. and two P.M. the sheriff will take you to that big *encino,* put a *chicote* around your *pescuezo* and *ahorcar* you until dead, and may the Lord bless you. *Entiende? Sabe?*"

"Oh, *sí señor, entiendo. Muchas mil gracias, señor juez.*" (Many thousand thanks, Señor Judge.)

"This court stands adjourned for the term." The Judge's spurs jingled out of the courtroom and soon the hoofbeats of his mount were heard pounding southward.

R. A. Redman, a son of this eminent jurist, one of the oldest barristers in California and at the present writing an honored member of the Los Angeles bar, inherits a great deal of his father's originality of character to which is added a rich fund of humor. How he became deputy treasurer of Santa Clara County is one of his best stories.

It seems that in the days when R. A. was a young man his father was the fortunate possessor of an old iron safe he had salvaged from a stranded whaler on the shores of Monterey Bay. This he had in his home in San José, county seat of Santa Clara County. A certain Murphy was county treasurer and coveted the old safe, the only one in town, as a repository for the official funds. So he approached young Redman and proposed that if he could procure the use of his father's safe he would appoint the boy deputy treasurer at a salary of two hundred and fifty a month. The deal was put through and young R. A. was installed in the office of the treasurer where as keeper of the safe he soon had opportunity to become acquainted with the remarkable financial manipulations of the county treasurer.

At times Murphy would bring a friend to his young deputy and say: "Look here, Red, my friend Jim has been in bad luck. He's been bucking monte and has gone flat broke. Give him a stake out of the safe, that's a good boy, and he'll bring it back to you in a day or two for his luck is bound to change."

So Red would hand over a thousand dollars or so of tax money and Jim would go back to break the monte bank. Maybe he would win and return the money in a day or two, and maybe he wouldn't. San José was the capital of the state at that time, 1850, the legislature was in session and the financial goose hung high, but one day the young deputy treasurer informed his chief that the old iron safe was about twenty-five thousand dollars short and that tax money wasn't flowing in just then to fill the reservoir up again. This caused Murphy to open his eyes and take thought. He was a rich man himself and dug down into his jeans. He made up the losses of his gambling friends to the people of the county then and there and started a life of financial reform, for be it known the Murphys of San José have always had a reputation for strict integrity. Generous and careless at times, perhaps, but always making good in the pinch.

I speak of the San José Murphys in the plural for there was a big tribe of them in and around the town in those days and they were all rich men. There is a generation or two of Murphys living there yet and some of them are very rich even for this day. A thrifty set were the Murphys that came to California in pioneer days. They all had an eye open to the main point. For one thing all the young men Murphys married Vallejos and the Vallejos were princely in their landed wealth. That fine old native, Gen. Mariano Vallejo, autocrat of the region north and northeast of San Francisco Bay, had a dozen or two Murphys for sons-in-law, brothers-in-law, cousins-in-law; but somehow or other the whole line of Vallejos went broke while all of the Murphys went rich.[1]

The former deputy treasurer goes on to tell how Treasurer Murphy went about collecting taxes when the county needed the money, particularly the time when they went down to the famous Gilroy Rancho, where the town of Gilroy now stands and where the old Butterfield transcontinental stage line left the coast and crossed over into the San Joaquín Valley via Pacheco Pass going south. This incident throws such a revealing light on the California of those days, when the state was just in its chaotic beginning as an American commonwealth, that I will try to relate it in the venerable jurist's own words:

"John Gilroy[2] was a familiar name in the early days of California long before it became American territory. Don Juan as the Californians called him was an English sailor that had come ashore at Monterey way back when this was a province of Spain and had remained to become a citizen of the far-away alien land. He had married a native woman and acquired a principality in the form of a great ranch thirty-five miles from San José.

"When the first California Legislature set the wheels of the anticipated state government in motion an election was held for county officers and John M. Murphy was elected treasurer and tax collector of Santa Clara County. He was one of the well-known Murphy family that came to California in 1844. His Spanish was fluent, he knew all the old families and was deservedly a very popular man. Though he did not want the office he consented to run for the good of his party 'to catch the vote for the Democratic ticket.'

"He certainly did catch the vote for his party but after election he was very little interested in discharging the duties of his office, being wealthy and occupied with large personal affairs. The quickest and most direct means of getting the tax money in and getting the trouble of collecting over with was all that interested him in the office.

"The state law permitted the tax collector to designate one day in each township for the collection of taxes, notice of date to be made public a certain time ahead. As an election was to be held on a date in the fall of 1850 for members of the ensuing legislature, Murphy appointed this day as tax day in Gilroy Township so that the population would be concentrated and the business thus more easily disposed of. The Gilroy ranch house, where the voting was to take place, was designated as the point where the tax money was to be rendered.

"The Gilroy house was one of those old sprawling tile-roofed adobes familiar to all old residents of California, with immense rooms and serapes or blankets serving as shutters and doors to exclude the heat during the mid-day hours. The election was held in the big central *sala,* where there was a long table at which sat two clerks and two judges of the election, with Don Juan Gilroy himself posing as inspector.

"There were only forty-five votes in the precinct and these were all in the Chinese teapot—the ballot box—on the long table by noon and everything had proceeded without excitement, even the tax gathering. The crowd showed plainly a craving for something to happen and a disposition to start something as the day wore on. There were present not only the forty-five voters but a throng of Indian, Mexican and half-breed vaqueros from the surrounding ranchos charging about with swinging reatas or stalking here and there with jingling spurs as they sought amusement inside the building. Numerous games of monte and short-cards were going on in the shade of the thick adobe walls, the players squatting around dried hides and Indian blankets that served as card tables.

"Pretty soon two well dressed men with the appearance of city merchants rode up, dismounted and mingled with the crowd. They said they were on their way to Monterey on business. But Murphy and I both recognized the new arrivals, the one as a professional athlete whom we had seen win some sensational footraces in Sacramento, and the other as his manager. And soon we understood why they were here.

"Nicodemus Gilroy, one of Don Juan's numerous sons, was a splendid specimen of manhood, about twenty-two years old, famed over the countryside not only for his horsemanship but for his fleetness of foot. Footracing was a prominent sport among the Indians but the Spanish Californians seldom became proficient in this sport, though they delighted in watching and betting on any kind of a race. The Gilroys and their retainers were proud of what they considered the great athletic prowess of Nicodemus and boasted a great deal about him. But Nicodemus had never had a moment of real training in footracing nor ever contended in a real competition, running down wild cattle being the rule by which his fleetness was judged.

"To shorten a long story, the professional athletes from Sacramento had learned that the Gilroys had lots of money, that they would bet on anything and that they were proud of their Nicodemus. They had picked out election day as a good moment to start a little excitement to their own profit and soon after their arrival there was a buzz of excitement, a rushing to and fro, loud placing of bets and every evidence that a footrace was being arranged between Nicodemus and one of the strangers. The latter, as I remember it, was the holder of the world's record at that time as the fastest human on foot; but that crowd at Gilroy's, in its exuberant ignorance, considered it just too bad for these strangers that they didn't know the truth about Nicodemus Gilroy. They were betting every cent they had on their country champion.

"Tax Collector Murphy's conscience felt uneasy as he watched developments. It was bad form in those days to spoil any sport that did not concern one directly and it wasn't supposed to be one man's business how another man bet his money; but finally Murphy called the Sacramento athletic manager aside and said: 'Look here, I don't like to interfere in your affairs, but these people are my friends and I don't like to let this matter go any further until I inform them who your runner is.'

"The manager was a very cool, deliberate, polite sort of a person and he replied with icy courtesy: 'Mr. Murphy, you can do whatever you think best; you may be able to stop further betting but as for the one thousand dollars already bet, that is in the hands of the stakeholder, and there will be a footrace or a fight.' He turned on his heel and walked away to where the race course was being cleared and Murphy, deciding that the possibilities of deadly trouble that would follow his interference with the excited crowd should not be risked, said nothing more.

"Just as the racers were about to toe the mark old Señora de Gilroy rushed from the house carrying a big red bandanna in which she jingled six hundred dollars and cried out in Spanish: 'Where is that man that thinks he can run faster than my Nicodemus? I want to bet this on Nicodemus!'

"Desirous of stopping the woman from squandering the

heavy bag of money, Murphy halted the señora and tried to explain to her privately who the challenging stranger was. This only roused her indignation and made her more determined than ever to place her bet. So Murphy covered her bet himself, planning to return the money to her after he had won it. Lady Gilroy's face lighted up in anticipation of triumph over the gringo who didn't believe in her son and the Tax Collector put up six hundred dollars of the county tax money.

"Murphy and I were the last to leave the house and go over to where the race was to be held, about three hundred yards distant. There was not a soul left within the walls; the ballot box, with its ballots, was left deserted in the center of the great *sala*. Every man, woman and child, Californian, Indian, Mexican, American, of that whole countryside, and every dog, was crowded around the scene of the contest.

"As we reached the fringe of spectators I noticed a man detach himself and saunter alone back toward the house. I recognized him as Grove C. Cook,* a well-known mountaineer who came to California in 1842. We knew him well for his ardent support of the Democratic ticket on which my superior had been elected.

"The racers started. The well-trained professional athlete flew away like an arrow. Nicodemus Gilroy seemed not only surprised to see a man run with such style and grace, it was a revelation to him. Then suddenly Nicodemus seemed to realize that this affair had something to do with him. With an amazing burst of speed he swept past the stranger, looked back at him with a grin, won the race and turned a handspring as he crossed the line.

"The ensuing frenzy of the crowd over their champion

* Member of the Bidwell Party of 1841, the first American emigrants to cross the plains for the purpose of settling in California.

need not be described, nor is it necessary to say that the Señora de Gilroy showed no scruples about taking the six hundred dollars of our tax money, the sum total collected by us that day. Murphy met the situation like the gentleman he was and the señora never knew that his bet had been a gallant gesture to save her from probable loss.

"Gradually a part of the crowd drifted back into the house and the election officials resumed their places around the ballot box, but no more votes came in and at sundown the counting began.

"Let me explain that when Mr. Murphy and I had arrived that morning we had noticed that every one of the election officials was a member of the Whig party. This looked bad to us, as Democrats, but there was really no other material to be had in the township and there was nothing we could do about it.

"However, as the count proceeded it became evident that the precinct had gone overwhelmingly Democratic! Slowly, one by one, the little bulwarks of human liberty were lifted from the casket, and every one was a Democratic vote. The judges looked at the inspector and the inspector looked at the clerks, glowering suspiciously, for all the political talk that had been bantered about that day was to the effect that everybody was voting Whig.

"Finally there was just one ballot left in the teapot. 'Well,' grimly said the Whig who was counting, turning the pot upside down with a bang to get the piece of paper out, 'the vote will not be unanimous, for I know that *I* voted the Whig ticket.'

"But that last ballot proved to be a straight Democratic vote!

"The only man in the room who did not seem flabbergasted was the lank mountaineer, Grove C. Cook. The true ballots that had been voted were in Cook's pocket. He had substituted a Democratic vote for every Whig vote while the election officers were watching the foot race. This was possible as the ballots were mere slips of paper on which the voter expressed his preference with a pencil. The election officers refused to swear to the returns and the whole vote of the precinct was cancelled; but the Democratic jokester from the mountains had still done in his party a service because the real vote had been almost unanimously Whig. The true facts of the case were afterward confided to me by the wily mountaineer, who trusted me as a true party member."

José Vejar

CHAPTER 17

Life and Death in the City of the Angels

THE first Los Angeles mob raised its horrid head in 1851 when a Mexican named Zavalete was hanged. From that time on mob rule and lynchings showed a healthy growth from year to year until in 1861 the great traveler, J. Ross Browne,[1] visiting here, was moved to contribute to *Harper's Weekly* in New York some astonishing observations on life and death in the City of the Angels. He said he was familiar with all manner of game hunting the world over—buffalo, bear and wild turkey in the West; tigers in India, lions in Africa and jaguars in South America—but that Los Angeles was the first place he had ever been where he had been honored with an invitation to go man hunting.

"Why," wrote the globe-trotting Browne, "you would sit at the breakfast table of the Queen of the Angels and hear the question of going out to shoot men as commonly discussed as would be duck shooting in any other country. At dinner the question would be, 'Well, how many did they shoot to-day? Who was hanged?'"

One evening this distinguished traveler was sitting under the *portales* in front of the Bella Union Hotel on Main Street, his chair tipped back against the adobe wall as he enjoyed his post-prandial cigar. Through the deeply-embrasured windows to either side of him could be heard the sounds from the barroom—clinking glasses, loud discussions in English and Spanish, the click of billiard balls. Outside the street seemed in complete siesta, thought Mr. Browne,

The Bella Union.
Los Angeles's first hotel and stage station. *From an old lithograph.*

"The Two Friends."
A native cantina of the 1850's in Los Angeles. It was located at First and Los Angeles Streets. *From an old lithograph.*

Chinese Gambling-house, San Francisco.

Dead Chinamen in jail yard after the great Los Angeles massacre.

and he was about to yield to that snoozy feeling himself when he noticed that a citizen had suddenly appeared close to him and without paying the least attention to Browne was dodging back and forth, peering into one window and then another, a double-barreled shotgun held at ready. Here in the *portales* there was deep shadow except for the yellow shafts of light from the windows. The citizen would raise his gun and aim carefully into the barroom of our leading hostelry, then apparently his game would move and he would "recover arms" and tiptoe to another window.

Finally Mr. Browne could restrain his curiosity no longer and ventured to ask the hunter what he was aiming at.

"Sh! Sh! you damn fool!" whispered Gabe, for this was no less than Gabe Allen, an eminent character of the Pueblo in those days. "Don't make a noise! I'm trying to bunch them fellows in there. I'd like to get a half dozen at a shot."

Before the amazed stranger could ask Gabe why he wanted to get a half dozen human beings at a shot the half dozen apparently bunched, for Gabe raised the gun to fire when J. Ross Browne's humanity compelled him to yell a warning which almost cost him his own life.

Such was the plane of civilization to which our people had attained in that early period of the city's American history. Thirteen years of American rule had certainly demonstrated to the benighted sons of Mexico the superiority of our civilization. We had evolved a very simple rule for the classification of the population. A man was either a manhunter, or he was one of the hunted. That is, if he amounted to anything at all. If in neither classification, then he was a mere nonentity. The decent minority—for there was such a group of nonentities—wondered when and where it would all end. It was barbarism gone to seed.

The momentous question of when and how it would all culminate was answered on the twenty-fourth of October, 1871.

Ever since that earlier day when the mayor of the town had resigned his position in order to go out and lynch a prisoner who was under the protection of the law of the land Los Angeles was ruled by a lawless mob. It must be acknowledged that the law as administed by the legal courts was not much better than that administered by the lynchers for the reason that the mob elected the judges and the sheriffs and all the rest of the county officers and if they failed to stand in with the rowdies, the gamblers, the saloonkeepers and the squawmen, they couldn't be reëlected.

All this is disagreeable to recall and to record, but it is a part of the city's history. The people of Los Angeles made that history. They sowed the wind and reaped the whirlwind. "As they sowed so did they reap." The harvest was gathered in on that twenty-fourth of October already mentioned.

It was on that day the mob rose in its maximum fury and turned itself loose on the hapless, helpless Chinese population.[2] It murdered, robbed, pillaged at will and gloried in it until the indignation of the self-respecting people of the town and of the outlying ranches and settlements brought an end to the orgy. On that October day barbarism rose to its full tide. From then on it began to ebb, very slowly at first, but perceptibly until, after the coming of the Southern Pacific Railroad from the north,[*] connecting Los Angeles finally with the rest of the world by modern transportation methods, the city definitely entered the list of orderly American municipalities. Ruffianism was put down with a heavy hand and most of the old mob leaders disappeared. Occa-

[*] September, 1876.

Los Angeles Star.

GEO. W. BARTER, Editor & Proprietor.

WEDNESDAY............OCTOBER 25, 1871.

For President of the United States in 1872,
WINFIELD S. HANCOCK.

DEMOCRATIC COUNTY COMMITTEE

W. Woodworth, Chairman	Los Angeles
B. E. Hewitt, Secretary	Wilmington
John King	Los Angeles
C. Aguilar	Los Angeles
Wm. M. McFadden	Anaheim
John D. Young	La Ballona
A. W. Ryan	Silver
Wm. Caruthers	Silver
F. Palomares	San Jose
T. A. Mayes	El Monte
E. Pollerano	Los Nietos

THE CHINESE OUTRAGE.

The horrible assassinations which were perpetrated in our city last night by the brutal, uncivilized barbarians that infest the country, is an indication of what the consequence would be were their race transmigrated in large numbers upon this coast. Upon all the earth there does not exist a people who value life so lightly, who practice so many horrors, or who are so unmerciful in their outrages. From their very mode of existence they have little regard for their own lives and none whatever for the lives of others. The shooting of four of our citizens upon the streets yesterday, ere daylight had gone, and the frequency of their horrible acts of a similar nature, has now, at last, set our citizens to thinking as to the best mode of ridding ourselves of such a living curse. Little doubt exists but that such measures will be immediately taken as will entirely rid the city of their accursed presence. In this matter we should little heed the opinions of those abroad, who are not familiar with the Chinese nature and our circumstances. Have we not seen—have we not sadly realized? During the excitement last night several methods were proposed, among which was one, that a brief period of time be allowed for every Chinaman to leave the county. The most moderate course which could be pursued, would be to withhold from them all business and all employment.

After the above was written, last night, eighteen Chinamen were hanged and shot to death. The friends of the killed and wounded Americans were exasperated to such a degree that all attempts to quell the hanging and shooting were without avail, until the very horror of the scenes became sickening to the participators themselves. Comment is useless.

The Great District Fair.

Already the busy hum of life and activity caused by the inauguration of the great District Fair, is heard and seen throughout six of the lower coast counties; and next

PRESIDENTIAL.

The Star of Hancock "lights the tropic skies" of southern California. The Los Angeles Star, one of the very best dailies—probably the best—south of San Francisco, declares in favor of the great soldier, statesman, and patriot, Winfield S. Hancock, for President, and places his name at the head of its columns. The Star is strongly opposed to Chase, and says that Hancock is the only available man... The Star will have the pleasure of seeing its choice nominated by the National Democratic Convention. The REPORTER, if we mistake not, was the first paper in California to declare for Hancock. We can name no other man who could carry the great State of Pennsylvania for the Democracy. The Democratic party can not be beaten if it secures the vote of the Keystone State, and it can not win without it. Pennsylvania secured, the battle would be won, for the following States will certainly give their electoral votes for the Democratic candidate, especially if that candidate be Hancock: Alabama, 8 votes; Delaware, 3; Georgia, 9; Kentucky, 10; Louisiana, 7; Maryland, 7; Mississippi, 7; Missouri, 13; New Jersey, 8; New York, 30; North Carolina, 9; Oregon, 3; Tennessee, 10; Texas, 8; Virginia, 10; West Virginia, 4. Here we have 146 votes, not counting California, Connecticut, Indiana, Arkansas, Nevada, or New Hampshire. To this number Hancock would add Pennsylvania, 25, making a total of 171 votes, 13 more than is necessary to elect. If Hancock should not be nominated, and, as a consequence, Pennsylvania be lost, Indiana would have to be carried. Her thirteen votes would give one more than would be needed, and Hendricks could very probably secure those thirteen votes to the Democracy. But just here we must remember that New York could not be counted on for Hendricks as certainly as for Hancock. The Empire State will be carried against the Democracy at the election on the 7th proximo, and who but Hancock could insure her redemption next year? If she should go for Grant one year hence, and Pennsylvania also, then the Democracy would have to carry at least three of the doubtful States named above. Could they do this? Would it be wise to experiment? If there is a man who would receive the support of the two most populous States, that man, if a good Democrat, should be the nominee. Is not Hancock that man? We are assured that his popularity is unbounded in New York, and that Pennsylvania, his native State, is alive with enthusiasm for him. We once thought, like the Star, that he was the only available man. This opinion has been somewhat modified. The figures we have given above show that it is possible for the Democratic party to elect Hendricks, or it might succeed with Seymour, or Adams, or Chase, or Parker, or Thurman. But we still adhere firmly to the belief that it would not be safe to nominate any other man than the distinguished son of Pennsylvania, whose claims we shall continue to urge with what

[Communicated.]
Los Angeles, October 24, 1871.
To the Editor of the Los Angeles Star.

DEAR SIR:—It having been currently reported that we are opposed to, and have been endeavoring to break up the movement that has been going on for some time to establish an opposition steamer on this coast, and several of our personal friends having called upon us for an explanation, we deem it essential, in justice to ourselves, to state the facts of the case, which we desire to do through the columns of your valuable paper as concisely as possible.

When this movement first originated, a committee, composed of Messrs. Peel, Wright and Wm. Workman, called upon us and requested our co-operation, and desired us to sign an agreement to ship our freight by the opposition steamer, at the rate of four dollars per ton for down, and two dollars and a half for up freight. Believing then that the sole object of putting on this steamer was to reduce the rates of freight and passage, which would be the only benefit the community could desire from it, and that the movement was *not intended as a personal advantage to any particular individuals*, we suggested to the committee that it might be advisable to consult with Messrs. Hulladay & Brenham, the owners of the regular line of steamers, and endeavor to procure from them an agreement to carry freight and passengers at the same rates proposed by the committee. They were in favor of this proposition, but nothing has been finally consummated with regard to it. We are of opinion that such an arrangement would have been the most advantageous to the community, as it would have prevented the losses likely to be sustained in maintaining an opposition to a wealthy line, and at the same time would have produced all the benefits sought for.

We most emphatically deny that we have ever been opposed to the purchase or establishing of an opposition steamer, but on the contrary, have always asserted that we were in favor of it, that we would patronize it in every way in our power, *in preference* to any other line, providing we can procure as low rates of freight. It would, however, work great injury to our business to be compelled to ship our goods at a fixed rate of freight for a length of time, thereby being deprived of the same benefits that other parties might have, shipping by other lines at lower rates.

We have been established in this county a great many years, and depend upon its prosperity for our success, and are at all times ready to aid any and all enterprises that may tend to the development of its resources, or the welfare of the community.

Respectfully,
H. NEWMARK & Co.

SUSPENDED.—The following dispatch of yesterday indicates the suspension of the Peoples' Insurance Company:

"The report that the Peoples' Insurance Company has suspended, is practically correct. It will go into the hands of the Insurance Commissioners, who will wind up its affairs."

How the Insurance Companies Stand.

The following approximate estimate of losses by different Insurance Companies doing business in Chicago was reported to a meeting of representatives of a number of Eastern companies held in Chicago on the

---

Editorial in the *Los Angeles Star* denouncing the Chinese and printed in the same issue that contained an account of the subsequent massacre

sionally an old resident may still recognize an ancient relic of those turbulent years hobbling around the Plaza or Chinatown, decrepit, wrinkled, wrecked and ragged; but his once incendiary call can never again thrill a throng to violence.

Los Angeles was for a long time beyond the reach of religious missionaries. Their influence was absolutely ineffective. But by and by there came a civilizer and this was the railroad. The Southern Pacific found its way hither across the high Tehachepi, down over the burning Mojave Desert, through the twisting Soledad Pass, under the sheer San Fernando mountains through a tunnel costing seven millions of dollars and burst like a white light upon this land of darkness. From the day the whistle of the first S. P. locomotive was heard in Los Angeles our civilization started on the upgrade. The missionaries of this civilization that redeemed us were Leland Stanford, Charles Crocker, Mark Hopkins and Collis P. Huntington. Whether it was their intention or not this was the result. They raised us from barbarism into moral daylight.

But now let us go back to the twenty-fourth of October, 1871, when the Angels turned themselves loose on the hapless Chinese. I will state what it was all about, what happened and who were to blame, and I will try to give the truth of it *which has never yet been put in print.* Hubert Howe Bancroft* in his so-called history gives a garbled statement and an untruthful narration of the Chinese massacre. He charges that the scruff and scum of the city rose on the excuse that American peace officers had been fired on by the Chinese and one of them killed while attempting to execute a warrant on a Chinaman and that no one was

* Compiler of voluminous histories of our Pacific Coast states, Mexico and Central America; collector of the material in the great Bancroft Library, University of California.

Los Angeles Star.

WEDNESDAY............OCTOBER 25, 1871

The following will show the changes in the temperature yesterday, as indicated by the thermometer at Brodrick & Reily's Book Store, Spring street, next door to the Post Office:

8 A. M.	60	3 P. M.	70
12 M.	68	6 P. M.	66
Average temperature yesterday			66

CITY AND COUNTY.

INCIDENTS AND AFFAIRS.

THE CIRCUS.—The Mammoth New York Circus of Messrs. Kinsley & Thomson, will arrive in this city next Friday, and on Saturday will give a grand performance. This is the show of 1871, and the brilliant reputation of its acrobats, riders and clowns has preceded it. The boys are "spoiling for a 'circus ;" havn't seen one since Lee left, last fall, and will throng the big tent in crowds. Los Angeles will be the liveliest town on the Pacific Coast Fair week, and the circus will contribute its share to the general amusement. Full particulars will be found in our advertising columns in both the American and Spanish languages; and it will be also seen that this circus is on a more extensive and magnificent scale than any which has heretofore visited Los Angeles.

COMPLIMENTARY DINNER.—Last evening the members of the Los Angeles Social Club, together with many of our leading citizens, attended at Eugene's, where a sumptuous dinner was served in honor of Mr. D. L. Walter, late of the firm of Walter & Smith, who leaves our city this morning to settle at Portland, Oregon.

The unprecedented excitements and scenes upon our streets last evening and consequent rush upon our columns, prevents our giving this affair the extended notice which it deserves.

THE INDUSTRIAL FAIR.—The Mechanical and Industrial departments of the Great District Fair will be located at the Turners double hall, above the store of Caswell & Ellis, commencing on the morning of the 31st instant. Applications from those wishing stands for exhibiting articles, should be made at the store of Rinaldi & Co. before the 28th, at 2 o'clock P.M. The Halls will be ready to occupy by 9 o'clock on Sunday morning next.

PUBLIC MEETING.—A meeting of citizens has been called by the Board of Directors of the Agricultural Association, to be held at the Court House Friday evening, at half-past seven o'clock, for the purpose of calling the attention of our citizens to the necessity of extending hospitality to visitors during the

MURDER!

TERRIBLE OUTRAGES!

FIENDS IN OUR MIDST!

AN OLD CITIZEN MURDERED!

POLICEMAN SHOT BY THE FIENDS

Fifteen Chinamen Hanged and Three others Shot!

THE KILLED AND WOUNDED!

INTENSE EXCITEMENT!

FULL PARTICULARS.

Yesterday evening about half past 5 o'clock the quarrel, which has been brewing for some days past, between the Chinese companies in this city, and which caused the shooting affair between Yo Hing and Ah Choy, on Monday, culminated in a shooting affray in Negro Alley between the Chinamen. When the first shot was fired in this affair, our reporter was near at hand and arrived on the scene of action in time to see officers Jesus Bilderrain, Sepulveda, and Esteban Sanchez, and several others rush in and seperate the combatants. Hardly had this been done when the Chinamen commenced an indiscriminate firing, shooting rapidly at the police, at each other and at every man in sight. One old heathen who did'nt seem to be taking a hand in the affair, was no sooner approached and advised to get into a house out of the way of

THE BULLETS

Which swept through the air in all directions, than he pulled a six-shooter from under his coat and discharged every barrel at persons in his immediate vicinity. Two others, one of whom is said to have been identified as Ah Choy, stood on the porch in front of Coronel Block, and emptied their pistols at the crowd, which attracted by the firing, had assembled on Los Angeles and Arcadia streets. After twenty-five or thirty shots had been fired, and officer Bilderrain

VIGILANCE COMMITTEE

was still in existence, and suggested that these members present repair to the headquarters of the organization. It was recommended that a strong guard be placed around the building, firing, so far as practicable, discontinued and the place stormed by daylight. The excitement intensified and the authorities were powerless to act, the crowd treating commands, entreaties, and expostulations with disdain and refusing to listen. At about a quarter to 9 o'clock a door in the eastern end of the building was battered down and a storming party rushed in

EIGHT CHINAMEN

Were found within and dragged out to the infuriated crowd. One was killed by dragging him through the streets by a rope fastened to his neck, on the way to the place of execution; three were hung on a wagon on Los Angeles street; four on the western gate of the Tomlinson corral, the gate upon which Lachenais, the murderer of Bell, met his fate. The crowd appeared maddened with the taste of blood, and clamored for "more." It is stated that several other Chinamen, not captured in the house where the murderers took refuge, fell victims to the thirst for vengeance. At this hour it is impossible to ascertain the exact number of casualties, but it is known that fifteen Chinamen were hanged, three shot to death, and that one of the wounded will die of his wounds. One Chinaman was cut down, and his life saved when nearly extinct. Numbers of Chinamen

FLED THE CITY,

And took refuge in the country; several gave themselves up at the county jail; others were captured by small squads, and placed in jail for safety; one or two were put in, in the face of the crowd, and with the cries of hang! hang! ringing in their ears. In many instances individuals expostulated and pleaded with the people, and not without effect. At about twenty minutes past 9 o'clock, Sheriff Burns addressed the crowd at the corner of Spring and Temple streets; commanded the peace, and called upon all good, law-abiding citizens to follow him to the Chinese quarter. There he ascended a porch, and, after stating that he had attempted in vain to check the affair in its incipiency, called for twenty-five armed volunteers on the order of law and order to preserve the peace and guard the building until this morning.

Ten were hung on the west side of Los Angeles street below Commercial. Five were hung at Tomlinson's Corral, and four were shot in Negro Alley and vicinity. One Chinawoman was shot at the commencement of the row by a Chinaman. Of the wounded at Jail, two will probably die. Two of the Chinamen hung, wearing of eighteen or nineteen years, one of them is said to have been

Courtesy Los Angeles County Museum Library

Reproduced from the *Los Angeles Star* of October 25, 1871, the day after the great Chinese massacre. Copies of this issue are very scarce

to blame because no one could help it. I know whereof I write and I am going to put my version into history, let it chafe whom it may. Here it is:

For a few days preceding the twenty-fourth of October, 1871, there had been some small disturbances in the Chinese quarter. Several arrests had been made, but the trouble was purely local among the Chinese themselves. There were two factions among the Chinese and they quarreled. Each faction had in its employ a certain class of white men, sycophants that sought to make money out of the Orientals.

Yo Hing was an enterprising and prominent Chinaman at the head of one of the factions. He was a fine fellow, had a large vegetable garden on the southwestern side of the city, a store in Chinatown and was already quite a capitalist. A. J. King, an attorney known as "Judge" King, was Yo Hing's lawyer.

On the twenty-third of October one Ah Choy was arrested by Emil Harris, acting constable in the court of W. H. Gray,[3] Justice of the Peace, on a complaint lodged by Yo Hing, and after examination before Judge Gray was held to answer to the Grand Jury with bail fixed at one thousand dollars. The examination took place on the twenty-fourth. A Chinatown merchant named Sam Yung and another Chinaman came forward and went on Choy's bond. King, as attorney for Yo Hing, objected to the sufficiency of these sureties. The Chinatown merchant stated in reply that he had a store in Negro Alley and that he considered his store worth at least a thousand dollars. King still objected that this alone would not qualify a man on a thousand dollar bond. Judge Gray took the merchant in hand and his questions brought the statement from the Chinaman that he had money in the store.

"How much?" asked the Judge.

"Seben t'ousan' dollah," responded the merchant. The Court looked surprised and asked him where he kept the seven thousand dollars. He answered frankly that he kept it in a trunk in the rear of his store. At this point King, attorney for Yo Hing, who had caused Choy's arrest in the quarrel between the factions, suggested that Constable Harris should go over with him, King, to verify the Chinaman's statement.

Returning, the investigators reported that it was true that there was a large sum of money in the trunk in the back room of the Chinatown store. Whereupon Sam Yung, the merchant friend of Ah Choy, was accepted as a surety and Choy was set at liberty temporarily.

This all occurred in the forenoon of the twenty-fourth. In the afternoon a complaint was sworn out, or pretended to be sworn out, against Sam Yung, charging him with some sort of an offense against the peace. What the charge was does not appear on the record. Now, strangely, this warrant was not placed in the hands of Constable Harris, whose regular duty it should have been to serve it, but was entrusted to a man named Thompson. This Thompson is the "officer" Bancroft says was killed while attempting to serve a warrant of arrest on a Chinaman in Negro Alley. As a matter of fact Thompson was not an officer and had no warrant. He was accompanied by a gambler that was connected with the police department. No return on the warrant was ever made because before he could make the arrest Thompson was killed and the terrible riot followed. Afterward a Chinaman that was present at the shooting of Thompson made a statement to the following effect:

That Thompson and his police friend came to Sam Yung's store and told him they had came to arrest him. Sam Yung objected to leaving the store unprotected and apparently was afraid to leave it long enough to call in a friend while Thompson and the policeman were there, for when they insisted that he go out with one of them he went into the rear of the store and sat down on the trunk where he kept the seven thousand dollars, obstinately refusing to move. Thompson attempted to pull him away from the trunk and in the ensuing scuffle the Chinaman shot Thompson dead. Some Chinese rushed in and barricaded the door with Bilderrain, the police attaché, still inside, and during the attack on the building by the mob Bilderrain was shot through the legs from the outside, not by the Chinese on the inside.

This was about four o'clock in the afternoon and in less than half an hour a surging mass of humanity surrounded Chinatown and filled Los Angeles Street and the Plaza, bent on the destruction of every Chinese resident. Contemporary writers say that it was the underworld part of our population that took advantage of the situation to start indiscriminate killing and pillaging. But they do not state that the police force of the city furnished the leaders of the mob; that the Chief of Police of Los Angeles stationed his policemen and the deputies he had mustered in for the occasion, at all strategic point with orders to shoot to death any Chinese that might "stick a head out or attempt escape from the besieged buildings"; nor that one of the leading members of the City Council participated in the slaughter. But all these were facts developed at the Coroner's inquest.

Prominent merchants in the vicinity dealt out rope to be used for hanging Chinamen and on the following day citizens, including policemen, publicly displayed their booty from Chinatown and boasted of the rewards of their valor.

The leading local newspaper of the day, *The Los Angeles Star,* edited by one George Washington Barter, printed a two page report of the "great victory." During the momentous war between the Northern and Southern states of our country no battle was ever pictured or painted with more exultation, with more flourish, than George Washington Barter pictured our "glorious victory" over the heathen of Negro Alley. He eulogized the leaders for their energy, bravery, determination and patriotism and raised one of them to the title of general in his newspaper columns by his praise of "a great act of bravery, daring and enterprise when General Botello surmounted the flat brea roof of the principal adobe in which the Chinese were barricaded," cut a hole through the brea and summoning his forces, poured volley after volley into a room filled with Chinese men, women and children.

On the morning of the twenty-fifth of October the heroes of the night before paraded the streets, received acclaim and displayed their booty. A great deal of money had been stolen that night in Chinatown, a great deal of jewelry had been taken from the persons of the Chinese, most of whom were defenseless. The town waxed rich over this victory.

But before the following nightfall a cloud began to settle over these high-spirited fellows. Honest men, men with a sense of right and wrong, who had slept through the night of horror in the suburbs, on the ranches and in near-by settlements, hearing of the tragedy began to gather in knots on the street corners and in public buildings denouncing the outrage and the men in power who had been involved. It was apparent that a counter move was imminent, that the turn of the tide had come and that it was going to sweep out with it as wreckage the political forces that had so long debauched the ancient and honorable Pueblo. The heroes of the night began to slink away from the daylight.

It is only fair to state that the sheriff of the county did make a futile attempt to stop the massacre but he was tossed aside like a feather in a whirlwind. The next day he paraded through the streets a little Chinaman he claimed to have saved from hanging and by relating the harrowing circumstances to the groups of decent citizens wherever he found them gathered, did some good in arousing shame over the affair. Emil Harris, before referred to as constable in Justice Gray's court, also attempted to do something to stay the fury of *The Star's* patriot army and its General Botello, but he was powerless.

When the sun set on the twenty-fifth of October the reaction had started in definitely. The decent members of the community assembled in a mighty protest meeting, after attending the Coroner's inquest. I was present at that inquest. It was a peculiar fact that every one summoned as a witness was a person that had participated in the affair on the side of the attackers. There were but a few examined that volunteered their testimony who were not of the active mob. Among these was Gen. John M. Baldwin, afterward City Engineer of Los Angeles. He was ill in bed when the riot started but along toward evening he got up and came down to the scene of the tumult.

Baldwin said: "I went down Commercial Street to Los Angeles Street and turned toward Chinatown. As I passed Mr. Hicks' store he was dealing out rope and others were hanging Chinamen to the high spring-seats of a big wagon that stood in front of the store. I protested and attempted to argue with the executioners, but I might as well have spoken to a cyclone."

There was a second newspaper published in Los Angeles at the time, *The Los Angeles News*. *The Star* hastened its issue in order to get all its glorious news to the public ahead of its rival. When the other paper did appear it spoke in forceful terms against the barbarism and inhumanity of the massacre, and, finding public sentiment taking the views expressed by *The News* the more hasty sheet began to modify its previous statements. *The Star* discovered that it had made certain mistakes; that its "General" was an assassin, that its heroes were murderers, that its patriot army was composed of thieves and cut-throats. But *The Star* was already growing dim; it never shone brightly after the twenty-fifth of October, 1871. In fact it went out.

I have since searched everywhere trying to find a copy of this paper containing its account of the victory of the patriots over the heathens, but without success. That issue has disappeared, perhaps burned to destroy its awful testimony to the shame of a community.

The subsequent Grand Jury found many indictments based on the massacre but somehow or other all of them were against poor Mexicans without influence, and a lone Irishman, a shoemaker. The merchants that furnished the rope with which to hang the Chinamen were not indicted. The policemen that participated in the massacre were not molested. The councilman, proved at the Coroner's inquest to have been a participant, was not interfered with in his legislative capacity.

There is no doubt that all those indicted were guilty. But there were so many others, persons of position and influence, that had boasted of their guilt while the affair was yet hot, left unmentioned by the law, that the indictments became a matter of jest. To heighten this effect those brought into court were tried before a real estate agent who, by some hook or crook, had been appointed by the Governor to fill a vacancy on the bench. Some of the accused were never brought to trial at all, but those tried were convicted of manslaughter and got, I believe, ten year sentences.

But—two very astute practitioners, the Colonels James

G. Howard and E. J. C. Kewen, had defended the prisoners at the trial and after the convictions they appealed the cases on writ of error and the record went before the Supreme Court of the State, with the result that the Supreme Court held that the real estate agent had proved to be a very poor judge and reversed the decisions of the lower court. The prisoners all came home and some of them were immediately appointed to office.

It was estimated that about forty thousand dollars was taken during the sack of Chinatown. For this the Chinese never received any redress except the convictions above described. Twenty-one Chinese were hanged. The number shot down could never be definitely ascertained because bodies and wounded were concealed by their countrymen.

I have gone into this matter at some length as a horrible example of mob law and as the climax of the turbulent record of the first thirty years of American rule in the City of the Angels. And I do not intend that the "smoothing out" the affair got by writers of the time shall be perpetuated as the truth. If Justice W. H. Gray issued a warrant upon complaint, which his record failed to show that he did, why was not the warrant given to the court's then acting constable, Emil Harris, who had acted in all the other Chinatown cases recently brought before that court? The fact is, no such warrant was ever issued by Justice Gray, who was an able and an honest man. Thompson (who pretended to serve the warrant), and his confrere, becoming aware of so much money in Sam Yung's store, went there for the purpose of stealing that money. The Chinaman suspected what they had come for and refused to be robbed. Result, the Great Chinese Massacre of 1871.

Yo Hing, the Chinaman who caused the arrest of his fellow-countryman, Ah Choy, and thereby inadvertently

Lynching of Lachenais for the killing of Jacob Bell, Los Angeles, 1870.
Most of the crowd has dispersed, leaving the victim hanging from the cross-bar of the corral gate (center of picture).

First house on the site of the present city of Pasadena.
Built in the 1830's by José Pérez on the Rancho San Pascual. It still stands, in renovated form, on the slope below the Hotel Raymond.

LIFE AND DEATH

started the fiery trail of events, had a sardonic appreciation of the technicalities of the white man's law. He was a suave, polished, educated Oriental, was liked and respected by all decent citizens and escaped the massacre. But not long afterward his skull was cloven by a hatchetman of a rival tong. Justice of the Peace B. L. Peel took Yo Hing's antemortem statement in writing, during which the Chinese dictated an indictment of his murderers with cool self-possession. When he had finished, as Justice Peel thought, the latter thrust the document forward hastily to get Hing's signature before he died. Hing, rallying and glancing the text over, remarked in a tone that conveyed a reflection on the Justice's professional ability: "Judge, I desire to remind you that you have forgotten something."

"What's that?" inquired the American in an agitated voice, for he was considerably shaken by the ordeal.

"Why, you have failed to have me state that I was killed in the City of Los Angeles, County of Los Angeles, State of California."

When this technical oversight was remedied Yo Hing signed the statement and died.

Now a word about the lynching of Lachenais by a Methodist mob. This was an affair referred to in Judge Sepúlveda's charge to the Grand Jury concerning the bringing of indictments against the perpetrators of the anti-Chinese riot. Lachenais was a Frenchman married to a Spanish Californian wife of considerable wealth, and he was a fellow of some influence in the community. He was a man really feared by a considerable element and he had a knack for killing that went all-too-long unchecked. But finally even his own countrymen and fellow-Latins became dangerously aroused against him by an unforgivable *faux pas* on his part. It was this:

An important French citizen had died and Lachenais and another Frenchman were appointed to sit up with the corpse. While engaged in this act of piety they disputed over a matter of French politics, probably concerning Louis Napoleon and the Maximilian usurpation in Mexico which was then a live piece of news. "One word led to another," as the reporters say, with the final result that Lachenais killed his fellow mourner and left his body lying across the principal corpse, or what we might term the legitimate corpse.

Such indignation was aroused by this show of bad manners that Lachenais took flight for the first time in his career and lay low in Lower California until the double funeral was a record of the past and the affair had blown over. Then he came back and settled himself on the bounty of his rich wife.

Way out in the southern part of town, near what is now called Agricultural Park,* Jacob Bell held a preëmption of eighty or more acres of land. Lachenais claimed the same land. The two disputed the matter hotly. One day I happened in at a lawyer's office in the Temple Block while Lachenais and a friend were in consultation with the lawyer. I didn't know at the time what it was all about but I heard the lawyer say, "My advice to you is to rely on the law of rifles." They were speaking Spanish. "The law of rifles it shall be," replied Lachenais in the same tongue, and abruptly left the office.

This was about two o'clock in the afternoon and at four o'clock I dropped in, on my way home, at John Schumacher's.* I found John in a great state of excitement. "What's the matter, John?" I asked.

* Now Exposition Park, site of the County Museum and the Coliseum.

"Why," he replied, "that bull-headed Frenchman has killed Jacob Bell."

John Schumacher's agitation was heightened by the fact that he was in partnership with Jacob Bell in a fine building they had recently erected at the southeast corner of Commercial and Los Angeles Streets, known as the White House.[5]

At the inquest next day it was established that Lachenais and Bell had fought. A pistol lay beside Bell's body when found and Lachenais maintained that Bell fired first.

During the day a mass meeting of citizens was called and I, being a friend of Jacob Bell and bearing the same family name, was invited to attend. I declined because as bad as was the administration of law in Los Angeles I preferred to bide a better day than to indorse mob action. The meeting was held in Arcadia Hall, at the southwest corner of Arcadia and Los Angeles Streets,* and it was a Methodist meeting. Yes, it was a Methodist mob. The proceedings of the meeting were secret, but the next day that mob took Lachenais forcibly from jail and hanged him by the neck until dead, in a corral at the corner of Temple and New High Streets. It happened that I had ridden into town in the morning and I saw the procession moving from the jail. I galloped north on Spring Street to Temple and there I sat my horse and reviewed the parade. A Methodist parade. The pastor of what is now called the First Methodist Church marched at the head with a double-barreled shotgun resting in the hollow of his left arm.

It was claimed that the real estate agent that shortly thereafter was made a judge was the prime mover in organizing the hanging party. He was a pillar of the Methodist

* The Arcadia Block, first two-story brick building in the city, erected by Abel Stearns in 1858.

church in question, but at the last moment, after the mob was incited, he dropped out and left his pastor to do the substantial work.

Now, I knew that Methodist pastor and always thought him a pretty good fellow. I frequently attended his services and liked his Christian discourses. But what a state of affairs, when a minister of the gospel descends from his pulpit to become himself a law-breaker and murderer in an alleged vindication of decency! There is no doubt that the fellow Lachenais deserved hanging but there was a doubt that he deserved hanging for the death of Jacob Bell. At least he was entitled to a hearing before a legal tribunal, but he was given no hearing at all, even by the mob, after the Coroner's inquest.

Andrés Pico

CHAPTER 18

Leonis the Basque, King of Calabasas

THE Kingdom of Calabasas [1] is bounded on the north and east by the San Fernando Valley, on the south by the Pacific Ocean and on the west by Ventura County. Its area is larger than some of the German principalities and greater than at least one state of the United States. This is one of the loveliest regions in Southern California, even to-day after thirty years or more of devastation by the woodchopper among its parks of noble oaks. Calabasas has towering mountains, verdant slopes, shady glens, meadows, brooks teeming with trout, woodlands filled with deer, wild hogs, mountain lions and all manner of smaller game. It is the paradise of the hunter and the elysium of the surviving frontier fighter.

For Calabasas succeeded to the martial fame of El Monte as a region of tough customers. At least it duplicated the Monte's notoriety as a danger spot and on a much wider scale, mile for mile. It has been estimated that a murder marks each freehold in and around El Monte. And undoubtedly each squatter's claim and each patented freehold in the Kingdom of Calabasas is saturated with human blood. Should future farmers ply the subsoil plow thereabouts they ought to turn up human bones in astonishing numbers.

Calabasas once had a considerable population but the inhabitants killed each other off so steadily that a human face is a rarity now anywhere off the main road, and if glimpsed is usually peering from behind a great oak tree or over a boulder, spying out the traveler, deciding whether he is a known enemy that should be perforated with bullets instanter or a stranger that ought to be shot on general principles as a possible disturber of shotgun land titles.

While the remaining male Calabasans are spying on each other and the stranger, the females supply the family larders by hook and by crook and also by raising poultry. Along about Thanksgiving and Christmas time it was no uncommon sight to see one of these wild hillmen herding a flock of turkeys to market in Los Angeles, one of the few occasions on which they emerged to mingle with the outside world. But precious little of the proceeds of the turkey marketing ever got back to the trusting women that had toiled all year to raise the birds and guard them from the animals of prey that infested the region, for the money was blown in at the cantinas and the sporting houses, and if the mountaineer survived to return home at all it was usually with empty pockets and a worse disposition than ever.

A squatter war raged throughout this region for thirty years or more until the name Calabasas—which signifies in Spanish pumpkins or squashes, certainly a mild designation —became a synonym for all that is ruffianly, lawless and associated with sudden death. The king of this kingdom for years was one Michel (or Miguel as the Spanish-speaking population knew it) Leonis, the Big Basque. This Leonis, known to the natives as El Basquo Grande,* started the land war in about 1870. El Basquo Grande had been born a French subject, just over the line from Spain in the Pyrenees, and in the early '50s had been a captain of *contrabandistas* or smugglers. Things were made so hot in the Pyrenees for Leonis by both French and Spanish customs officers that he migrated to America and settled in Cali-

* A local term. The Spanish word for Basque is *Vascongado*.

fornia. He was a giant in statue and strength, a perfect savage in nature, besotted in ignorance, so illiterate that he could not read a word in any language.

Still, the Big Basque was in a way a great man. He was of indomitable will, industry and perseverence, was a great business manager and became rich. When he was killed in 1889 he left a half million dollars, the most of which was inherited by the lawyers.

He first became a sheep herder in the San Fernando Valley. About 1869 he married a half-Indian woman at the head of the valley whose father was owner of Rancho Escorpión. Once married Leonis calmly squatted down on the old father's land, took the management of the property into his own hands and gradually possessed himself of all the cattle, horses and sheep of the rancho, thus laying the foundation of his future wealth.

El Rancho Escorpión bounds the Calabasas country on the north and as Leonis's herds grew he extended his dominion southward into the vales and meadows of that delectable land. It was practically all government land and the Big Basque simply appropriated it to the use of his flocks and herds without legal formalities. By 1875 or '76 his sheep numbered not less than thirty thousand while his horses and horned cattle ran into the thousands of head. By this time he dominated the whole country south of the Ex-Mission San Fernando grant, west of El Encino and north of El Malibu, a really vast domain.

All this government land was of course tempting to the new American settlers coming into California and they in their innocence supposed they could squat on it as well as could any one else. Leonis disposed of the first installment of squatters in short order: he would get criminal complaints filed against them on some charge or other, they would be thrown in jail in Los Angeles and if they gave up their ideas of wanting to live in the kingdom of El Basquo Grande they would be let off easy, if not the charges against them would be pressed.

With his numerous Mexican and Indian retainers the Big Basque could place in the field an armed following that made him equal in power to some of the feudal barons of the Middle Ages. He was liberal in feeing his lawyers and in spending money on the elections and he dominated most of the courts. He ruled his country with rawhide, rifle, revolver and bribery. He was a tyrant pure and simple. No Mexican or Indian in the region dared oppose his slightest wish; if one did dare he was soon missing from his family circle.

About 1875 there appeared in the Calabasas region an American named Banks, an ex-Union soldier, a harum-scarum, dashing, devil-may-care fellow. He liked the country and determined to settle in it. Instead of retreating before the threats of the Big Basque he gathered around him a set of Americans who, like himself, wanted land and besides liked adventure—a venturesome, brave bunch, many of them discharged Federal soldiers.

With Banks at its head this band marched into the Kingdom of Calabasas, picked out the most likely locations and each member, according to his choice, pitched his tent or built his cabin. All were sworn to brave the wrath of King Michel to the end.

There were about thirty in this Banks party. Leonis could muster at an hour's notice a hundred armed men. And he did. The skirmishing began almost immediately. The war was on and El Basquo Grande thought that he could run the whole group out in one attack with rawhide, rifle and revolver, scorning the slower method of complaint and arrest. But so well organized was the little Banks army that when

Leonis started to eject the first settler he came to in his line of march all the rest rallied to this one's aid with a rapidity and valor that sent the bully and his henchmen fleeing from the field carrying their wounded with them.

After this a bitter, relentless guerilla warfare was carried on by Leonis. Scarcely a day passed that a settler was not killed from ambush; yet the Banks outfit held on and gradually gathered replacements from newly arrived land seekers. All this time there was no interference by the legally constituted authorities; the opposing forces were left to fight it out between themselves.

This went on for about a year when finally Michel Leonis, desperate at the sight of his toppling scepter, decided on a final grand muster and attack. The increasing number of settlers interfered with the pasturage of his great herds; he had to either diminish his stock, move elsewhere or drive the locaters out. So the King of Calabasas sent a message to the untitled but unafraid Banks that on the coming Sunday he was going to sweep the range with every man that he and his wife's family could muster; that this was to be war without quarter and that the Banks ranch was the first point he intended to clean up.

But not a settler fled; every one stood his ground and Saturday night they all rallied on the Banks cabin and awaited the attack, after sending out scouts and throwing out pickets in approved military fashion. It was toward the end of the afternoon of Sunday before the Leonis army attacked. A real battle waged until dark. After two hours, during which several of the settlers were killed outright and others wounded the army of the Big Basque was routed and left the field carrying its dead and wounded.

Michel Leonis was driven from the field but alas, fate designated him the victor nevertheless. The brave Banks had fallen, mortally wounded. He was brought to Los Angeles by some of his followers. I was called to take his ante-mortem statement, and he no sooner gasped out the last word than he died. Left without a leader the settlers became disorganized and within two weeks there was not one left in the Calabasas.

Despite representations made to the authorities no inquest was held over Banks's body, no judicial inquiry was organized, no arrests were made. Yet the battle occurred within thirty miles of the Los Angeles County Courthouse.

How many were killed and wounded in the Leonis forces was never known exactly because they concealed their losses. From one of the Banks men, Yarnell, a brother of the so-called "Apostle of Temperance," Jesse Yarnell, I obtained a description of the encounter which would indicate that the Leonis losses should have been considerable, or else Yarnell saw double. It was Yarnell who called me to the side of the dying Banks and solicited my legal counsel on behalf of the settlers. I asked Yarnell:

"How comes it that we don't hear of your having killed anybody up there in this great fight while on your side you lost so many good men?"

Yarnell answered: "Why, Major, I never killed so many men in one day in my life! I had my old army Spencer, and at every one of sixteen shots I fired without moving from behind a tree, I saw a man drop. I think we killed enough Indians and Greasers to load a railroad car."

It was six or seven years before settlers began to percolate into the Calabasas country again. But the old contest was bound to be resumed because wherever the United States Government owns good lands the American people will possess them, whatever the odds. You might as well attempt

THE KING OF CALABASAS

to stop the current of the Mississippi as to keep the American people off the public domain.

The leaders of the next invasion were Sansome and Davis. Elias Sansome was a squatter from way back. He was as tall as Leonis of Calabasas, was born and reared in the mountains of West Virginia, and was the equal of Leonis in mulish illiteracy. He had started West at an early date and had squatted all over Missouri, then all over California. There wasn't a county from Del Norte to San Diego where he hadn't squatted a half dozen times; and as far as my knowledge goes old Elias Sansome has squatted on at least twenty pieces of public land in Ventura and Los Angeles counties. Now over ninety years of age, he is still squatting.

His partner, Davis, was a novice squatter; a pupil of the veteran Squatter Sansome, and the two came over from Ventura County to squat on the range of the King of Calabasas. But, my goodness, what a surprise was in store for Squatter Sansome! Always hitherto such a successful squatter! The Big Basque just hitched a team to a wagon, took along a dozen retainers, drove over to the Sansome-Davis camp, lassoed them both, tied them neck and heel, tumbled them into the wagon, kept them over night in his stronghold and the next day hauled them to Los Angeles. There he went to his lawyers and got out complaints charging his prisoners with the crime of burglary in having burglariously entered upon the domain of the United States of America, at which crime they had been detected by the loyal public guardian, Michel Leonis.

The trussed-up prisoners were thrown into jail and I was called in, as an attorney, to defend them.

Can you imagine such a charge as the above being entered and entertained in any court in the United States of America? Yet it was so entered and entertained.

Well, to continue to relate the unbelievable, one John Trafford was Justice of the Peace then and he conducted the examination into this strange charge of burglary. He conducted this examination business for twenty-one days and the attorneys for the prosecution got more free whiskey, free lunches and season meal tickets during that period than they ever saw during the rest of their natural lives. A saloon adjoined the courtroom. Recess would be declared about six times each day and there would be a migration from the courtroom via the back door to the saloon. El Basquo Grande dispensed coin all the time without stint. It was a judicial bonanza and His Honor got so drunk he never got sober again until he died.

After the prosecution had rested we brought in sixteen of the most reputable and opulent Frenchmen and Basques of the county, all of whom, though in fear of their lives, testified to the evil character of Leonis. All asserted that they would not believe him on oath.

Garnier, lordly owner of El Rancho Encino, when he had testified, was asked by the prosecution: "You are an enemy of Leonis, are you not, and that is the reason you are here to testify against him?"

Garnier replied: "Yes, I am his enemy, but I did not volunteer to come here; I am afraid of Leonis and am only forced to tell the truth under oath."

"What are you afraid he will do to you?"

"I fear he will burn my house and barns. He burned my fields of wheat and barley one year."

Jean Goyeneche testified to the same effect as Garnier and related how the Big Basque had stolen one thousand sheep from him. And so it went through the whole sixteen that were brave enough to tell what they knew about Michel Leonis. The fact was brought out by some of the witnesses

SOME REMARKS

Major Bell, of the Los Angeles PORCUPINE, is one of the most invincible martyrs of this southern country. He persecutes thuds and rascals, reveals and airs the rendezvous of thieves and murderers, and is likewise prosecuted. His PORCUPINE is conducted on the fearless plan—as the old soldier fought so he writes. Would the country had more Bells and less Baldwins, Wells and Cheneys. We admire tho gentleman's pluck and honor his humane principles. He is truly one of God's noble specimen of men.—*Murietta Era.*

Horace Bell, editor of the Los Angeles PORCUPINE, has recently been fined and imprisoned for contempt of court by Judge Cheney. That is to say he told damaging truths about the contemptible court and made comments upon the public actions of its different members. For thus availing himself of the rights of an American citizen he was dragged into court, fined and imprisoned and as a result the "court" is held in as great contempt by the people as some of the blackleg members of Washington Territory courts. This contempt of court is becoming a tyrranical weapon in the hands of corrupt judicial knaves, with which to silence free speech and comment on their rascally actions. It must go along with the Chinese.—*Co-Operator.*

The people's advocate THE PORCUPINE.

Some press comments reprinted in *The Porcupine* after the editor had been imprisoned for contempt of court

that some years before Leonis had engaged in a lawsuit with Jean Etchemende, and knowing that Etchemende possessed certain documentary evidence locked in his safe that would be of value to him, he, Leonis, broke into Etchemende's store in Los Angeles one night. He was discovered removing the safe bodily. In the chase that followed Leonis, carrying the safe on his shoulder, ran across a large open space between Negro Alley and Alameda Street, pitched the safe over a nine-foot adobe wall and sprang over after it. In falling the safe burst open and Leonis possessed himself of the coveted papers and all of the money in the safe, said to have been thirteen hundred dollars. He then pitched the safe into the great water canal, or *zanja madre* which flowed along the western border of Alameda Street and furnished the town with water. Then he made his escape without particular hurry, having already far outdistanced his pursuers, even with an iron safe on his shoulder. To give some idea of the giant strength of this Pyreneian smuggler, seven men were required to fish that safe out of the *zanja* and get it back into place in Etchemende's store.

That's all that was done about it; they got the safe back into the store and let it go at that. Leonis got away with the documents and the swag but was never prosecuted.

It was a common thing for the Big Basque to go out on the range with a wagon, shoot down a thousand-pound steer, pick it up bodily and lay it in the wagon; and he would do this without greater effort than an ordinary man would put forth in handling a sack of grain.

The final outcome of the trial of Sansome and Davis, whom I defended through the twenty-one days above described, was their discharge. I then immediately brought action on their behalves against Leonis for malicious prosecution and false imprisonment. Fortunately, by the time this came to trial, a competent judge, Volney E. Howard, had been raised up by the people, and after a hotly contested jury trial old Elias Sansome and his partner were actually awarded damages against the Big Basque totaling fourteen thousand dollars. This was the first setback that Leonis had ever received in his lawless, domineering career in California. It made him very, very mad. Becoming suspicious that John Lazzarovich, a rich citizen of the Pueblo, had backed the prosecution of this case Leonis assaulted Lazzarovich on the street and inflicted on him serious injury. For this I immediately brought another suit against Leonis on behalf of the injured party and actually recovered from the great man an item of two thousand dollars damages for my client. This sum was paid down by the Big Basque in twenty-dollar gold pieces and he retired to his Calabasan stronghold in sullen dudgeon. We had him on the run!

Sansome and Davis returned to their locations in Calabasas, others followed them and civilization began to press in again harder than ever on the harassed Basque. He fought back but not with the savage confidence he had before exercised. This time he waged war by driving his cattle onto and over the lands which the settlers were trying to cultivate. He forced many of them out this way because they were as yet too poor to fence their lands adequately. Finally a game young Californian, Meza, who had been made a victim of this trick, drove the Leonis cattle off to the four winds, whereupon Leonis, forgetting for the moment his recent reverses in the courts, resorted to his old method of getting his enemies thrown into jail. He charged Meza with larceny of the cattle. The courts now being out from under the Leonis influence Meza was discharged and the author of these lines once more went after El Basquo Grande with a damage suit on behalf of the falsely imprisoned Meza. Again we collected gold twenty-dollar pieces from the treasure chest of the now pretty-thoroughly discredited King of Calabasas.

By this time suits had cost the great man twenty thousand dollars, which had a noticeable tendency to modify his aggressive barbarism. At the same time the settlers were mightily encouraged and the Calabasas became a habitable country.

This brings us down to the middle '80s. The tables are now completely turned. It is the squatters that have become arrogant and somewhat savage. El Basquo Grande scarcely dares to ride along the highway in front of settlers' locations but chooses the byways. A leader of the settlers has risen up, by name Harvey Branscomb. He is not averse to winning a reputation as a frontier fighter and he takes an occasional shot at the Big Basque just to show who is boss. Leonis is afraid of his neighbors now. His herds have diminished and he tries grain farming, but that is a dangerous business for a man with so many enemies for grain fields burn so easily.

Finally, in desperation over another damage suit with which he had been pestered, the shorn giant came to my office and begged *me* to defend him in court! I took the case and won it for him. So rejoiced was he at winning his first damage suit that he went on a big drunk and while driving his wagon homeward through the Cahuenga Pass fell out and his head was crushed under one of the wheels. At least this was the common report, though it was pretty well believed that he was assassinated.

This Michel Leonis had peculiar qualities aside from his savagery. He claimed before his Mexican and Indian followers that he dealt in the occult. They said he could disclose the future, unravel men's secrets, discover stolen property and foretell to a certainty rain or drought. An instance which they relate of his mysterious powers, which is really an instance of a gleam of Solomon-like wisdom, is this:

There were a hundred or more shearers engaged in shearing sheep in his pens when the foreman's watch was stolen from a vest left hanging on the limb of a tree. Receiving his complaint, Leonis had all the men lined up and demanded that the thief forthwith bring the stolen watch to him. There was no response. "Very well," said Leonis, "I will now proceed to discover the thief and recover the watch." He went from man to man holding his ear down near the mouth of each as he passed along the line. But no man spoke. This done he called for a burro. Then he led the ass along the line of men, demanding that each whisper his innocence or confess his guilt into the donkey's ear. After the passage of the line and the whispering in the donkey's tall listener, Leonis led the animal aside and pretended to commune with it for a long while. Then Leonis returned to the uneasy sheep shearers and said: "Yes, one of you confessed to the burro and now I know the thief. But the principal object is to recover the watch. I will not expose the thief if he will return the stolen article. I now hang the vest back on the tree and to-morrow morning I expect to find the watch reposing in the pocket. If not I shall hang the thief on this same tree until dead." The gang was dismissed to supper.

The next morning the watch was in the vest pocket.

After the death of Leonis, Harvey Branscomb constituted himself a sort of successor to the Basque as a ruler of the settlers and more bloody trouble blighted the region; quarrels and killings revived and made it a dread country again. Then drought fell upon it, and quietude. Now it is waiting, in all its beauty, for a revival, and may its future history be peaceful and productive as befits such a naturally glorious region.

CHAPTER 19

Spit in the Mouth of Hell

I HAD often wondered over the possible origin of a perfectly graded but utterly abandoned turnpike road extending in a straight line from where the Soledad Pass * opens onto the Mojave Desert to Elizabeth Lake, fifteen miles to the westward. In places the drifting sands of the desert have obliterated the mysterious road but where the earth is hard and flinty and the sand cannot take hold it shows as plainly as it did over one hundred years ago when it was cut, filled, graded and smoothed by the Devil himself. For *El Demonio,* I finally learned on most excellent authority, was the builder.

In explanation of how I came by this astonishing revelation let me say that some years ago I edited "The Spiritual Conquest of California" from the manuscript of Don Guillermo Embustero y Mentiroso, and the publication of this document was the cause of much interest among historians and students of Catholic history. The manuscript was placed in my hands by a lineal descendant of Don Guillermo Embustero now residing in Los Angeles and known as a man of scientific distinction.

Considerably later I was in conversation with this Don Guillermo of the fourth generation and referred to the *milagro* † of the desert's border. He surprised me with the

* Through which the Southern Pacific Railroad now passes from Los Angeles into the Antelope Valley, a westward extension of the Mojave Desert.
† Miracle.

SPIT IN THE MOUTH OF HELL

reply: "There is no need to wonder about it. Did I not give you a manuscript of my ancestor relating the true history of the Devil's Turnpike?"

I replied in the negative and he promised to bring me the document. He fulfilled his promise, and here is a translation from the old Spaniard's yellow pages:

In the year of Our Lord 1780 and in the tenth month thereof the Holy Father and President of all the Missions of California, the illustrious and Most Reverend Junípero Serra, with an escort of dragoons under command of the valiant veteran, the Sergeant Arguello, engaged in an expedition of discovery to the great valleys of the north. On his return journey he was pursued, attacked, harassed and finally surrounded by hostile savages and besieged at a point that was afterward called La Laguna del Diablo.

The beleaguered Spaniards were reduced to most direful distress but happily an Indian neophyte escaped through the besiegers with a message to the commandant of the guard at San Gabriél. The latter at once despatched the valorous Lieutenant Pico with every soldier that could be spared to the rescue of the Christians. The brave lieutenant and his *mando* * pushed forward in hot haste but most unfortunately became lost in *las soledades* † of the desert. For three days and three nights they wandered in search of the forlorn Christians, their countrymen. On the eve of the fourth day the distracted Pico, suffering from hunger and thirst, found himself back again at the site of the camp he and his companions had made three days previously, that is, at the mouth of the Cañon or Pass of Soledad, that gives out onto the boundless desert.

* Command.
† The solitudes.

The horses were utterly worn out, the troopers famished for food and drink. The sun had set and darkness was casting its mantle of charity over the despairing warriors when the frantic Pico raised his eyes, crossed himself desperately and said, "Ay, *Diablo,* what would I give for a good road direct to the camp of the besieged Christians, my countrymen! I would not only give my soul but I would pledge the soul of all my kith and kin for generations to come!"

" 'Tis a bargain!" A demon stood before the desperate Pico. But the lieutenant of San Gabriél Arcángel feared nor man nor devil nor chimera dire. He always backed up his word, and with a gesture of accord he replied promptly to the demon, " 'Tis a bargain!"

Immediately a legion of demons bearing picks, spades, axes, hammers, prying bars and torches appeared upon the scene.

"Go!" said the Devil (for the first demon proved to be no other than El Demonio himself) and the division with axes cleared a way through the brush.

"Go!" said the Devil, and the ground was leveled and graded by the pick and spade demons.

"Go!" said the Devil, and the demons with iron bars pried out the great rocks.

"Go!" said the Devil, and the huge stones were beaten into pebbles by the hammer division.

"Go!" said the Devil, and the spade demons returned to work, spreading the pebbles and pounding them down into a hard surface as the torch bearers reddened the encroaching night with their flares. Magically a broad finished road began to stretch straight into the west.

"Ready?" asked the Devil, bowing to the undaunted Lieutenant Pico.

"Ready!" responded the brave lieutenant.

"Go!" said the Devil.

"Forward Fours! Trot! Gallop! Charge!" shouted the officer, driving the spurs into his horse's flanks and dashing along at the swift heels of the Devil whose whole legion of demons swarmed on ahead creating the road with demoniac magic as they flew along, the brush cutters followed by the imps with picks, who were followed by the spade wielders and they by the division with iron bars and they by the rock pounders and they by the smoothers, the whole fiendish horde led by the bearers of sulphurous torches. On rushed the infernal road builders with terrible swiftness and on followed the Chief Demon with the Lieutenant Pico at his heels and at his heels in turn the loyal troopers whose valor and discipline would have caused them to follow their commander into the fires of Hell.

"Level that hill!" shouted the Devil as Pico, thinking to evade his bargain at this point, now that he knew the right direction, circled away around a hill that stood in the way. The demon legion leveled the hill in a twinkling and suddenly there seemed to be no other way except straight through the cut they had made.

"A bargain's a bargain!" laughed the Devil. "Follow the road, my good lieutenant!"

On they dashed with the road still unrolling magically before them.

"A fraction of a league more and my contract is fulfilled," coolly remarked the Devil to the breathless Pico.

"I shall arrive at the end of the road but you shall not!" cried Pico, making a thrust at the Devil with his Knights Templars sword. The point of the sword proved harmless to the Arch Fiend and the latter grinned defiantly. But he paled as his flaming eyes rested on the hilt of that sword.

Quickly the lieutenant, who was both learned and pious

and knew of those instances in history when the sight of the Cross has sent the Devil slinking back into Hell, held aloft the silver hilt. "Behold the Cross of Christ!" he pronounced.

The Devil trembled in mute despair. The legion of demon road builders ceased their labors and shrank into the shadows as they gazed on the symbol of Redemption glittering in the sulphurous glare of their hellish torches.

"Out of the way!" commanded the brave Christian Spaniard. Holding the hilt of his Knights Templars sword always towards the Arch Fiend the officer ordered his troops forward while he himself covered their rear. The demoniac road crew broke and fled, the Devil with them.

Spurring forward to rejoin his command Pico found his soldiers already at the camp of the intrenched Sergeant Arguello and the precious Father Serra.

Turning a triumphant look back into the valley where he had escaped the infernal horde the incomparable Pico saw the demons huddled around El Demonio himself in the light of flames that licked out from a fearsome hole in the ground. Suddenly volumes of black and yellow and red smoke arose and enveloped the demons in a horrific pall. A livid lake of fire spread out all about them and down through its crimson surface the infernal band sank from sight.

In the morning when the happy Christians, rescued and rescuers alike, started their return to San Gabriél Arcángel they found that the lake of fire had been replaced by a lake of beautiful pure water, whereupon Father Serra, with a beatific expression, fell on his knees and gave thanks to God for this His gracious sign of safety to unworthy sinners.

When I submitted my translation of his ancestor's manuscript concerning the origin of Elizabeth Lake to Don Guillermo of the fourth generation, he said:

"That is fine. You did your part well; but the inference made by the original chronicler at the end of his legend, that the Divine Spirit overcame the influence of the Arch Fiend at that spot by turning the lake of brimstone into a lake of pure water, though a beautiful idea, does not conform to the subsequent history of Elizabeth Lake. By all reports that is a horrible, haunted body of water. It is a mouth of Hell. For the century since the birth of that *laguna* as narrated in the manuscript, frightful and unearthly noises have emanated from those depths. Screams, shrieks, groans, as though Hell itself and its congregation of the damned might lie directly beneath the lake."

"I had never realized that," I replied in amazement.

"Why," returned my informant, amazed in his turn at my ignorance, "it is all common knowledge among the natives, at least common tradition among them. And it is an actual fact that in the past no one could be found who would accept permanently a grant of that valley, despite its beauty and fertility, its succulent grasses, cool springs, purling brooks, shady groves. And even when American squatters began to come into the country they soon gave up their desire to possess the region. You may judge by this that there must have been something to the stories of its horrors, for the American squatter is hard to scare from good land.

"I'll tell you about Don Pedro Carrillo's experience. You of course know the Carrillo family, perhaps the most prominent of all the old line in California, the men all brave and the women all beautiful. This Don Pedro was as brave as the Carrillo tradition, absolutely free from superstition, a disbeliever in things supernatural. In the middle 1830's, when in the full prime of his manhood, he procured a grant of many square leagues of land radiating from the Laguna del Diablo. He built a house by the lake, stocked the vast domain with horses and cattle and settled down to a life of pastoral independence and baronial pomp.

"He was in his new home just three months. He fled one night, his pathway lighted by the conflagration that consumed his house, stables, corrals and storehouses. He abandoned his grant, and all he will give as the reason if you ask him is, 'It was because of the hell raised in and around Laguna del Diablo. Conditions there made me prematurely old.'

"From that time the beautiful lake and surrounding lands remained a desolation until the invasion of American squatters in 1855. They thought they had found a paradise but they didn't stay long. It is the only instance in the history of California where the squatter yielded up a good location without a fight. They withdrew in a body, saying simply, 'The whole infernal region is haunted.'

"Afterwards Chico López yielded to the lure of the valley and settled down on a piece of the property out of sight of the *laguna*. Another Chico—Chico Vásquez, brother of the notorious bandit of the '70's, Tibúrcio Vásquez—was mayordomo del camp or boss of the ranges for López. Once I was a guest at the López house when the mayordomo dashed up on horseback in great excitement and exclaimed, 'For the love of God, *mí patrón,* go with me to the lake. Surely all the demons of song and story have come to the surface. Such an uproar and lashing of waters one never heard or saw before!' The excited mayordomo crossed himself piously and offered up an *oración* from his seat in the saddle.

"We went immediately to the lake, the two Chicos and I.

"It was mid-day and the sun shone benignly on the mirror-like surface of the *laguna,* which was as calm as a sleeping infant. Everything was delightfully quiet except the temper of Chico the master, whose choler rose as he concluded that he had been tricked by Chico the servant.

" 'What do you mean, mayordomo,' he began, 'in bringing us on this two-league gallop just to satisfy your idea of a joke?'

"The poor mayordomo was trying to find words to cover his confusion when, as terrifying as a peal of thunder from a clear sky, a great whistling, hissing, screaming roar issued from a growth of tules growing on the margin of the lake and so near to us that we could smell the nauseating, fetid breath of the monster emitting the sound. So sickening was the foul effluvia that we reeled in our saddles and no doubt would have been overcome had not our horses dashed away with us in fright.*

"After bringing our horses under control we turned and gazed back at the lake. From our position we could discern the outlines of a huge monster, larger than the greatest whale, with enormous bat-like wings. At times it would flap these wings as though attempting to rise from the mud where it lay. It would roar and splash the water with what appeared to be great flippers or legs.

"Night came on and we returned to the ranch house and tried to eat supper, but found no relish in it. Neither could we sleep that night. In the morning all the vaqueros were mustered and armed with rifle, revolver and reata. With them we returned to the lake.

"The monster had disappeared. Whether it had flown away or sunk beneath the mud we could not determine but the foul odor, in diminished strength, was still evident. We returned to the house for breakfast to speculate over this astounding *milagro*.

* It is a fact that until recent years Elizabeth Lake gave off a foul odor at certain seasons.

"Said Chico López: 'That water is certainly well named Laguna del Diablo, but how do you suppose its evil history originated? Is that slimy water spit in the mouth of Hell, or what?'

" 'I can probably arrive at the historical facts in a very short time,' said I, remembering the yellowed old manuscripts still lying unread in the treasure chest of my ancestor, Embustero y Mentiroso. 'That forebear of mine wrote down everything of importance in the beginnings of California.' And my surmise proved correct for you have before you now the document bearing on the origin of the lake you Americans call Elizabeth."

Continuing the story of the two Chicos and their horrific monster, Don Guillermo the Fourth said that for a while nothing more of it was seen, but the López horses and cattle began to disappear. First the owner thought grizzly bears were responsible, but this opinion proved unreasonable in view of the volume of devastation among the herds. Finally one night a great uproar was heard in a corral and by the time the vaqueros reached the spot ten mares with their foals were missing. And against the night sky was seen an incredible griffon winging away, heavy with feasting.

This was in 1883, the year in which Don Chico López sold out cheap to El Basquo Grande and left the accursed spot.

In October, 1886, one of our Los Angeles papers published the following, which was undoubtedly as true as anything else contained in this chapter:

> A python, or at least a monster of some kind most terrible to behold, has made its appearance at Elizabeth Lake and has caused more terror and excitement among the people of that locality than did the great earthquake of 1855 which rent the earth asunder, leaving the present appearance of an old canal or the grade of a cyclopean

SPIT IN THE MOUTH OF HELL

railroad. The earthquake did not frighten the lake people to any great extent for the simple reason that in 1855 there were no inhabitants in that windy locality.

The python or whatever it is, is not alone because there are many cattle, horses, sheep, pigs, chickens and people at the laguna now off which the python delights to feed. We don't know positively that the monster has yet gorged itself on *corpus humanus,* but it is attested that at night he comes out of the water, visits the corrals and fills up with sheep and calves, a half-dozen at a time. Upon one occasion the monstrosity tried the temper of a regular Texas long-horn steer, which made such a kick and bellowing as brought Don Felipe Rivera to the *locus in quo.* He saw the python which at that moment had swallowed the bronco steer to the middle. But after a terrific struggle the victim freed itself and the monster, in disappointment and alarm, betook itself to the lake.

Don Felipe describes the monster as about fifteen varas (forty-four feet) long and as large as four elephants. Large enough, indeed, to make a saddle horse for Gen. Brierly. It had a head very much like a bulldog, and Don Felipe thinks it had six legs. Of wings he is positive, which lie flat on the monster's back when not expanded.

Don Felipe Rivera, as his name indicates, is a don of the true Castilian blood who fears not hippogriffes, dragons nor devils, so he ran alongside the python as it floundered toward the lake and emptied his .44 caliber old-fashioned Colt into its side. "The bullets striking the monster's side sounded just as if they were striking against a great iron kettle," said Don Felipe. "One bullet bounced back and hit me and the next morning I picked up four that were as flat as coins. This is all true, on the honor of an hidalgo."

We learn that Don Felipe has come to town at the instance of the terrified Laguneros to consult and adopt ways and means to capture the python. The Sells Brothers have already sent an agent to the lake to report upon the best means of securing the monster alive and to decide if it is possible to handle it in the circus. The contract which Don Felipe has been astute enough to demand from Sells Brothers is on record and can be seen. It covenants as follows: "That if the python is such as the party of the first part describes it to be, and if the party of the first part succeeds in taking it alive, then the party of the second part agrees to pay the party of the first part the sum of $20,000."

This flying amphibious monster was seen several times from 1881 to 1886 and once El Basquo Grande, with his well-known aversion to any rival in his domain, got after it as it betook itself to the lake. Before he could come to grips the terrible Thing sank without leaving a trace, as had the Devil himself once upon a time at that very spot. But not long thereafter it was seen emerging and flying away eastward. Since then it has never been seen in its native valley because it was found and killed eight hundred miles from Lake Elizabeth, as is proved by the following article that appeared in *The Epitaph,* Tombstone, Arizona:

> A winged monster resembling a huge alligator with an extremely elongated tail and an immense pair of wings was found on the desert between Whetstone and the Huachuca Mountains last Sunday by two ranchers as they returned home from the Huachucas. The creature was evidently greatly exhausted by a long flight and when discovered was able to fly but a short distance at a time. After the first shock of wild amazement had passed the two men, who were on horseback and armed with Winchester rifles, regained sufficient courage to pursue the monster and after an exciting chase of several miles succeeded in getting near enough to open fire and wound it. The creature then turned on the men but owing to its exhausted condition they were able to keep out of its way and after a few well directed shots

SPIT IN THE MOUTH OF HELL 205

the monster rolled partly over and remained motionless. The men cautiously approached, their horses snorting with terror, and found that the creature was dead.

They then proceeded to make an examination and found that it measured ninety-two feet in length and the greatest diameter was about fifty inches. It had only two feet, situated a short distance in front of where the wings were joined to the body. The beak, as near as they could judge, was about eight feet long, the jaws being thickly set with strong, sharp teeth. The eyes were as large as dinner plates and protruded from the head. Some difficulty was encountered in measuring the wings as they were partly folded under the body, but finally one was straightened out sufficiently to get a measurement of seventy-eight feet, making the total length from tip to tip about one hundred and sixty feet. The wings are composed of a thick and nearly transparent membrane and are devoid of feathers or hair, as is the entire body. The skin of the body was comparatively smooth and easily penetrated by a bullet. The men cut off a small portion of the tip of one wing and took it home with them. Last night one of them arrived in this city for supplies and to make preparations to skin the creature. The hide will be sent to eminent scientists for examination. The finders returned to the kill early this morning, accompanied by several prominent men who will endeavor to bring the strange creature to town before it is mutilated.

Commenting on the story in the Arizona paper, a Los Angeles paper in May, 1890, said:

Such a bird, reptile or monster was seen about three years ago by three Mexican rancheros living near Elizabeth Lake. When first seen it was lashing itself about in the deep waters of the lake. The men took it for a bunch of cattle that had mired down and approached to see if they could save them when a winged creature of huge proportions rose into the air and flew heavily out of sight. The Mexicans' story was told here and greatly ridiculed at the time.

It may prove, however, that in the desert fastnesses some of the prehistoric reptiles, supposed to have become extinct ages ago, still exist. The traditions of the Indians would seem to point to such a possibility.

Thus runs the legend of Elizabeth Lake and I beg the reader to believe every line of this chapter because it is founded on the word of an Embustero y Mentiroso, hidalgo of the old blood, and others of equal credibility.

Francisco Rico

CHAPTER 20

A Malay Yankee and the Great Peralta Land Fraud

IN a former book of reminiscences I painted a word picture of a man whom I believed to be perhaps the most remarkable that ever came to California and I called him simply Bill. That Bill was Major William P. Reynolds, son of a Massachusetts sea captain and a Malay or Malay-Chinese mother, and the man primarily responsible for the first raising of the American flag over Monterey. He was born in Manila, raised in Honolulu, educated in Boston and settled in California.

We first hear of Major Reynolds' father from Commodore Wilkes, U.S.N.,* in the late 1830's when with his flotilla this naval officer rounded Cape Horn, explored and surveyed most of the South Sea islands and laid up for a cleaning spell at Honolulu. The Commodore in his great book descriptive of his explorations speaks of a controversy he had with the royal authorities of the Hawaiian Kingdom, the result of which was that they would not furnish him with a pilot to take his ships to sea through the reef that encloses Honolulu harbor. "Fortunately," comments Commodore Wilkes, "there was a Mr. Reynolds, a Massachusetts man resident at Honolulu, who volunteered as pilot, and I went to sea without the consent of the mighty powers that were. I did this in contempt of the King."

* Lieutenant (later Commodore) Wilkes, U.S.N., sailed in the flagship *Vincennes* from Hampton Roads Aug. 18, 1838. In 1841 his exploring expedition was on the California coast.

Major Reynolds arrived at Monterey, California, some years before the outbreak of the war with Mexico. He came as mate of the Hawaiian brig *Eama,* was later wrecked on the Southern California coast in the bight where Redondo is now located, barely escaped with his life from his demolished ship, went to Santa Bárbara awhile, then to Monterey, where he enlisted in Fauntelroy's Dragoons, a company that went to make up the Frémont Battalion in the march on Los Angeles.

In 1849 Reynolds returned to Los Angeles and became the original proprietor, the founder, of the historic old Bella Union Hotel.[1] In 1858 he entered the service of the United States as a surveyor and draughtsman in the office of the Surveyor General in San Francisco and became one of the most eminent authorities on the vexing question of the old Spanish and Mexican land grants. He was a man of wonderful mind and most fertile imagination. He was such a skilled romancer that he would absolutely captivate any audience with his marvelous yarns. Certain qualities of the Oriental mind which he inherited made him a superlative story teller. In appearance he was quite lordly and in manner most impressive; his head was larger than Daniel Webster's but well shaped and contained a tremendous intellect. With this intellect went a trenchant sense of humor.

One day during the height of the Denis Kearney campaign in San Francisco against the Chinese in California,* when the union workingmen were being inflamed against coolie labor, a delegation of so-called workingmen called at Major Reynold's office in Los Angeles. The Major was doing some work in Southern California at the time for the Surveyor General and maintained an office in the old Temple

* A campaign that culminated in the new state constitution of 1879 and the Chinese Exclusion Act.

Block, near my own. I said so-called workingmen because the agitators that made up the visiting committees in those days were merely windjammers that did no work except with their voices.

The Major and I were enjoying post-prandial cigars and some gossip in his office when in walked the delegation, requesting a contribution to the "Workingmen's Fund," to be used to bring about legislation for the expulsion of the Chinese from California. Reynolds listened respectfully to their speeches and when they had finished this was the answer he shot back at them:

"A fine set of statesmen you are, picking me out to insult me. You come here asking me to put up money to enable you fellows to commit outrages on my countrymen!"

The leader of the delegation asked in astonishment: "What do you mean by your countrymen?"

"What do I mean? Don't you know that I am a Chinaman? I am not only a Chinaman, sir, I am a Mandarin! At my father's house such miserable trash as you are would not be permitted to pick up the crumbs that fall from his table. Get out of here and don't assume to mix with Chinese gentlemen."

Utterly flabbergasted by the Major's lordly manner the Kearney delegation withdrew in sullen confusion. As the door closed Reynolds laughed and turned to me with the question: "Say, Bell, do I *really* look so much like a Chinaman?"

William Toler, who died comparatively recently in Oakland, is the man credited in history with having first raised the American flag over California. He was a midshipman in the U. S. Navy in 1846 and when Commodore Sloat took possession of California July 7 of that year in the name of the United States, Midshipman Toler is recorded as the individual who actually hauled the Stars and Stripes up the flagstaff over the old customs house at Monterey.

But four years previously William P. Reynolds had caused the American flag to be raised over the same building. In 1842 Commodore Ap Catesby Jones, U.S.N., on board a man-of-war lying in Monterey Bay, was visited by Reynolds, who was then mate of some sailing craft in the Pacific trade. Bill Reynolds gave the Commodore a whole lot of romance, the gist of which was that England was about to seize California; that he, Bill Reynolds, had discovered through intricate diplomatic intrigue that a British man-of-war was expected at Monterey any moment to take possession to forestall the possibility of American ownership in the future.

Whereupon Commodore Jones, U.S.N., not to be outflanked by any maneuvers of John Bull, landed marines, hoisted the American flag over the government building and formally took possession of California in the name of the United States of America.

Twenty-four hours thereafter despatches arrived which convinced Commodore Jones that he had been the victim of a romantic imagination, no war having been declared yet by Mexico and no British ships appearing in the offing with shotted cannon; so he hauled down Old Glory, apologized to the indignant and haughty representatives of Mexico, up-anchored and sailed away in humble disgust.[2]

As a matter of fact Reynolds was right, except that he was four years ahead of his time. His keen mind foresaw the coming conflict with Mexico and the British desire to get in on the ground floor in California. He was a patriotic American who didn't want to see his country out-jockeyed and figured that a sensational yarn was justified if predicated on the possible truth and if it would serve as a warning for the future.

In 1876 I suggested to Major Reynolds that he should turn to writing romances. "Romancing is your forte, Bill," said I. "Eugene Sue, Victor Hugo, Captain Marryat, Washington Irving couldn't hold a candle to you if you once got started. Write a romance and make your fame and fortune."

So Bill, in the course of four years, wrote a novel; and could you believe it, this romantic tale which Bill Reynolds wrote was the cause of the launching of a tremendous land fraud case that cost the United States Government tens of thousands of dollars and years of litigation to quash!

The plot of the novel centered around the Casa Grande, a famous and monumental ruin, like the ruin of some great baronial stronghold, in Arizona. There have been many differences of opinion among scientists and historians as to its possible origin, but it is generally believed to have come down from times prehistoric. Bill Reynolds, however, in his capacity of author brought there in the early days of the Spanish conquest of the Southwest a great Spanish nobleman, a conquistador, called him Miguel Peralta and designated him Baron of Arizona. Then he mixed up a lot of highfalutin' Spanish names as followers of the Baron, had them all get together in the wilderness where the Baron had taken up a tremendous land grant, a domain of a hundred square leagues or so, and had them all build a baronial stronghold. The ruins to-day known as Casa Grande[3] were no more nor less than the ruins of the palace of Miguel Peralta, Baron of Arizona, according to this fiction.

The author went on to relate the contests the Peraltaites had with the savages, the final conquest of sword and cross over paganism, the desperate conflicts with jealous fellow-conquistadores who came into power in the government of New Spain and tried to betray the Baron; the love affairs of the master and his men, and so forth, at fascinating length. It was a wonderful production. Bill Reynolds brought it to me, written in the clearest and roundest style of penmanship. He wanted me to read it, review it, criticize it. This was along in 1879 or '80.

In 1881, after my first book of reminiscences had appeared and Reynolds was chiding me for some of the yarns I told on him in that work, though I did not disclose his full name then, I asked him: "When are you going to publish your Casa Grande romance? That one about the Peralta barony?"

"Why," said Bill, "the truth is it's lost."

"You *lost* it? How in the world did that happen?"

"Well," began Bill, "you remember that old school teacher from Downey named Reavis? He was employed by you once as a writer on your paper *The New Constitution.* You know when he lost his job he went out to live on Bill Jenkins' ranch. Bill Jenkins, the fellow you call 'Baron of Alcatraz y Casteca.' Well, I used to go out to Jenkins' ranch to rusticate every now and then and once I had my manuscript out there with me. Reavis wanted to read it. He was supposed to be a man of literary education, a good critic, so I loaned it to him. Left it out there with him. Afterward, when I saw him in town and asked for it, he put on a terrible long face and said that he hadn't had time to read it, that he had brought it back to town to give to me, but had lost it."

Now let us outline as briefly as possible the long and intricate string of events that resulted from the "loss" of the Reynolds manuscript. Reavis, the itinerant school teacher and writer, read it thoroughly, got a great idea from it, drew Bill Jenkins into his scheme, the latter probably not realizing

THE PERALTA LAND FRAUD

its fraudulent nature, and with the fictitious details of the novel as a basis, laid claim to the Barony of Arizona!

Reavis had married a half-breed squaw away up in Mendocino County, California. In the case which he prepared with much legal skill he set her up as the sole surviving direct heir of Miguel Peralta, original proprietor of the hundred square leagues in Arizona; the sole surviving descendant of the union of the Baron of Arizona and the native woman whom he, the Baron, was supposed to have espoused.

Reavis sought powerful help in financing his case, and he got it. He drew into his scheme the Southern Pacific Company, Robert G. Ingersoll, Roscoe Conkling, Collis P. Huntington, William S. Wood, Reuben H. Lloyd, John E. Mackay, Ed S. Stokes, Charles Crocker and others. The Southern Pacific Company, according to Reavis' confession, advanced some two hundred thousand dollars and all together there must have been half a million dollars put up to cheat the United States out of one hundred leagues of government land in Arizona and New Mexico.

Reavis was finally convicted of fraud and sent to the penitentiary in New Mexico. He wrote a confession in which he claims that the government, though it spent a hundred thousand dollars in defending its interests against his conspiracy, never hit upon the true facts of how he built his case. He tells how he conceived and executed the fraud, how he supposedly met and married an *Andaluza* (girl of Andalucía), parentage unknown, and built up for her a mythical lineage proving that she was the descendant of one of the noblest families of Spain, sole heir to the Peralta grant in Arizona. For it is a fact that the Peralta name is prominent in the early annals of California and the Southwest. He tells how he took his wife to Spain, where they were received into the noblest families and where he searched the ancient archives, stealing some documents, forging others. Document by document, by twisting them to fit his needs and getting them falsely certified, he built an apparently perfect title to millions of wealth. Not only large financial interests took stock in his claim but a great many individuals here in Los Angeles County contributed small sums each, expecting to draw great dividends when the claim was proven.

The *Andaluza* he said he married and took to Spain was no other than the Mendocino squaw.

I have before me as I write several great volumes of transcripts and briefs all neatly printed and published, supporting the claim of James Addison Peralta Reavis to that Arizona land, through marriage and through consanguinity with his wife's family. They contain a great array of pictures of Spanish grandees, supposed forebears of himself and wife. One of these is of a Peralta I knew in Los Angeles in early times. He is all rigged up and pictured as the heir should-have-been immediately preceding Señora de Reavis, but who died, alas, unconscious of his noble heritage. When I knew the little scrub he was a hanger-on of the gambling tables. A squatty, black—well, I might as well say greaser. He was not a genteel Mexican nor was he a Spaniard, nor an Indian nor a negro, but all mixed together. He was known around the Pueblo simply by the name "El Español," why, I don't know, for, as I have intimated, he was anything but pure bred.

I have omitted to state that a great deal of money was realized by the combination pushing the claim, before the dénouement, through the process of quitclaiming lands in Arizona. For instance, the city of Phœnix and other prosperous communities came within the limits of the "Peralta Barony." The Reavis claim looked so plausible that the holders of lots and ranches within the disputed territory, to safeguard valuable improvements they had made, thought it safer to get deeds from the Peralta interests then and there rather than await the decision of the courts. So they put up the price the grant claimants were willing to take to quiet their titles in advance. It has been stated that some three hundred thousand dollars were collected in this way.

And all of this originated in the romantic brain of my old friend Bill—Major William P. Reynolds—whom I urged to pen a romance!

This Reavis served out his time in the New Mexico penitentiary and has since been admitted to the bar. If he lives long enough perhaps he will be elevated to the bench.

Before leaving the subject of the Great Peralta Fraud I want to say that I do not believe that Bill Jenkins, who was an old Ranger comrade of mine in the days of Murrieta, knowingly assisted Reavis in framing a fraud. I think that Reavis imposed on the "Baron of Casteca" as he did on some much more prominent men.

A word more about the illustrious Major Reynolds. He had a very dark complexion. As I have said, his mother was a Malay and his father an American, and he was even darker than ordinary half-castes. He was sensitive about this and said that he had been as white as any man until he had been artificially colored, and this is the story he told of how he had become colored:

"When I was twenty-five years old I was supercargo of a trading vessel in the South Seas. A hurricane struck us and piled the ship up on a reef where she was torn to pieces. Myself and three or four others escaped to the island and were made prisoners by the natives, who proceeded in detail to barbecue my companions, leaving me for the last.

"Can you imagine a man's feelings when he knows he is going to be spitted and roasted? When he knows that he is going to have his bones gnawed by a horde of hungry cannibals? Well, I knew I was in for an *auto da fé* and that's all that need be said about my emotions. I brought all my philosophy to bear and just waited quietly for my day to come, for they didn't rush things, but waited for a good holiday to roast a prisoner.

"One day the chiefs gathered around me and held a great pow-wow. The other white men they had simply knocked in the head, one by one, when they needed a feast, and roasted them without any pow-wowing at all. I began to wonder why they were giving me such marked attention; but after a while I was made to understand that I was not to be cannibalized. No, sir, the women had taken a great shine to me. And the men allowed that I ought to make a pretty good native and that if they were successful in smoking me to the proper color of a native they would not only spare my life but make me a chief.

"Well, sir, I was put into a smoke house, much like a house for smoking hams, and subjected to the smoking process for three weeks. During that time I was taken out several times, washed off and examined to see if the coloring had set into my skin, and each time I was shoved back in again as underdone. They gave me plenty of food and water during the process but I tell you it was a tough proposition. When they got through with me I was as dark as any cannibal on the island and not just on the surface, either."

"Why, Bill," I laughed, "then you must be the original smoked Yankee."

"Yes, sir, smoked Yankee and no mistake about it. I was three years on that island and raised myself from a mere village chief to Lord Paramount. I was King."

"How did you get away?"

"Well, there came a vessel that landed men for the purpose

of trading for copra. I made myself known to the captain, but I tell you I had a hard time getting a word with him. My wives guarded me every moment for fear I would escape."

"Wives? How many?"

"Oh, just as many as I wanted. I think that day I had thirty."

"And you finally managed your escape?"

"Yes, I arranged with the captain that the last time the boat shoved off from the shore, after it was out a ways in the water I would make a rush and swim to it. So I did; I outran my wives to the water's edge and made my getaway."

"Did you ever try to whiten yourself, to get the smoke off?"

"Smoke *off?* Out, you mean. Yes, I tried everything in the world—sweating, hot water immersions, solution of oxalic acid and every other possible chemical, but still I'm a smoked Yankee."

Major Reynolds died at Los Angeles in 1889, thoroughly lamented.

Abel Stearns

CHAPTER 21

"The Law West of the Pecos"

THE reputation that California had for "killers" in the early American days has hardly been exaggerated. Texas probably led us in that respect, but we certainly had our share and they kept on drifting through clear down to the days of the big Southern California boom in the '80's. This boom, too, brought hordes of men that were fugitives from justice elsewhere. They sank their identity under assumed names in the excitement of the times, manipulated real estate or preyed on the speculators in other financial ways and sometimes became well-to-do, staid citizens ultimately, handing down family names that did not belong to them.

The "killers" of the early days were a queer study. Mighty good fellows to meet, many of them, without fearsome aspect or manner. We had a class of men in and around Los Angeles, and in fact scattered up and down California, largely from Mississippi, Arkansas and Texas that were jolly good fellows, honorable in their every day dealings with those that met them in the same spirit and wonderful campfire companions. But each one of them was rather proud of having killed his man, or men. They liked to reminisce over these affairs. I have sat down in camp with these men and listened to their after-supper conversation as they smoked, and often it would run like this:

"Have you heard of Bill Magee recently?"

"Oh, yes. The last I heard of him he killed Jake Sipes up on the Trinity, then went over into the Pitt River country, staked a claim, found that a man had got in ahead of him so he killed him."

"I knew Bill Magee's father in Arkansas," volunteered some one else.

"Yeah. He killed old man Hunter. Hunter had killed one of Magee's sons-in-law. Now let's see—who was it killed old Magee? Some one did, but I can't seem to remember who."

"Say," broke in some one else, "do you remember Sam Brown? Sam killed a couple of men down in Texas before he came to California. How many has he killed here, anybody know?"

"Oh, three or four so far as I know. Who was that last man he killed in Texas and what was it about?"

Here the conversation would become involved in the intricacies of why somebody killed somebody else and the individual opinions concerning the merits of the fatal dispute.

When I was in Texas after the close of the War of the Rebellion in '65 I commanded a cavalry patrol for a while on the border. One night I stayed at the house of old Johnny Sansome out on Mason Creek. That was way up toward the old Dutch town of Fredericksburg. Johnny Sansome was a pre-historic Texan. He had fought at the Battle of San Jacinto during the war for the independence of Texas from Mexico. His son John had been a captain in the First Federal Texas Cavalry during the recent war, serving in Louisiana and Texas, was a fellow scout with me during the campaigns in that region, and that is why I had stopped at the Sansome ranch, because John had just come home from the wars.

Old man Sansome was a great story-teller. Among other things he told me about Three-Legged Willey. This fellow was a politician in the Texas Republic, an Alabaman originally, who sought a Congressional seat in the republic of which Sam Houston was president. The reason he was called "Three-legged" was that one of his knees had been shattered by a bullet and when the bone knitted the lower part of his leg stuck square out behind at right angles with his thigh. This was of no use to him of course so he had a wooden leg from the knee down to walk on.

Willey had several opponents for Congressman and at a mass meeting at Victoria they all made speeches. Those who preceded Willey on the platform all took the old-fashioned course of righteously defending their past lives, denouncing as slanderous the rumors being spread abroad by their enemies that they had killed men in their home states and were in Texas as fugitives. Then each went on to explain how justified the killing had been.

At last it came Three-Legged Willey's turn to talk and when he got up he ridiculed the other candidates for all the oratory they had put forth to refute such unimportant accusations as having killed only one man apiece. Then he launched forth thus:

"I killed a man in North Carolina and then crossed over into Tennessee. I killed a man there. Then I went to Alabama and there I laid low my third man. This occasioned my visiting Mississippi, where I killed the fourth. Only after this fourth, gentlemen, did I consider myself sufficiently practiced to claim the honor of becoming a citizen of Texas. And now I ask you, the voters, to consider if I am not four to one more distinguished than any one of my opponents, each one of whom seems to be ashamed of his trigger-finger."

"I hardly need to tell you," finished Johnny Sansome, "that Three-Legged Willey was overwhelmingly elected."

In the '50's there was quite a conspicuous character in

Southern California named William Nelson. He got into a dispute and was perforated with a bullet. The wound was very serious and laid him on his back for almost three years. He was absolutely bedridden. Then suddenly, to the amazement of everybody, he recovered. In 1859 he went to Texas, got a wife, returned to Los Angeles, resumed the business which had been interrupted by his long confinement on a bed of pain, became a thrifty citizen and lived long and prosperously.

Down to the time of Nelson's death people were still marveling over the miraculous recovery he made from the old wound that had been apparently killing him. Here is the sequel, or the explanation or whatever you want to call it, concerning this miracle: When I was on the Texas frontier in April, '66, I visited the ranch of a Mr. Woodward away out on the Leona near its junction with the Rio Grande. In our conversations around the fire in the evenings we talked of various Texans that had gone to California and Mr. Woodward asked me if I had ever known William Nelson. I said that indeed I did and was present at the time he was shot. Then Woodward told me a very strange story concerning William Nelson. He said that along in '52 or '53 a murder was committed in San Antonio. McMullen, the victim, was found in his room with his throat cut, weltering in blood. He was a single man, a small-fry Shylock, a title fiend, so nobody grieved about his death and very little attempt was made by the authorities to solve it. The only clew discovered was the bloody imprint of a man's hand on the wall near the door, and it was remarked that it must have been made by a very tall man groping his way in the dark from the scene of the murder.

"On the last day of the year 1859," continued Woodward, "I was in San Antonio from my ranch. Meeting some friends I was informed that William Nelson had just arrived in San Antonio from California. Nelson and I had been fellow soldiers in the same company in the United States Army some years previously and I wanted to see him, but I put off looking him up until the following Monday. To my disappointment I found that he had already departed on the stage, accompanied by a wife, bound for Indianola, there to take steamer for New Orleans. That same day I met the sheriff and was surprised to find that he was looking for Nelson. Asking what he wanted Nelson for, the sheriff showed me a letter from Los Angeles, written by one who professed to have nursed Nelson during his long illness from the gunshot wound, saying that Nelson had confessed a murder to him. Nelson had called him to his bedside, said the writer, and confided to him that he believed he could get well immediately if he confessed a great crime he had once committed. He then confessed the murder of McMullen in San Antonio, saying that after a dispute with McMullen over money matters he had stolen into the latter's room and cut his head off with a bowie knife.

"Strange to say, the letter writer stated, Nelson showed improvement from the time of his confession and in two or three months was walking the streets a well man. The letter writer then explained that the matter now lay on his own conscience and knowing that Nelson intended visiting San Antonio, where he apparently dared to go now that his mind was free, he, the letter writer, felt that he ought to report the confession to the Texas authorities, though he did not know whether the confession was just the vagary of a sick man or whether there really had been committed a murder in San Antonio on a victim named McMullen.

"I told the sheriff what I had learned of Nelson's departure for New Orleans, but apparently no serious effort was made to apprehend him at this late day and he returned safely to California."

I was of course very much interested in Woodward's story and on returning to Los Angeles I questioned Nelson for the details of his marvelous recovery, without telling him of what Woodward had confided to me. Nelson's explanation was this: That during his long confinement he had experienced many spiritual manifestations and had been led to study the teachings of the spiritualists. That a spirit had finally told him that there was a gun wad in his wound that the doctors had overlooked, told him just where it was lodged and said that he must have it removed in order to get well. He had called in a doctor, who refused to believe it or to probe. "Then," said he, "I got a piece of wire, bent a hook on the end of it and knowing exactly where the wad was situated I drove the wire into the old wound and pulled out the wad. Whereupon I got well."

Now, Nelson's statement could not have been true because he had been on his bed for three years and that gun wad could hardly have persisted in there for that length of time without disintegrating, nor could the man have survived the probing of an old wound in such a crude manner. The only theory that I can accept is that he did kill McMullen, that in his low condition following his own wounding the crime preyed upon his mind to the extent that it kept him from getting well, that the fact of mind over matter was proven in his case in that his confession so relieved his mind that he was able to build up a faith in his recovery that actually resulted in a cure.

There is a character mentioned in my first book of reminiscences that deserves further notice. This is Roy Bean, he who kept the Headquarters Saloon at San Gabriél Mission in the early '50's and who in later years became famous as the

Justice of the Peace of Langtry, Texas, known as "The Law West of the Pecos." Roy came from a highly respectable family; had one brother, Josh, who was a captain in the army and another, Sam, who was a freighter and trader in the Santa Fé and Chihuahua trade.

When Roy was sixteen or seventeen his brother Sam took him to Chihuahua and put him in his store as clerk. A Mexican desperado came into the store and attempted to terrorize the place. Roy ordered him out. With drawn knife the desperado advanced on the American youth, who kept warning him to stand back. The Mexican kept coming on, leering and wielding his knife, until within three or four feet of the boy. Then that boy put a bullet square between the bully's eyes.

A Mexican mob gathered, bent on lynching Roy Bean. His brother and a few other Americans in the place rallied to his defense until they were able to slip him out of town. He was taken to Jesús María, a large mining town in the northeast corner of Sonora, but the news followed him there and a second attempt was made on his life by a mob. Again Americans rallied to his support and a conflict ensued with the final result that the Americans in Jesús María were driven out. Their stores were sacked and they barely escaped with their lives. They finally found refuge in California after a terrible journey.

Among those pillaged and driven out was William B. T. Sanford, who became a prominent merchant in Los Angeles and was a member of the old Ranger company during the bandit reign of terror. He lost his life in the explosion of the tug *Ida Hancock* in San Pedro Bay.[1] Frank Carroll was another. He became a saloon keeper out at the Mission in competition with Roy Bean's "Headquarters."

On arriving in California from Sonora Roy Bean first

stayed in San Diego. He was quite a dashing figure of a young buck and was soon prancing around the old town appareled in all the gay trappings of a Californian caballero, on a spirited steed with silver-mounted saddle and bridle, and became the beau ideal of the aristocratic señoritas of California's original white man's settlement.

One day he had a famous adventure that came very nearly ending much too seriously. There was a gay, rollicking son of Gaul in San Diego who prided himself on his horsemanship and his ability to shoot from the saddle with a revolver. He bantered Roy for a match, shooting at a target from horseback at full charge. Roy promptly accepted the challenge, on the condition that each should be the target for the other. This was probably just a counter-banter on the part of Roy, but the Frenchman accepted the condition and the two heroes prepared for the desperate encounter.

It was common practice for Californians and Mexicans to fight duels for the fun of it with lances or with the swords they usually carried on their saddles beneath one thigh; but a revolver duel on horseback was a new sport and when the news got out that such an encounter was to take place in the principal street of Old Town there was great excitement near and far.

Harathzy was sheriff of San Diego County at the time—the well-known Count Harathzy who later became the great vineyardist and winemaker of Sonoma and also served as superintendent of the U. S. Mint at San Francisco. In connection with the mention of the Count it may not be amiss to recall here that when Harathzy was called upon to settle his account with the government at the end of his term in the mint, he was forty thousand dollars short. He claimed the deficiency was due to a defect in the chimney flues of the mint which carried off the smoke from the molten gold; in other words that the shortage went up the flue in smoke. There was a great deal of public amusement at the superintendent's explanation at the time and it was then the expression originated that a thing has "gone up in smoke" or "gone up the flue." However, scientific tests proved the mint superintendent's contention true, he was exonerated, the flues reconstructed and the drain on the mint stopped.

To return to San Diego: Sheriff Harathzy pretended to regard the approaching duel between Roy Bean and the French gallant as a sort of joke and took no steps to prevent it. Indeed, it would have been quite an impolitic act to call it off because news of the impending show brought rancheros swarming to town, the rancheros patronized the stores and cantinas and there ensued lively prosperity, for the moment at least.

Seconds were appointed and the sheriff did exercise his authority by insisting that the firing be so arranged as not to endanger—at least, not much—the innocent bystanders. If either of the combatants shot an onlooker the law would step in with a penalty; and on this basis the fight took place.

The two heroes maneuvered their spirited horses, each jockeying for a position that would enable him to fire in the direction of the open plain where the crowd was not permitted to gather. I am indebted for a particular description of this combat to the Hon. Guadalupe Estudillo, an honored resident of Los Angeles at the present time and formerly Treasurer of the State of California.* He was living in San Diego then and says it was surely a most exciting affair. Each one strove desperately to get to windward of the other, as a sailor would say, because the one to

---

* The fine old adobe home that is shown to visitors in Old Town, San Diego, as "Ramona's Marriage Place," was built by the Estudillo family about 1820.

leeward could not fire without shooting toward the crowd.

Finally Roy plugged the Frenchman, and as the latter reeled in the saddle Roy plugged his horse to boot. Down went rider and mount in a heap in the middle of the street and young America was proclaimed winner. The señoritas cheered him as boldly as they dared from the sidelines and for the moment he was the hero triumphant.

The Frenchman was not killed, only sorely wounded; but now that the show was over and could no longer be construed as a valuable attraction the sheriff decided to vindicate the law and threw Roy into jail. Count Harathzy had just built a new jail, not of adobe but of a new mixture called concrete which was a seven day wonder to the natives, and he was proud of it. It was fine to have a hero to incarcerate in there because it certainly made the new edifice a center of attraction. The señoritas no longer hung back in maidenly modesty to cheer only faintly for their idol, but they stormed the jail with baskets and shawls filled with flowers, cold chicken, tamales, enchiladas, dulces, wines and cigars and crowded for position at the gratings to hand their gifts through to their Adonis. Those warm-hearted little California beauties just went wild over the handsome fellow; for, as a matter of fact, Roy Bean was as handsome as an Adonis. His complexion was as fair and rosy as a girl's. Hair black and silky, figure above medium height and perfect. In manners a Chesterfieldian gallant.

No jail could hold a hero whom so many beautiful women were passionately determined should be freed. Not even Count Harathzy's new concrete jail, the first in Southern California. Concealed among the fragrant petals of the bouquets, or maybe imbedded in the succulent hearts of tamales, were tools of escape. Roy cut his way through that miraculous concrete in less than no time. True gallant that he was he afterward denied that the ladies supplied him with contraband and claimed that no tools were needed to burrow through that public contract job. However, some one had seen to it that his horse stood all caparisoned behind the jail, with holster and pistol swung at the pommel, and the young gentleman cut stick for Los Angeles.

In 1857 or '58 Roy went to Piños Altos, New Mexico, and thenceforth was lost to California although his fame was destined to shine forth in years to come more brilliantly even than it had among his admiring circle at the "Headquarters" in San Gabriél or among his sportive cronies in the Pueblo de los Angeles.

At the outbreak of hostilities between the North and the South, when the Texans invaded New Mexico and were so roughly handled by General Canby, Roy Bean assisted in organizing a company of Confederate sympathizers that called themselves the Free Rovers. Others called them the Forty Thieves. After the failure of the Texan campaign in New Mexico the Forty Thieves disbanded and Roy engaged in running cotton into Mexico and bringing out supplies to San Antonio for the Confederate army. He was well paid, apparently, and made a lot of money that way. When I was in the service at San Antonio in '65 Roy was there with his wagon train. He was still freighting to Mexico, in business for himself.

When the Southern Pacific Railroad was built from El Paso to San Antonio a certain station near the Río Grande, which is the border line between the United States and Mexico, was named Langtry. It is just west of the Río Pecos. Roy Bean opened a saloon there and called it "The Jersey Lily." This saloon and its keeper made the station of Langtry, Texas, almost as famous as the Jersey Lily herself, the beautiful Lily Langtry. It was here that the dashing youth of yesteryear became Justice of the Peace, an office which he has held continuously down to the time I am now writing, with one brief exception. One time as an election approached some boosters for another settlement that had sprung up down nearer the river put up a rival candidate to Roy. The latter feeling so sure that his re-election was automatically assured, gave little attention to the rival claimant, with the surprising result that the upstart was actually elected and the judicial seat moved down to the river bank.

"But I am the only man that could ever make anything out of the office," said Justice Bean to me when he was laughing about that political slipup, "and in a little while the Río Grande judge came up to propose to me that I buy him out. He brought his commission along with him, his docket and all his papers, and dickered with me. He was sick of the job. So I gave him a demijohn of whiskey, two bear skins and a pet coon for the right, title, honor and emoluments of the office. I've run the thing ever since without opposition."

Roy's court is held in the bar-room of "The Jersey Lily" saloon. The bar, or counter, is the judicial bench, and whiskey barrels set up on end in front of it constitute the legal bar. The opposing lawyers, if there are any, use the heads of the barrels as desks. From this courtroom in the desert have issued decisions that have carried the fame of Justice Bean the world 'round. Judge Bean and Coroner Bean, for he also occupied the latter distinguished office.

While the railroad was under construction beyond Langtry a section boss killed a Chinese laborer. He was arrested and brought before Judge Bean. The boss was a popular man in that section and valuable to the railroad authorities so the latter exerted strong pressure on the court to get him acquitted. Judge Bean proved very patient in his examination of the case. He examined a great many witnesses very solemnly. He consulted his book of law often. This book, the only one he ever consulted in running his court, was a compilation of the laws of the State of California published in 1856.

"They send me the Texas statutes, codes and so forth every year," Judge Bean once explained to me, "but I never read them. All the law I want I take from the compiled laws of the State of California. They are good enough for any state, they are good enough for anybody, they are good enough for me. I administer the law upon the authority of that book and don't need any other."

After the testimony in the trial of the section boss was all in, which showed conclusively that the accused had murdered the Chinaman, the Court opened the compiled laws of the State of California, spread the volume before him with great ceremony and delivered this opinion:

"The Court has been very patient in inquiring into this case. It is true that the defendant shot the Chinaman and killed him. It seems as if there ought to be some sort of punishment meted out, but there doesn't seem to be any provided for. What they don't know about Chinamen in California they don't know anywheres, yet I've looked this book through and can't find any place where it is named as an offense for a white man to kill a Chinaman. So far as the feelings of this Court goes it would be the greatest pleasure to hold the defendant for murder, but the situation is not the fault of this Court. Therefore the judgment of the Court is that the defendant be discharged."

A case that came before "The Jersey Lily" bar, with the proprietor acting this time both as judge and coroner, was that of a man accidentally killed by one of the Southern

Pacific trains. On the body at the time were found forty dollars and a revolver. The judgment of Coroner Bean was that no fault attached to the railroad company for the unfortunate occurrence. The judgment of Justice of the Peace Bean followed, and was this: "Yet the Court must take into consideration another feature of this case. That is to say, a concealed weapon was found on this person. He was therefore violating the law at the time of his death and the Court is driven to the disagreeable necessity of imposing on the deceased a fine of forty dollars. The weapon will be confiscate to the Court."

A wiry cowpuncher rode in one day escorting a buxom prairie lass and applied to Judge Bean for a marriage license. It was issued and the ceremony performed on the spot. After paying over a liberal fee the cowboy and his bride dashed away into the wilds on their mustangs to enjoy the delights of matrimony.

About a year later the pair came back and complained to His Honor that they couldn't get along together and wanted a divorce. The Judge told them that divorces were very expensive. The cowpuncher thought he could stand a pretty good pull on his resources to get relief, so the Judge named his price, received it, pronounced the pair divorced and they rode away, each in a separate direction.

The judge of the District Court in El Paso had heard tales of queer decisions issuing from the Justice of the Peace at Langtry but paid no attention to them until he got wind of this divorce proceedings. Then he thought he would go down and have a talk with the Langtry justice. Said the District Judge to Justice of the Peace Bean over the bar —the social bar—of "The Jersey Lily": "Justice Bean, the question of separating a man and wife by divorce assumes a degree of gravity that precludes hasty treatment. I have come down to talk to you about this matter. What have you to say in regard to your jurisdiction to grant divorces?"

"Why," answered Justice Bean, "I'm the only jurisdiction west of the Pecos—if I can't grant a married couple relief from each other who can? And besides, I'd like to ask you this: When you commit an error in your court and it is brought to your attention, what do you do about it?"

"Do you mean to ask me, do I correct an error in some case that has been before my Court?"

"That's what I mean, Judge."

"Why, certainly, if I commit an error I correct it if it is called to my attention in the proper way."

"All right, that's just what I did when I divorced that cowpuncher and his woman. I had issued the license and I had married them. They brought to my attention the fact that I had made an error in those matters and I corrected that error."

The District Judge allowed that Justice Bean had the better of the argument and it is to be presumed that the two judicial wiseacres thereupon turned their attentions exclusively to decisions concerning the choice of liquors.

I last heard of Roy Bean through an Associated Press despatch in a newspaper. The despatch was dated Langtry, May 27, 1901, and read as follows:

> Judge Roy Bean, notorious throughout western Texas and many times the subject of magazine articles, also known as "The Law West of the Pecos," again distinguished himself last night by going through a Pullman car while the westbound Southern Pacific train was stopping at Langtry and, with a .45-caliber Colt in his hand, collecting from an eastern tourist thirty-five cents due for a bottle of beer. The tourist had bought the beer at the Judge's saloon but had rushed off without paying for it. Going through the car Bean peered into each

passenger's face until he found his man when he said, "Thirty-five cents or I press the button." He was handed a dollar bill and returned the correct change.

As the Judge left the car he turned in the aisle and said to the frightened passengers, "If you don't know what kind of hombre I am, I'll tell you. I'm the law west of the Pecos." The passengers thought it was a holdup.

At the time of this "holdup" Roy Bean was over seventy years old.

In the days of Joaquín Murrieta Roy was a Ranger along with the author, and after he left San Gabriél it was my pleasure to correspond with him from time to time. The last letter I received from him was on May 21, 1898. Since then, as I have said, my only news of him was through that Associated Press despatch from Langtry.

They were queer letters that Justice Bean and I used to exchange between us. His were short and laconical, but from me he expected a full line of gossip about the doings of the old-time families he used to know when he enlivened Southern California by his presence; all the personal news of the Pueblo and the Mission. For some reason I kept a copy of one newsy letter I sent him from Los Angeles, and as it contains an account of a court decision very much akin to some of the decisions that issued from the mouth of "The Law West of the Pecos," I will venture to quote from it:

> In this letter, Judge, I am only mentioning those prominent persons that I know you will remember. The Nietos, for instance, you knew them all. Don Diego was a way up caballero, in your time and long before, but unfortunately he got sent to the penitentiary. Not for the usual thing, cattle stealing, but because he stabbed a man and the man laid down and died. Don Diego plead guilty to manslaughter, made a statement

in mitigation of sentence and threw himself upon the mercy of the Court. The mitigation consisted in this: a low down cholo, a pelado, assaulted Don Diego with vile words. He used on him all the vile and profane epithets of which the Spanish language is so prolific. What a beautiful language is that of Spain anyway, Judge, when it comes to real low-down, genuine cuss words! It beats English all hollow. But all that Don Diego would answer to the vile names the cholo called him was, "I am a caballero! I can't be insulted by a low-down pelado like you. Say what you please, your words do not penetrate my consciousness."

That pelado had about given up trying to insult the caballero when suddenly he had an idea and burst out with, "Yes, a fine caballero you pretend to be, but you are a bigger scoundrel than Bill el Molacho!"

"That," said Don Diego in his plea to the Court, "was more than any gentleman could stand. I killed him."

The judge agreed with Don Diego and would have let him go scot-free except that some sort of a reform movement was on just then and he had to give him a minimum sentence of three years. The caballero was soon afterward pardoned by the governor and allowed to go free.

You remember El Molacho, don't you, Roy? I won't call him by his family name even in this letter because he is now a man of prominence among us. Of course you know my horror of hurting the feelings of any of our leading families!

You will recollect that we had Bill el Molacho and we had Bill el Tuerto. Both Americans. El Molacho's reputation was such that—well, you see what a caballero like Don Diego Nieto thought of it. El Tuerto left New Mexico ahead of the law after some transaction in mules, landed in Los Angeles and became a banker. That is, he opened a monte bank. Then he got to be a kind of constable, then got into the legislature and afterward came very near being elected judge in Los

Angeles. Jack King beat him; Jack King got to be the judge.

You remember Jack King and the other King boys? They killed Bob Carlisle in a free fight in the old Bella Union. Jack married Miss Laura Evertson. You knew the Evertsons out at San Gabriél. I saw you there at the time the Ranger company came out to take the bandit trail. It was during the heated time of the Murrieta régime and a raiding party had entered the Evertson house over across the arroyo from your "Headquarters." The head of the house was away and the only male person about the place when it was attacked was little Evert, about sixteen years old. Do you remember how that boy took down a pair of old percussion-lock holster pistols that belonged to Doctor Sturgis, who lived there, and turned loose on those thieves? The first bandit had Mrs. Evertson by the throat, about to kill her. Evert actually drove those fellows away and when the alarm was given the Rangers took the trail, you and I among them. Great days, those were. Evert was a fine fellow, died at San Francisco eight or ten years ago.

It was Evert's sister Jack King married, and they still reside here. Jack is the oldest lawyer at the Los Angeles bar unless it is myself. He reared a most talented family of boys and girls.

Roy, you wouldn't believe it, but it is almost a continuous town now from San Gabriél to Los Angeles and from Los Angeles to Wilmington and San Pedro. You know Phineas Banning, afterwards General Banning, founder of Wilmington. A great man, a great citizen. He is dead and his sons have succeeded—

So ran the letters that used to keep Justice of the Peace Bean, "The Law West of the Pecos," in touch with his early cronies of La Misión San Gabriél Arcángel and El Pueblo de Nuestra Señora la Reina de los Angeles while he was growing famous behind the bar and on the bench of "The Jersey Lily," down by the Río Grande.

Recalling the San Gabriél days of the Bean brothers ("Los Frijoles," the natives used to call them) prompts me to mention the terrific treasure trove excitement that broke out only a few years ago in the region of the old Mission. There have been many stories circulated of buried treasure left by the padres when they were forced out of their establishments but they are mostly great exaggerations. There never was very much money in California before the Americans came and what existed was kept in violent circulation on the gambling table or in betting on horse races. Rawhides, tallow and soap formed the currency of the country. Yankee ships came to the coast to trade manufactured articles from the American east coast for the products of the slaughtered cattle and it was in this way that the Californians of the Mexican era bought practically all their imported goods.

But the individual rancheros were only small fry in this trade in comparison with the Franciscan padres, up to the time of the secularization of the Missions. In spite of all the laws that were aimed at keeping the friars from trading with foreign ships their vast herds were the principal source of supply for the Boston hide droghers that came round the Horn and that have been made familiar to the American reader by Richard Henry Dana's "Two Years Before the Mast."

Now, this old hide, tallow and soap trade has a direct bearing on the mining excitement that had all the tenderfoot Americans in the San Gabriél Valley by the ears not so long ago. When, in the 1830's, the Mexican Congress passed an act secularizing the Missions and it became apparent that the padres must soon relinquish all temporal control of their vast properties to civil administrators appointed by the government, which would thenceforth pocket all income from the properties, the padres got busy in an attempt to save what they could before the storm struck. They organized great *matanzas,* or slaughters, and killed their cattle by the thousands in order to reduce them to a marketable product that might be disposed of to trading ships before the government took hold. Each rawhide represented at least a dollar; the tallow from each animal was worth so much according to the degree of fatness of the creature, and other parts were boiled down for soap. The tallow was ordinarily packed in rawhide bags called *cerónes,* containing a weight called *arroba,* or twenty-five pounds, and stored temporarily in the Mission warehouses to await the arrival of a Yankee trader.

But the wholesale slaughter now undertaken made it impossible to find room for the product in this way so they dug immense pits, poured in the molten tallow or soap, covered it with a surface of earth when it had cooled, and so had it safely in cold storage for an indefinite period. The intention of the priest was to mine out the product, sack it and sell it to the ships as they arrived. However, the agents of the Mexican government fell upon the Missions like a horde of hungry wolves before the buried treasure could be shipped out, and it was overlooked in the scramble for the assets that still appeared on the surface.

The San Gabriél Valley settled up pretty fast with Americans in the '80's, once the boom got under way, and cellars and wells were dug here, there and yonder. One day a settler rushed into Los Angeles with the information that he had discovered a new resource in the soil of California that promised to yield inestimable wealth. He had found a soap mine—a great vein of natural soap. He brought samples with him and the Chamber of Commerce experts pronounced it veritable soap, no mistake. What a sensation it produced! A solid lode of beautiful soap, of what extent no man yet knew, right at the city's door! The newspapers took it up and published sensational articles about the San Gabriél soap mines.

Right on the heels of this excitement came more sensational mining news. A citizen had located a mine of pure tallow! Why brag about this being a land of milk and honey when tallow and soap deposits were so much more valuable? Well, well, this certainly was a country worth coming to. Dig, burrow, gouge and tunnel was the order of the day until the vicinity of old San Gabriél Arcángel was pitted deep and pitted wide.

Then, wonder of wonders, a great aerolite was reported to have fallen west of Los Angeles during a rainstorm. This fact could be proven by viewing the steam it sent up through the soft moist earth as it cooled down there, nobody knew how far beneath the surface. Pure iron probably! The scientific world of Los Angeles was agog. Committees were sent out to locate the spot. Yes, steam was issuing from beneath. Some eminent professor was telegraphed for, from the Lick Observatory, I think. They awaited his arrival before beginning to excavate, so that the great savant might be the first to feast his eyes on the marvel from the skies.

The professor arrived, the stage was set and the earth was opened. The miners soon struck into a bulky mass, but it was soft and foul. They dug up the remains of a big fat horse; an old family horse, as was afterwards learned, cherished by the Valdez family of the Rancho Rodeo de las Aguas * and interred out in the pasture just before the great rain storm. Some one riding along to town during the storm had seen a flash from the skies that looked like a meteor fall-

* The highly developed Beverly Hills district of to-day, home of movie stars.

ing; then returning into the country after the storm, when the sun had come out good and hot on the wet earth, he had noticed the steam rising from the spot where he had certainly seen an aerolite strike! From such small rumors do mighty movements grow, in a new and miraculous land.

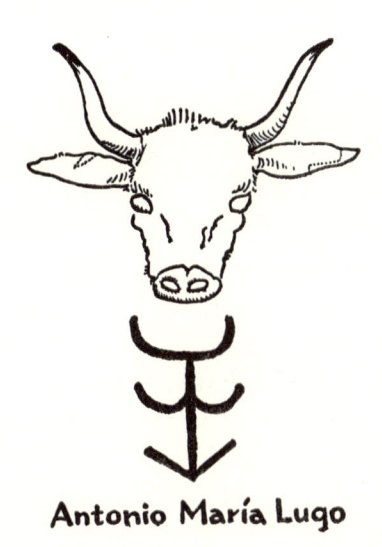

Antonio María Lugo

CHAPTER 22

Some Early Mayors

STEPHEN C. FOSTER [1] became mayor of Los Angeles in 1854; the third mayor of the new American municipality and the first one to distinguish himself in office.

About the first thing this Maine Yankee did after arrival in the Pueblo with the army was to become a Mexican by marriage. He married a rich widow, daughter of *el viejo* Lugo, the greatest land holder in California, a patriarch who numbered his horses and cattle by the tens of thousands. Before becoming a regular mayor Foster had been First Alcalde of Los Angeles under appointment by the American military government; also a delegate to the constitutional convention of 1849 and a state senator.

The Lugo family was rich, numerous and influential and by marrying into the fold Foster acquired a power among the Californian-Mexican population that was almost unlimited. In addition Foster was personally attractive, persuasive and educated—a graduate of Yale, I believe—and was a fine-looking, dashing fellow in those early years, wielding a greater influence for good or bad than any other twenty men, nay fifty men, in Los Angeles County.

A good man naturally was Stephen Foster, of kindly disposition, sensitive, personally honorable, but the wealth and influence which this adventurous young Yankee found thrust upon him, as it were, caused him to lose his head and his importance wrought his ruin.

His fatal mistake was made in the case of Dave Brown.

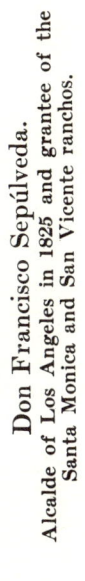

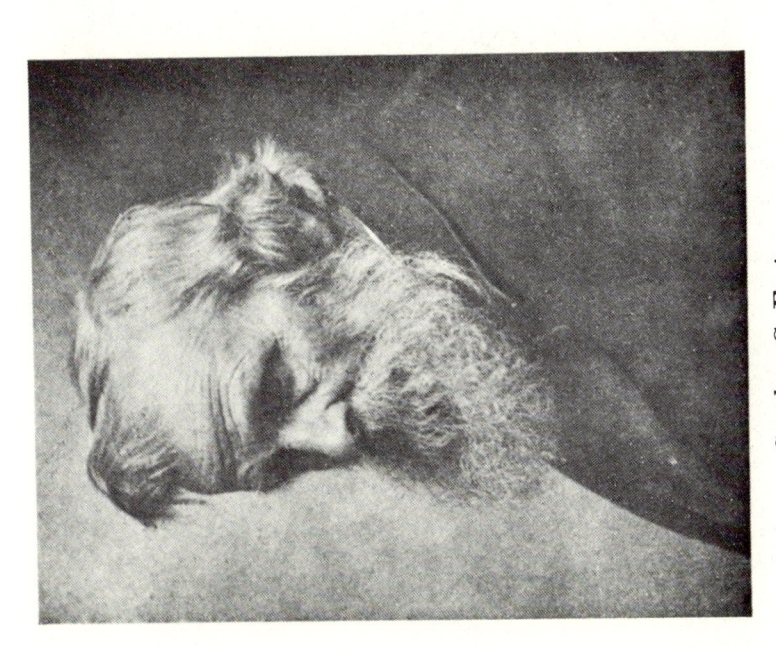

Don Francisco Sepúlveda.
Alcalde of Los Angeles in 1825 and grantee of the Santa Monica and San Vicente ranchos.

Stephen C. Foster.
First American alcalde of Los Angeles, later mayor and state senator.

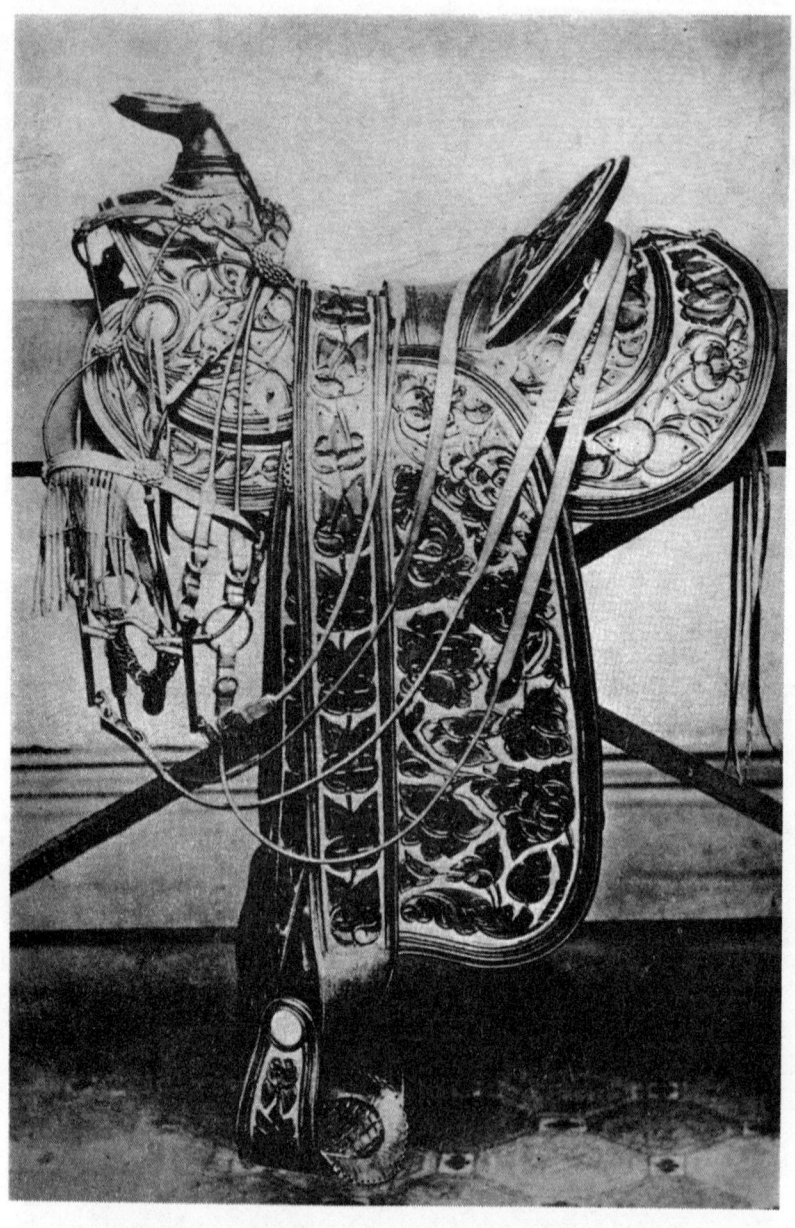

Famous saddle and bridle of General Andrés Pico, valued, when he owned them, at $5,000.

SOME EARLY MAYORS

Dave was what is now called a cowboy, and when not at work among the cattle could be found in the saloons and gambling houses, as, for that matter, could almost every other citizen. Not a particularly hard case; had never killed a man until his first, which proved to be his last as this story will show. In fact Dave Brown was a red-headed, good-natured, hail-fellow-well-met who never meant any particular harm and had never been up for stealing or any of those baser crimes. He was chief cowboy for John Rains, cattle drover mentioned in previous pages.

One day in the summer of '54 Dave got on a drunk that ended in delirium tremens. In this condition he met Pinkney Clifford, his most intimate friend. He asked Pinkney for a loan of five dollars. Observing Dave's condition Pinkney refused. Whereupon Dave stabbed his chum to death.

Great excitement ensued. A mob assembled. Mayor Foster appeared on the scene and advised the mob to leave the murderer to the courts. Good advice, but given with this proviso: "If the courts fail to hang him I will lay down my office and will lead you myself to hang him."

Dave Brown was tried, convicted and sentenced to be hanged. A defense lawyer took an appeal to the Supreme Court on the ground that the evidence showed Brown to have been irresponsible at the time he killed Clifford. The governor of the state granted the condemned man a respite until the appeal could be decided.

About the time Dave Brown killed Pinkney Clifford an hidalgo of Mission Vieja named Alvitre assassinated an American named Ellington, a citizen of El Monte. When Alvitre was arrested he admitted his guilt and in explanation simply said: "I killed him because he was an American." Alvitre was tried and convicted in the same court that had passed on Brown. The caballero, after the fatalistic way of his kind, had no particular objection to hanging, apparently, so there was no appeal entered in his case. He was sentenced to be executed on the same date set in the case of Dave Brown. When the day came Alvitre was hanged alone and Brown continued to live under the terms of his reprieve.*

This made the Mexican population very mad. They raised a public clamor, claiming that when a Mexican was convicted of crime he was always promptly punished but that an American in like circumstances always escaped punishment. As a truthful historian I must confess that there was a good deal in this argument, because the American always had a better knowledge of the judicial ropes and was wise enough to hire lawyers who could do him the most good.

Mayor Foster responded to this clamor on the part of the natives, resigned his office, called a mass meeting and announced himself ready to make good his promise to enforce equal justice by hanging Dave Brown. If one's sympathies are inclined off hand to approve this stand, let it be remembered that the convicted man was still under the protection of the Supreme Court of California. Its decision on the appeal had not yet been handed down and Brown remained under sentence of death by legal execution.

On the day originally set for the double execution the sheriff of Los Angeles County hung Alvitre and Stephen C. Foster hung Dave Brown. In response to Foster's call a horde of horsemen, Californian and Mexican, assembled from far and near, filled the streets of Los Angeles, surged around the adobe jail. Strange as it may seem a valiant Californian, who had commanded his countrymen at the Battle

* As a matter of fact some appeal seems to have been taken on behalf of Alvitre for a stay of execution did arrive from the higher court, but almost a week too late! (See *Pioneer Notes from the Diary of Judge Benjamin Hayes*. Privately printed, Los Angeles, 1929.)

of San Pascual in a desperate effort to turn back the American invasion of his native land and to save the provincial government headed by his own brother, fought now against the mob in defense of American law and government. This was General Andrés Pico, at this time Brigadier General of California Militia. In an attempt to stem the tide of trouble that Foster, an American, had set running among the Mexican population, General Pico promptly organized a body of fellow-Californians in whom he could trust and formed them in front of the gates to the jail yard, where he sat his magnificent horse, sword flashing as it plied about him, and held the mob at bay for an hour. However, the odds proved hopelessly against him as the well-armed mob increased. An ultimatum was issued by the crowd that unless Pico withdrew his force the sheriff and his deputies who were inside the jail with the prisoner would be strung up with the latter when the inevitable success of the mob should have been achieved. Pico continued to hold off the attackers until he had sent word to the sheriff and his men that they had better get out as the jig was up; and after they had withdrawn in safety he bowed to the superior force led by the very recent mayor of Los Angeles. In short order the jail doors were battered down with sledge hammers and crowbars, the prisoner was dragged out and hung to the cross beam of the corral gateway. A notorious Mexican gambler was master of ceremony and Juan Gonzalez, one of the late Joaquín Murrieta's outlaws, acted as hangman.

It may be comforting to mention here that these two desperados were soon ground up in the judicial mill. Within a few months Gonzalez was sent to the penitentiary for a bloody crime, escaped prison with the notorious Juan Flores of the subsequent Barton war, and both were hanged by the law a few years later.

But it is very depressing to think of an educated American, mayor of an American city, resigning his office to head a Mexican mob to hang an American who was under the protection of the courts. In my opinion Stephen C. Foster committed a fatal mistake; he died morally on that day as surely as Dave Brown died physically. However, after the hanging an election was called and Foster was immediately reëlected mayor. The American portion of the population was against him, but his countrymen and the law-abiding element of Californians were greatly in the minority. Foster's portrait hangs to-day in the City Hall. Just as reasonable to hang Benedict Arnold's in the capitol at Washington.

Lynch law as administered in Los Angeles in the early times was not a marked success and after a half century of observation I have found that most of the people who indulged in that passionate pastime came to untimely or miserable ends. When the usual high sense of honor, the sensitive nature and the conscience of Stephen C. Foster reasserted themselves he seems to have realized the enormity of his mistake. He broke down under a brooding remorse and became an unhappy misanthrope to the day of his death, forty years after the hanging.

Joseph Mascarel was mayor in 1866, a plain, honest Frenchman turned into a good American. He fought on the American side in the war with Mexico. Mascarel did not distinguish himself particularly while mayor but he did in '69, when Turner was mayor, as will be hereinafter related.

Mascarel did get for Los Angeles some world-wide publicity, however. While he was mayor some Parisian journalists on a tour of the United States honored our Angel City with a visit. Learning that our mayor was a son of Gaul they lost no time in calling at our *Hotel de Ville* to pay their respects. His Honor was out so they hunted up his residence. It was in Sonoratown, an old tumble-down adobe with barred windows and dirt floor. Conducted by a Spanish-speaking guide the party of Parisians, with gloves, canes, tail coats and top hats, entered the *Palais Royal*. In the middle of the room their astonished eyes rested on a fat old Indian woman on her knees before a big flat *metate*, grinding corn. The upper part of her body was nude and reeking with perspiration.

Without interrupting her grinding she turned her head indifferently toward the Parisian gentlemen who had darkened her doorway so unexpectedly and snapped at the native who had brought them in: *"Que quieres?"* (What do you want?)

The guide wasn't sure himself what it was all about, so a spokesman stepped forward from among the visitors and, bowing low, attempted to make known that the distinguished party wished to pay his respects to the mayor of Los Angeles.

"El no está aquí. Vayanse!" (He isn't here. Get out!)

"Ah, oui, certainement, but where then is his lady, the Mayoress?" persisted the French journalist.

"Yo soy, pero tengo muchos negocios. Vayanse!" (I'm she, but I'm very busy. Get out!)

Crunch, crunch, crunch, went the *mano* against the grains on the *metate*, preparing meal for the evening *tortillas*, while the skin of the Lady Mayoress glistened as her shoulders rose and fell. The distinguished Parisian journalists raised their eyebrows, shrugged their shoulders, twirled the points of their mustaches, looked at each other indignantly and departed.

But their silent, well-bred departure from the doorstep in Sonoratown was not the end of the incident by a long shot. When those journalists got back to Paris they wrote about everything they saw in Los Angeles "that astonishing town in one of the southern *comtés* of the province of California," and recounted with pointed Gallic humor their attempted call on the Mayor and their reception by the Lady Mayoress. They mailed copies of their papers back to Los Angeles, to the chagrin of many a voter who had cast his ballot for a good, honest, vigilant mayor but one who proved a little short in training as a glad-hander.

Damien Marchessault * succeeded Mascarel in '67. He was a New Orleans gambler before he came to Los Angeles, a professional gambler here, and greatly distinguished himself by committing suicide. He was reputed to be an absinthe drinker. There was nothing strange in our having a gambler for mayor, as in the good old times the gamblers were the cream of society and filled most of the offices of honor, trust and profit.

Marchessault's principal contribution to public service was the laying of the first water pipes under the streets of Los Angeles, in partnership with Louis Sainsevain. These water mains consisted of hollowed logs fitted together. They burst so often and aroused the indignation of so many citizens by jetting them with sudden geyserings as to humiliate the mayor to the point of suicide.

Joel H. Turner succeeded Marchessault and won such distinction as to render his name forever famous. Joel Turner was a statesman, a politician, a perpetual office holder. Joel was a hanger-on with all the tenacity of a Southern seed tick. Leech or snapping turtle would not express this particular trait in the gentleman's character strongly enough, neither would barnacles. Barnacles can be scraped off, snapping turtles and leeches sometimes let go,

* Commemorated by Marchessault Street, which bounds the Plaza on the north and runs eastwardly through Chinatown.

but ticks hang on to the end of their lives and so did the Honorable Joel.

For many years Joel was Justice of the Peace at El Monte and elsewhere. In connection with his court room Joel always conducted a whiskey mill, and while Justice of the Peace at El Monte the whiskey mill paved the way for his elevation to the seat of mayor of Los Angeles.

Besides, the Hon. Joel H. Turner was a great conventionist. From the time he fixed himself on Los Angeles County until the day he died he never missed being a delegate to every Democratic convention. If Joel couldn't get into a convention any other way he would explore the mountains, find a district where man abideth not, and elect himself a representative from that district to represent himself.

Here is how the whiskey mill at El Monte helped Joel become mayor of Los Angeles: Along in '65 and '66, red hot political years, free drinks began to run short in Los Angeles for the politicians and they would go in crowds out to El Monte. Under pretense of having weighty matters of state to lay before him they would insinuate themselves into the hospitality of Judge Turner and gratuitously drink his whiskey. Joel would not demean himself by demanding money for whiskey from a fellow statesman.

But economically speaking there are certain cruel natural laws which make no allowances for a man's noble intentions, and Joel's generosity broke him. But the sponging statesman in their turn showed their nobility—a rare instance in political history, I'm sure—by banding together to make Joel mayor of Los Angeles as a sign of their gratitude. They said, said they to themselves and to Joel, in convention assembled over the last drop: "People are beginning to visit our fair city from afar and to write about it; Pixley has been here, also Rosecrans; some distinguished Frenchmen came all the way from Paris to see Los Angeles, and what sort of mayors have we had to receive all these celebrities? Not one of them has been equal to the occasion. Not one of them has been high-toned. Not one of them has done us proud in receiving high-toned visitors. Some of the mayors couldn't even speak English. Now, sirs, Joel H. Turner is high-toned. He can speak English, he has the social manner, he's out of a job and the city will soon be out a mayor. Joel just fills the bill. If El Monte will spare him we will see that he is elected to that high post."

The El Monte boys spared him and in 1868 Joel H. Turner was elected mayor of Los Angeles. Unfortunately a slight mishap befell His Honor the Mayor during his term of office, the particulars of which may be found in the 37th Cal. Reports p. 370. Briefly, a jury convicted the mayor on certain matters and a court sentenced him to ten years penal servitude in the State Penitentiary. But that is a small matter about which to interrupt our story of a rising career; let us drop it for the moment and take it up again, if necessary, hereafter.

Soon after Mayor Turner took office an opportunity was presented to him for winning distinction, and he won it. He made himself forever famous.

It was like this: United States Secretary of State William H. Seward, that great statesman, was on his way to visit Los Angeles and the City Council ordered the mayor to give him a grand public reception. Joel had heard of public receptions to secretaries of state and so forth but he didn't know exactly how they were gotten up. However, it would never do for the mayor of Los Angeles—the high-toned, imported (from El Monte) mayor—to confess ignorance of such matters. So he kept his own counsel, made his own dispositions and awaited the great man's advent.

Secretary Seward was coming down from Santa Bárbara via the Calabasas road by stage. Mayor Turner, mounted on a little white mustang and accompanied by a musical escort, lay in ambush for the important arrival just where the coach would emerge from the Cahuenga Pass,* bowling downgrade hell-bent for election. High, yellow-blooming wild mustard bordering the road was the hiding place for the reception committee, to wit: Joel Turner and his mounted band of troubadours consisting of a bare-foot Indian drummer, a ditto fifer, a mestizo flageolet player, an old cholo named Piñacarte with his flute, a skinny fiddler and a fat fellow with an accordion. Every member of the band was tricked out in ribbons and spangles in old-time Californian style.

The committee had not long to wait. At about 4 p.m., the great "Overland" came thundering through the pass behind its galloping, lathered horses.

At the order to "fall in" the drummer and fifer plied their bare heels on their horses' ribs and took position on each side of the prancing stage leaders, plying drumstick and wind for all they were worth. Old Piñacarte and the flageolet player ranged up on the flanks of the coach and the accordion man pounded along in the dust behind, pumping his bellows while the sweat cut watercourses through the silt on his face. With jingling spurs and gay equestrian trappings Joel charged along side Crandall, the stage driver, and shouted a plea to "hold down your horses a bit and give the boys a chance."

It is an eight-mile run from Cahuenga into the Pueblo and when, at about sundown, the escort and the escorted drew up in front of the Bella Union Hotel amid a wild scattering of pups, pigs and pelados † the musicians were desperately

* About the junction of Cahuenga Avenue and Hollywood Boulevard.
† Men of the lowest class; literally "hairy ones."

blown. Nevertheless Joel, with Spartan firmness, formed them in line from stage coach to portal and reining his heaving mustang front and center, gave the signal for a blast of dusty music in salute to William H. Seward, Secretary of State of the United States of America as that great man passed from vehicle to veranda.

The mayor dismissed his parade after making a speech, the public reception was over, a precedent had been set for high-toned welcomes by the city of Los Angeles and Mayor Joel H. Turner had won undying fame. It is this truthful historian's opinion that Joel's reception of Secretary Seward was perfectly planned and executed; indeed, a model of its kind and that he deserves his fame—because he saved a distinguished visitor from being bored. First impressions are the ones that count.

What a truly great man was William H. Seward. His wisdom and foresight in purchasing Alaska is almost without parallel in our national history. He had just been on a voyage of inspection to the new territory and was on his way to Mexico on a diplomatic mission when he dropped in to take a look at our Angelic selves.

Before he is through with the famous Turner administration this truthful historian must tell how it came to pass that the city of Los Angeles was despoiled of its great communal domain of 20,000 acres, title to which came down from His Most Catholic Majesty King Carlos III of Spain.[2] To come quickly to the point the method was that the Mayor and Council would conceive it necessary every so often to have a ditch excavated to extend the water system over the city lands. Some certain person would be given the contract for the job, worth perhaps from one hundred to two hundred dollars. What the contractor would actually receive in payment would be anywhere from a few hundred to a few thousand acres of municipal land. The city chain gang would be loaned to do the actual work. Upon receiving conveyance of his specified quantity of land the contractor would reconvey to the mayor, and to each member of the Council personally, a number of acres previously agreed upon. Thus the city's ancient domain—at least most of it, except what was already in private hands and under cultivation—was handed out.

Once upon a time the city engaged the late George Hansen to survey and map certain portions of the municipality. Hansen was a man of integrity, a civil engineer of high standing and also a master of sarcasm. When his tract maps were completed, paid for and finally hung on rollers on the walls of the council room at the City Hall the dignity of the Municipal Corporation was considerably impaired by the discovery that an inscription had been written across the face of each plat in bold red ink, reading like this: "This tract stolen when A—— was mayor." "This tract stolen when B—— was mayor." "This tract stolen when C—— was mayor." And so on. Then across the largest map of all, representing thousands of acres, was written: "This tract stolen when Joel H. Turner was mayor."

In his first and only message Mayor Turner congratulated himself on the high character of his councilmen, his honorable co-workers for the public weal, and promised the people wonders to be performed in the way of public improvements. The era of progress started at once. The first thing was to sewer the city. The exact extent of this work was the digging of a ditch beginning on the west side of Main Street exactly opposite the center of Commercial Street, thence down the middle of Commercial about five hundred feet or so to a point just east of Wilmington Street. Twelve thousand feet of lumber was used (these were wooden sewers) costing two hundred and fifty dollars. The whole improvement cost about four hundred dollars. This great sewer, three feet wide, one foot deep and laid one foot underground, dumped into a cesspool, and only one man's property was connected with it. It was really built for him. The sewer and cesspool soon choked up and became a terrible menace to health, so much so that the courts ordered the whole public improvement abated and the cesspool filled with earth. After the chain gang had conducted the burial the sheriff stuck a cross into the mound of earth where the cesspool had been, bearing this inscription:

> "Beneath this sand, mid fumes and gasses,
> Lie the souls of nine municipal asses."

The Council paid for this famous Commercial Street sewer the sum of $32,000 on a gold basis with a scrip issue at the rate of fifty-five cents on the dollar. That is to say, this little four-hundred-dollar job was made to cost $52,800 and the tax payers of Los Angeles to-day are paying the same with interest in our municipal bonded debt.

But this was not half. With whetted appetites the high-toned Council proceeded to issue warrants to the amount of $150,000 and to sell them for cash. These warrants are included in our bonded indebtedness and oppress us in the payment of onerous and increasing tax rates. For this $150,000 deal no stubs were kept to give evidence of issue.

Here is where ex-Mayor Joseph Mascarel comes again into the picture, and in a most favorable light. Shrewd, vigilant and honest he got onto the details of the great financial schemes of the City Fathers, and without revealing his attitude toward them watched developments and took notes until time for the Grand Jury to meet. Then he appeared before that body with the result that the whole high-toned batch, mayor and councilmen, were indicted.

And now, can you believe what that city administration did in answer to public clamor against them? This is the remarkable gesture the threatened officials made: They cut the dam where the water was taken out of the Los Angeles River to supply irrigation in and around the city. Many people depended on the ditches for their domestic supply also. A million's worth of immediate damage was threatened.

A meeting of the landed proprietors was called and the author of these lines was made chairman of a committee to wait upon the Mayor and Council to demand that the city immediately repair the ruptured dam and main canal. This was the answer received: "Procure those indictments against us to be dismissed and we will grant your request; otherwise every vine, tree and spear of grass in this city may dry up, or you can fix it yourselves."

Crops were threatened with total ruin within a short time, immediate action was necessary and the affected citizens had to organize and do city work at their own expense.

It happened that the State Legislature was then in session, the month being February of 1870, a dry year. The irate land owners called another meeting and again chose the author chairman of a committee, this time to go before the Legislature and petition for permanent relief from such a state of affairs in the future.

Benjamin D. Wilson—Don Benito—himself a vineyardist, was our senator. Through his efforts and ours a bill was drawn taking the management of the Los Angeles River and the distribution of its waters from the hands of the Mayor and Council and substituting a board of Water Commissioners. The bill was hastily put through, the indicted city administration was deprived of power over the water situation, permanent repairs were made to the water system, and the orchards, vineyards and truck gardens, to say nothing of horses, cows and humans, were saved from drought.

The indictment against the mayor was pressed, he was tried, convicted and sentenced to ten years in the penitentiary. We then had a Mexican for a judge, a notorious corruptionist and afterwards a fugitive from the state. The indicted councilmen were before this court and used some potent arguments, for they procured the dismissal of their indictments.

And don't think that Mayor Turner served his ten years in prison. Not at all. His lawyers appealed, secured an order for a new trial—and that was the end of it. The mayor continued in office just as if nothing had happened, as did the councilmen, and the taxpayers went on footing, as they still are footing, the bills incurred in this devil's dance.

After retirement from the mayoralty the Hon. Joel H. Turner was again appointed Justice of the Peace by the Board of Supervisors of the county and continued in office to the end of his life. And he lived a long time.

Francisco Ocampo

CHAPTER 23

Matrimonial Sharks as Bad as Shylocks

IN a previous chapter I referred to the loan shark curse that stripped so many of the Californians of their possessions in the early years of the American occupation. I described how not only the Spanish Californians but American-born rancheros that had settled down in this Mexican province previous to our war with Mexico were victimized and ruined by financial sharpers of their own race. There was an allied affliction visited upon these unsophisticated pastoral provincials, and that was an army of matrimonial speculators. Marrying a daughter of one of the big land owners was in some respects a quicker way to clean her family of its assets than to lend money to the "old man." And, of course, a much simpler process for the young sport who had no money to loan.

A rancho girl with a thousand or more head of cattle in expectancy and her share of a huge ranch thrown in was a rich catch for one of those matrimonial sharks. There were many marriageable girls in California in the early days whose expected inheritance went up into the hundreds of thousands of dollars. For instance, when Stephen C. Foster married the daughter of Don Antonio María Lugo she was already a widow rich in her own right, having received a big slice of her father's holdings, while Lugo himself was a millionaire. Not in cash, for that was always rather scarce among these people, but in the potential wealth of land and cattle. The two daughters of Isaac Williams of Chino were worth each at least three or four hundred thousand dollars on their marriage day. They were granddaughters of old man Lugo. The one that married John Rains inherited that part of the vast Lugo holdings known as Rancho del Chino, while the other sister was given the Cucamonga. I have already mentioned that John Rains was murdered. The husband of the other half-American Lugo granddaughter was killed in a bar-room fight. Both the girls married badly and were soon widowed, but their experiences with American husbands did not deter other native daughters from following in their footsteps. The señoritas were greatly attracted to stalwart young Americans. They seemed to be especially attracted to the smooth-spoken fellows of Irish extraction.

The daughters of that famous Californian, Gen. Mariano Vallejo of Sonoma, all married Americans, and proved the exception to the general rule by marrying well. One of them married Captain Frisbie,[1] a member of the old Stevenson Regiment of New York Volunteers, and Captain Frisbie is at this writing living in Mexico City, a very wealthy man. But against the successful matches made by the Vallejo daughters we could mention hundreds of failures. Mostly the native daughters married good looking and outwardly virile but really lazy, worthless, dissolute vagabond Americans whose object of marriage was to get rich without work. I know of four sisters in Los Angeles each of whom came into a fortune in both city and ranch property. Each married a fine-looking, well-educated American and each one was brought down to absolute poverty by her husband. Those men squandered their wives' fortunes in all manner of gambling and dissolute living. They brought those good wives, and they were all good and beautiful women, with their families of children, down to poverty. And these instances

The Presidio of San Francisco.

San Francisco Beauties—the Celestial, the Señora, and Madame.

Interior of El Dorado, San Francisco.
Most famous of the lavish gambling halls of the Coast.

First Presbyterian Church, San Francisco.

could be named over and over again at San Francisco, San José, Monterey, San Diego.

There were several reasons why these Spanish Californian girls were inclined to marry outside their own race. The more sensible and far-seeing of the heads of the old families felt that the future was in the hands of the invading race, that the old easy methods of business and life were no longer of avail and that it was a protection to family interests to have an American son-in-law, one who could give advice in the new business methods and have an authentic voice at court in legal and political affairs. And the girls felt that they acquired prestige by marrying into the dominant race. They were sensible to strange charms, as is true with women and men for that matter the world over, and found the foreigners better educated, more worldly-wise, than their own countrymen.

I do not mean to infer that all these self-seeking and often dissolute husbands were Americans. Among them were Frenchmen, Germans, and Englishmen and occasionally a European Spaniard. They all had the same idea. Even the Mexican sometimes learned to emulate his foreign rival and would put on a brassy front and run through his bride's fortune without regard to the old-time respect for wife, family heritage or children. Such an one was Don Pancho Ocampo, a big, handsome, elegant fellow who came up from Mexico, saw what the foreign boys were getting away with and put himself in the way of doing likewise. He laid siege to the heart of Doña Francisca, widow of one Leandri, an Italian, who was so rich in the old days before the Americans came that he operated one thousand ox-carts, necessitating two thousand peons to manage them in caravan, to carry on his commerce in hides, tallow and imported merchandise. Doña Francisca was the richest widow in California, owner of

Rancho de los Coyotes. Pancho Ocampo, the Mexico City gallant, married her and what he did to her fortune was just a shame. He blossomed out in the early-day costume of the Californian hidalgo, blue broadcloth and green velvet with red facings, gold and silver buttons, fine white linen, embroidery and gold lace. I used to meet Don Pancho in San Francisco in those flush days when he was dallying with the delights of that rip roaring metropolis, and how he was making Doña Francisca's money fly! Wine suppers, theater parties, *meriendas* in the country with refreshments by expensive caterers, boats chartered for trips on the bay, balls and *filles de joie*. What a following he had, while he lasted! The assets of the Coyotes Rancho just dripped off his finger tips. Bull-fights and cock-fights in Los Angeles and great bear hunting expeditions, all organized just to entertain his friends. Gambling halls chartered for the evening. Cafés too. Private race meets. What a beautiful bird of gay plumage was Don Pancho Ocampo! And what of the once richest widow in California? When Don Pancho had run his course, Doña Francisca sold and pawned the thousands of dollars' worth of fine silk shawls—gorgeous long-fringed shawls of the old Manila and China trade days, heritage from her Spanish past—and finally the family income was reduced to ten dollars a month allowed Don Pancho by the supervisors of Los Angeles County.

Doña Francisca's sister, Carlota, married one Eschrich, a Württemberger who had come to California as a musician in Stevenson's Regiment. He was a high-roller, that German, and Doña Carlota's possessions suffered the same fate as Doña Francisca's. It killed the wife of the Württemberger, and he followed her to the grave some time afterwards utterly impoverished.

Not every señorita succumbed easily to the marriage pro-

MATRIMONIAL SHARKS

posal and many a scheme was concocted by designing fortune hunters to trap the richest girls. It is reported that one enterprising individual entered into a contract to pay a priest ten thousand dollars out of the fortune of the girl he desired to marry for the priest's aid and influence in arranging the match.

After the professional Shylock the matrimonial shark was the worst infliction that fell upon the hapless Californians. He brought a lot of misery in his train, but also a lot of fun for the wags of the day. We had in Los Angeles in those times a talented and humorous character named Frank Ball, mentioned by me in a previous volume in connection with his fondness for lampooning prominent people in amusing doggerel. Frank was employed in my office for a long time, and it was while he was with me that his fame made him known as the funny man of the Coast. Nothing appealed to Frank's funny bump more than the Californian matrimonial adventures of some of his Yankee acquaintances of the gold rush days. He could never see much romance in a Mexican señorita, who, in his opinion, was quite low in the social scale in spite of her potential wealth. Or else he was jealous of the success of some of his rough companions in acquiring native wives and leagues of land along with them.

At any rate an example of Frank's state of mind on the subject is contained in a famous doggerel, "That Fine Young Señorita," dedicated to one Obed Smith. The verses are ragged and badly balanced yet it went the rounds of the theaters and saloons in the mid-fifties to the delight of all the sports of the Coast. This Obed Smith was a companion of Frank's in the voyage to California around the Horn, in the steerage. After arrival in San Francisco the two parted and did not see each other for several years. Finally one day

Frank ran across Smith at the old Union Hotel in the city where they had last parted. Smith was having a good time in the same lavish style as Don Pancho Ocampo. Frank was delighted to discover his old shipmate enjoying such apparent affluence and concluded that he must have been one of the lucky ones in the mines. But when he offered his congratulations he found Smith rather cool, rather socially superior. A great man he seemed to consider himself and looked down, so Frank felt at least, on an humble scribbler who was picking up a living writing verses for the press and songs for the theaters and saloons. Inquiring into the status of his erstwhile friend he found that he had married a rich Mexican girl at San José and had set out, on the strength of this really lowly social alliance, to play the part of a Spanish grandee. Moved to poetry by the situation Frank set this song loose in all the music halls and saloons of California:

That Fine Young Senorita
or
The Deplorable End of Obed Smith

Air—*"That Fine Old Irish Gentleman"*

I will sing you a little song that I heard the other day
Of a fine young señorita that dwelt in San José.
Her heart was light, her eyes were bright, her skin was
    somewhat yellow;
Her hair was black and shone like glass when she
    smoothed it down with tallow.
She was a fine young señorita of the California kind.

She never wore a bonnet on her pretty little head,
And her naked feet were sometimes seen 'neath petti-
    coat so red;
But on Sundays and on holidays she used to dress quite
    fine

With a brand new tortoise-shell comb that cost about a
    dime—
That fine young señorita of the California kind.

Her parents were respectable, her father a ranchero;
Although his acres were very wide his purse it was quite
    narrow.
He dwelt in his family castle, a one-story *adobe,*
And sometimes sold *frijoles* at four dollars the *arrobe*—
A fine old Mexicano of the California kind.

The way he lassoed horses to a stranger was surprisin',
And the way he hated Yankees was the rankest kind of
    pisin;
For when he met a Yank who says, "Sir, how do ye do?"
The only answer he would make was a muttered *"Cara-
    joo!"*
That fine old Mexicano of the California kind.

He believed in Jesu Cristo and the general resurrection,
And he had assisted slightly in many an insurrection;
So for his many services old Pico, out of gratitude,
Gave him a little piece of land—about four degrees of
    latitude;
That fine old Mexicano of the California kind.

The señorita met a Yankee at the end of a long lane
Who says, "My name is Obed Smith, from the eastern
    part of Maine,
And I rather like your looks, young gal, and I think I'd
    like to have ye."
But the only answer she did make was that old reply,
    "Quien sabe?"
That fine young señorita of the California kind.

So he *hablade* and he *porquede* and when he came
    again
He says, "My dear, I'm desperatee." Say she, "*Y yo
    tambienee!*"

And so you see it came to pass in spite of kin or kith,
That fine young señorita became Mrs. Obed Smith—
That fine young señorita of the California kind.

So Obed calmly squatted down upon the old man's land,
And went to breaking horses till he couldn't hardly stand.
The last time I heard of him, 'tis true upon my life,
He was doing nothing better than just living off his wife—
That fine young señorita of the California kind.

That line, "a little piece of land—about four degrees of latitude," is a dig on the part of our poet at the lavish manner in which Pío Pico, last of the governors under Mexican rule, gave away land to friends and relatives, especially as he saw the end of his sway approaching. A wise old coon was Don Pío. A man of real ability, a shrewd man, yet the Shylocks got him. Originally he was a Yankee hater. He didn't want to see his native province—for he was an *hijo del pais,* born at San Gabriél—come under gringo rule. Once, several years before the American occupation, when a provincial political convention was in session at Monterey, there was heated discussion of the probability that England was about to seize California. General Vallejo, a far-seeing man whose views were ahead of his time, dared to rise up and make an eloquent speech recommending annexation to the United States rather than surrender to England. This brought the stocky, swarthy, bearded Pico to his feet in violent denunciation of the gringos. "Look eastward toward the Sierra Nevada at this moment," he cried, "and watch them already descending into the valley of the Sacramento taking what they wish without so much as asking leave. The gringos come not to share, but to possess. *Los hijos del pais* will be driven completely from their native land. Better any alternative than this."

But when the hand writing on the wall had grown still plainer Governor Pico was wise enough to trim his sails to the rising wind and to favor his American friends equally with his native friends in the wholesale granting of public lands. These were his last acts of authority. All who had assisted him a couple of years before in his revolution against the then governor, Micheltorena, he liberally rewarded, and among them were several gringos who settled here in the Mexican days and have left well-known family names to the present social and financial roster of California. For instance, John Rowland and William Workman got Rancho Puente of about forty thousand acres for their services as riflemen at the battle of Providencia. William Wolfskill got his Puta Creek grant, eight leagues, in Napa County, for similar service. In fact all Americans in Don Pío's army at that battle were rewarded with land except Alexander Bell, the author's uncle, who possessed enough of the old Scotch-Irish virtue to refuse to forswear allegiance to the United States for the sake of a land grant.

When the United States Land Commission was in session in California in 1852 investigating the legality of land grants the claim was made that Governor Pico made many of his grants after he had fled as a fugitive to Mexico. That is, that he had pre-dated the documents and left them in the hands of his friends when he jumped the country so that they were really invalid, having been made after his authority had been displaced. That they were cooked up for the occasion to enrich his friends and to feather his own nest against such a time as he should return to his native haunts after the conclusion of peace between Mexico and the United States. It was claimed that the most flagrant example of this sort of thing was Pico's grant of the Ex-Mission San Fernando Rancho jointly to a relative and to a friend. These assertedly fraudulent grants extended all the way from San Juan Capistrano Mission to Shasta.[2]

All this, however, was a libel on Pío Pico. These grants were made while he had power to make them. They all turned up to be genuine. While still in power he rewarded his friends. It is a pleasure to me to speak well of old Don Pío and his virtues, among them the great gift of friendship; and of the chivalry and charm of his brother, General Andrés Pico. In their time and considering the limitations of their advantages they were great men. But they lived two hundred years behind the modern age that was introduced overnight, as it were, by the American occupation. Modernism was imposed suddenly on a social and political life that was almost medieval, and this must be remembered in rendering judgment on the representatives of the old régime.

Certainly some of the officials of the new régime, after California became a sovereign American state, were not paragons of virtue. Their methods were more modern and straight to the point, to be sure, than those of the Mexican politicians, but also often far more petty. We had some queer fish here in Los Angeles, especially among the lawyers and not so long ago either. I will cite as an amusing illustration a certain great lawyer (great because he thought so himself) that was more or less prominent in the '80's. He had been a prosecuting attorney in a county in Illinois where he was indicted for receiving bribes, forfeited bail, ran away to Missouri and there robbed the post office at Cape Gerardeau. What he stole from the postmaster just enabled him to reach Los Angeles and here, lo and behold, he became a prominent citizen, a statesman. But principally, as far as this story goes, he became Prosecuting Attorney. Together with his friend Justice of the Peace Ranney, in whose court he plied his business of prosecutor, he certainly made things lively in our town. By way of identifying this character more closely for those readers that may be able to recall those times and faces, I will say that he afterward became famous as Jim the Penman and that a grateful constituency sent him to the State Legislature, where he was on the high road to gubernatorial honors when an incident occurred that caused the Penman's retirement to the shades of the county bastile. Any one that wants to know still more about him can refer to one of those histories of Los Angeles which so many grateful subscribers have in their private libraries, where he will find Jim the Penman eulogized under the name of the Honorable James D—m, as one of the greatest and most prominent men of the Pacific Coast.

But to return to Jim the Penman when he was our Prosecuting Attorney: There occurred one day in Judge Ranney's court an incident that became quite notorious and went the rounds of the Associated Press. That is, in newspapers elsewhere than in Los Angeles, for the local press had been subordinated by Jim and his henchmen. Here is what happened: One day two Arizona miners, in town to see the sights, called at my office and told me they had been robbed the night before on the street. They didn't know who to go to about it; they may have had something on their consciences that kept them from wanting to go direct to the police about it and somebody had given them my name as a lawyer who might help them out.

I was leaving for San Francisco the next morning so all I could do for the two shy miners was to take them up to the Prosecutor's office and help them tell their story. I introduced them to George Watermelon, a deputy in the Prosecutor's office, one who, so far as I ever knew, was a willing and honest public servant, albeit he was in the office of Jim the Penman. I assured the Arizonans that Mr. Watermelon would do right by them, and excused myself from further service in the matter.

Watermelon drew a complaint for the two miners and went with them to Justice Ranney's court to procure a warrant before starting out on the trail of the two robbers described by the victims. Two John Does were charged with relieving the Arizona tourists of a quantity of gold by force and violence.

As the deputy and the two Arizonans entered the court the Judge was on the bench and the Prosecuting Attorney was making an argument to the Court. Mr. Watermelon begged the indulgence of the Court for a moment, requesting His Honor to swear the complainants on a complaint so that the warrant might issue without delay. The Prosecuting Attorney stopped his argument and His Honor took the complaint in his hand. Just then one of the Arizonans, who had been whispering with his companion while the two of them glanced dumbfounded from Judge to Prosecuting Attorney, grabbed Deputy Watermelon by the arm and broke out with, "Say, that fellow there" (pointing to the Judge) "and that fellow there" (pointing to the Prosecuting Attorney) "are the two thieves that robbed us!"

CHAPTER 24

Oranges on Joshua Trees

LOS ANGELES was the largest town in California at the time of the American occupation. It was the native metropolis, on a small scale, to be sure, but still the metropolis. It took on growth from the time it became an incorporated American city in 1850, but for some years the gold excitement in the north held down the increase of population in the south to an insignificant figure. From 1850 to 1856 the old Mexican town was very loosely, very informally governed by its new masters, as may be inferred by accounts of the free and easy—or rather free and strenuous—conditions that existed there. This was due to an excessive expression of individualism rather than to organized political corruption. But from 1856 on to and through the great real estate boom which began in 1885 and lasted three years, the banner of organized rascality floated over the municipal hall of Los Angeles and its rulers were banded together in a speculative conspiracy against all that was honest.

The city began to increase its rate of growth about 1875, but it was still a slow movement until the boom struck in '85. This boom was one of the crimes of the age. Only a few people profited by it while hundreds of thousands were trapped into insane purchase of property and crazy speculation, and finally ruined. The daily press of Los Angeles boomed the boom from the word go. The writer of these lines was the only person having access to printer's ink that published a word of warning to the credulous. I was publishing a weekly paper then and did all that was possible to save people from ruin.

At the height of the boom I printed a carefully written article calling attention to the great number of lots that had been cut by the boomers from orchards, vineyards, barley-fields and vegetable gardens in and around Los Angeles—acres and acres of productive, income-paying land suddenly reduced to waste. A vineyard that was worth three or four hundred dollars an acre as a horticultural proposition they would figure would be worth ten thousand dollars an acre cut up into lots. This jump in value was entirely false, of course, just a speculative inflation that worked for the moment if people believed it. As the result of the uprooting of these productive plots we had for years the unsightly waste places in and about the city, scars from the exploding boom that it will take years more to heal over. I showed in this article that in case all these lots were sold and a house built on each, as promised by the boomers, Los Angeles would then have a population greater than London. But mighty few of the investors seemed to think that this was a preposterous possibility at all.

I will give a few instances of the wildcatting during those memorable years. All the land from Redondo-by-the-Sea to Widneyville-by-the-Desert they cut up into town lots. They built cement sidewalks for miles into the desert fastness. They built railroad lines, where the main line did not run through, and took out train loads of crazy people with their pockets full of cash. Bands played gay music as they traveled. From the trains they herded them into wagons, tally-hos or stages and hauled them to the heart of the proposed new "city." Here a vast array of refreshment tables would be set up in serried ranks, covered with cold lunch, while barrels of beer, whiskey and wine would be tapped to the

ORANGES ON JOSHUA TREES

blare of the band. All free of course, and most stimulating when the hour arrived for bidding in lots. Lots selling on those feast days for thousands of dollars apiece were afterward assessed for taxation at two dollars a lot and many of them reverted to the tax collector. My goodness, the colleges they proposed and sometimes actually built! A college for at least every thousand acres. The college seemed to be a big selling point. And hotels! Magnificent structures were actually erected that never held a guest after opening day and were later dedicated to the insurance companies by the fire route.

"Widneyville-by-the-Desert" was a prize exhibit of those days. The promoters referred to it as "the modern Elysium," I believe, or some such high-toned Greek brag. A tremendous excursion was organized to conduct the speculative hordes to the site of the proposed ideal city on the opening day. A natural and to the Eastern tenderfoot a rather appalling growth of cactus and yucca palms, commonly called Joshua trees, covered the desert hereabouts. These spiny, writhing Joshua trees are really a horrific sight if you are not used to them, but the promoters of Widneyville had a bright idea that saved them the expense of clearing the growth off. They did a little judicious trimming on the cactus plants and yuccas, shaping them up into a certain uniformity, then shipped out a carload of cheap wind-fall oranges and on the end of each bayonet-like spike on the yuccas and on each cactus spine they impaled an orange. Suddenly the desert fruited like the orange grove! Down the lines of the proposed streets staked out in the desert, and around the great square outlined by the surveyors, crowded innumerable orange trees loaded with their golden harvest. The Easterners stood agape at the Elysian sight, hardly listening to the salesmen as they described the college, the several churches, the great sanitarium and the magnificent hotel—temperance hotel—that would so soon surround the central plaza of Widneyville.

"Here, you see, ladies and gentlemen, is the natural home of the orange," said the conductor of the excursion as he addressed the assembled multitude. "These beautiful trees, so prolific of fruit, are a natural growth. This is the only spot west of the Rocky Mountains where the orange is indigenous. In a little while we will have irrigation canals all over the tract and when these orange trees are irrigated their fruit will grow as big as pumpkins. There'll be a fortune in every block, ladies and gentlemen."

Blocks and blocks were sold from the plat of "Widneyville-by-the-Desert," at boom prices but no house was built on the actual site.

On the sea coast the boomers discovered some imaginary natural advantages in a bight or curve in the shoreline, laid out a city and called it "Redondo-by-the-Sea." Redondo [1] was advertised as the greatest and safest harbor in the world. The boosters hired engineers and got them to certify that it had limitless possibilities as a safe shipping point. As a matter of fact Redondo is an open roadstead, to-day as it was then, a pocket that catches all the force of the northwest wind, bringing the rollers in with crushing violence when it blows. But on a calm day the water looks pretty smooth and in such weather the eminent engineers and other eminences would say: "You see, there is a submarine oil well in the offing that spouts oil perpetually. This keeps the waters of Redondo as calm as a millpond. It will be the great harbor of the Pacific Coast."

The Redondo boomers organized several steamship lines, on paper; one to China, one to Australia, another to South America. Great cargo carriers from the ends of the earth were to cast their anchors in the oil pond of Redondo. There was a little old salt pond not far back from the beach where the Mexicans and the American pioneers used to go and boil the water down into salt. This pond was about as big as a garden in the backyard of a Dutch tavern. Well, the promoters blazoned the news that this pond was to be dredged out, surrounded with docks and connected with the ocean by a great canal. The canal was to have locks and all that sort of thing and by an astounding feat of engineering arrangements were to be made to let the water out of the basin when desired so that ships, while resting at their docks, could be standing high and dry, which would give a fine chance to scrape the barnacles off their bottoms. Lots of overland railroads, so it was claimed, were eagerly awaiting the opportunity to extend their railroads directly to the sides of these docks so that they would be in immediate touch with the whole United States. While a ship's bottom was being scraped her cargo would be passing directly into the railroad cars alongside. Not a moment wasted.

Elaborate maps and sea charts were prepared showing that the Asiatic trade was bound to center at Redondo. Redondo was nearer China than any other spot on the American coast. It was nearer to every other place, including New York.

The daily press of Los Angeles blazoned the great future of Redondo-by-the-Sea. Every person investing there would be sure of a fortune even if he or she never wanted to live there. You could get a pretty good waterfront lot for from twenty thousand to fifty thousand dollars. Villa lots back in the bleak dunes could be had for from one thousand to ten thousand dollars each. People bought them, too, and a few foolhardy sea captains brought their ships to the wharf that was built into the open sea and some of these vessels were dashed to pieces on the shore. But nothing came of the great commercial project which had furnished the basis for the ridiculous valuations on property there and the place lapsed into the status of an indifferent bathing beach.

We had another great city projected and called Pacoima. It was in the San Fernando Valley, on the slope east from the old mission town of San Fernando. The slope was just desert with a scant growth of cactus and sage, but Pacoima looked great on paper. They built a Methodist college there, or at least projected one, and projected a whole lot of other things of like pious character. They built a submerged dam at the mouth of Pacoima Cañon to catch the water that escaped underground from the mountains and force it to the surface for irrigation. When they got their submerged dam done they found it was not sufficiently submerged and the water continued to escape underground and leave the tract a desert. However the promoters made a lot out of the dam project for while the work was going on they pointed to it with pride and sold property to the gullible on the strength of what the irrigation project was *going* to do for the country. I knew one poor old Frenchwoman who bought three blocks in the projected business center of Pacoima. The first one she bought she paid sixteen thousand dollars for and as a favor the promoters allowed her to buy the two contiguous blocks for eight thousand apiece. There never was and never had been a day since the sun first warmed the earth that these blocks had been worth more than five dollars apiece. They were not worth anything so far as utility was concerned. Pacoima always was a desert, is a desert to-day and will be a desert for all future time, unless some one can find water somewhere, and then these blocks might be worth one or two hundred dollars apiece. But where is the water to come from?[2]

While the Pacoima project was in full force and effect I was riding down town from my home one morning on the street car and entered into conversation with a stranger. He had come, it seemed, from the Dakotas to pass the winter in our pleasant clime, and he remarked to me, "You have quite a real estate boom on in these parts, I see."

"We certainly have," I answered.

"Well," he continued, "I saw the most curious performance yesterday. My wife and I attended the Methodist church out on Pico Heights. After the sermon the preacher descended from the pulpit and spotting me right in the front row said, 'You seem to be a stranger here.' When I had acknowledged the accusation, he said, 'Going to stay here long?' When I told him we would be here through the winter, he said, 'Wouldn't you be interested in investing in real estate while you are here?' I answered that I couldn't say, but that I would look the field over. Right away he pulled a lot of circulars from his pocket advertising Pacoima. 'Now,' said he, 'before you buy anywhere I want you to go look this project over. Pacoima is going to be the great educational center of this country. A great Methodist college will be built there and the faculty is already elected.' Then he went on scattering circulars through the congregation.

"It seems to me," continued my street car acquaintance, "that this boom business is being carried a little too far when the preachers become boomers and set about to catch their Sunday congregations. I'm afraid it will burst one of these days."

We had still another "city" on the desert. It was projected by two great temperance oracles, ex-Governor St. John of Kansas and Jesse Yarnell of Los Angeles. They procured some land somehow or other, by hook or by crook, or perhaps both, mapped it out and advertised it widely as the coming great temperance colony of all time. Not a drop of wines or liquors even to enter the sacred precincts of this St. John-Yarnell heaven. Only pure, God-given water to be quaffed. Now, I doubt whether either of these apostles had ever actually laid eyes on the land they had mapped and put on sale. My opinion is that they never really owned the land on which they projected their colony.

I ridiculed their proposition in print. I told the public that the tract never would be worth more than three dollars an acre. I knew every foot of that land because I had ranged my sheep over it a quarter of a century before, and I told them that there was not a drop of the pure, God-given water that was to be such an important item in their lives within miles of the region, straight down or sideways. It was a poorer place than "Widneyville-on-the-Desert" because it didn't even have a Joshua tree on which to stick oranges. A temperance colony on a waterless waste was a stunner, indeed, and I warned the suckers that if they moved out there they would have to order beer to sustain life.

There were a few poor, hardworking men made rich overnight by the great boom, but usually their sudden wealth slipped through their fingers almost as rapidly as it had slipped into them. These were fellows that didn't know what the boom was all about until it struck them and left them near-millionaires; fellows that had taken up claims on almost waterless, unproductive lands and had put in years trying to make a living from the soil. I knew one such fellow that took up a government preëmption at the foot of one of our mountain ranges and toiled there for a long time trying to support a family. The boom hit right where his land was and he sold his one hundred and sixty acres for $160,000 in gold coin.

He came to town to enjoy life. A presidential election was approaching. One day I met the man—John, I will call him, without identifying the family, other than to say he was the first American child born in the city of Los Angeles—and he was on his way to Republican headquarters. He had two servants at his heels carrying bags of gold. He had been drinking and he wanted to talk. "Major," he said to me, "I'm going down to make a contribution to the cause."

"What cause, John?"

"The Republican cause, Major. I'm going to give this to the executive committee. I have some pride in Los Angeles. I was born here."

"How much have you got there, John?" I asked.

"Oh, just a starter, Major. There's five thousand in each of these bags."

John staggered on down the street carrying his load of alcohol as best he could and his servants carrying his bags of gold. It wasn't long before every penny of his $160,000 boom money was gone, his beautiful wife had divorced him and taken the lovely little children with her and this initial son of American Los Angeles was submerged in the drift.

I could name a dozen or more others that I personally know of the small honest class that got windfalls out of the boom, who sank right to the bottom along with John the First. That kind of money seemed to carry a curse with it.

We had an old Mexican silversmith in Los Angeles, a very ingenious and talented craftsman well known to the old-timers. He owned a little low, flat adobe on a lot in Sonoratown, with about sixty foot frontage on Upper Main Street and a depth of about one hundred feet. There he had been born and lived all his life, there he had reared a large family of most accomplished daughters whom he had caused to be educated in the modern style with the proceeds of his laborious craft. During the boom he contracted to sell his old adobe homestead for twenty thousand dollars and got two thousand down. A few days after making the contract he died. The widow took out letters of administration and consulted me as her lawyer. She wanted to bring suit to set aside that contract for the sale of the property. I advised her that the price named was just twenty times more than the property was worth, that now was the time to get that money if she could. The contract called for the payment of the remaining eighteen thousand dollars within thirty days. I knew that the capitalists behind the offer were financially responsible and would go through with the deal, even if the boom weakened within that thirty days. But so inflated was the old Mexican lady with the gambling spirit of the boom that she thought she could get twice as much for the house and lot. She dispensed with my services and went to two other lawyers. They advised a suit to break the contract on the ground that the husband had not been of sound mind when he entered into it.

The widow put up with the court the two thousand dollars paid her late husband by the capitalists and, in order to raise the two thousand more demanded by her lawyers for prosecuting the suit and to cover other expenses, she mortgaged some other property she had in that part of town for eight thousand dollars. She borrowed the money from a banker. The capitalists that had made the original offer to buy, instead of contesting the suit jumped at the chance to take up the two thousand she tendered them through the court and willingly cancelled the contract. The boom was bursting. The result to the widow was that she got back her old rookery, surrendered the down payment of two thousand dollars and lost the eight thousand dollars borrowed and all the property that secured it by the time the lawyers and the banker got through with her. The family was left in dire poverty. Boom insanity.

I had an old soldier friend. He was a stone cutter. He cut stone for a rich French Canadian here in Los Angeles named Beaudry.* Beaudry let him have ten acres of land on the western margin of the city on easy terms. When the boom came the stone cutter sold this ten acres for fifty or sixty thousand dollars. Immediately he styled himself a capitalist and put on airs, and his wife became one of the leading speculators of that hectic period. She was the "head man" in a series of big schemes. She went in for high society. One day I met her and she said, "I've made five thousand to-day and I will make ten thousand to-morrow."

The stone cutter and his wife bought a lot on a fashionable street and built a mansion and the lady became a leader in circles she could not have entered before. She was prominent in Grand Army circles as president of one of the women's auxiliaries and once I made the trip to a G.A.R. encampment at Santa Rosa with an excursion of which she was a member. As the train swept through the beautiful country above San Francisco Bay, up toward Petaluma, the scenery was gorgeous. It was springtime and those grand evergreen oaks that cover the hillsides and make parks of the valleys presented indescribable vistas. One superb oak stood alone and rising from beneath it was a great fragment of gleaming granite like a rough monument. Somebody exclaimed over the perfect picture the oak and the granite made with the foreground of verdure like a perfect

* Prudent Beaudry, several times mayor of Los Angeles. Beaudry Street runs through a portion of the city once largely owned by him.

lawn and said, "How beautiful that would look in front of the mansion of some rich person."

Mrs. Stone Cutter, the boom queen, immediately turned to me and said, "Major, how much do you think it would cost to have that granite bowlder set down on my lawn in Los Angeles?"

"Oh, it would cost you at least five thousand dollars," I answered.

"Well, I'm going to have it on my lawn if it costs ten thousand," she answered. And it was laid down there, at a cost that may have been nearer the maximum than the minimum. Two years later her husband was cutting stone again, when he could get work, and she was dying of a broken heart. The Boom Queen was a mere commoner once more, yea, almost a mendicant, and life was no longer worth living. Boom! Boom! Hear the boom burst! And the wounded cry out!

I had a Mexican friend, a good-hearted, industrious, honest fellow, a widower with several children and an aged mother. He owned thirteen acres of land on the edge of town for which he had paid a total of two hundred and fifty dollars. He raised watermelons, corn, beans, chile peppers and made a fair living. Quite a thrifty fellow was Jesús. The real estate boom began to grow louder and louder and my friend began to believe that it was the sound of salutes from castles in Spain. He decided that he was very rich and walked in the clouds. To him the conclusion in his own mind was sufficient; it wasn't necessary to do anything about it; utterly silly to rush around like these land speculators, making deals. One could easily calculate with a sliver of charcoal on a sufficiently clean cornhusk, even if one were not well educated, that thirteen acres of land within sound of the booming of the boom made one wealthy. That was a beautiful, effortless fact.

One day I said to him: "Jesús, haven't you sold your land yet?"

"No, not yet."

"What do you think it's worth?"

"Oh, to-day worth one hundred thousand dollar. To-morrow, *quien sabe?*"

That poor Mexican actually refused an offer of $150,000 for his thirteen acre truck patch. He thought he would wait for $200,000 *mañana*. And in the meantime, being already worth that two hundred thousand in his mind, Jesús decided that he was putting forth needless effort in raising watermelons, beans and chile. Instead of that he would go to the bank and get a little spending money to play with while he waited for the two hundred thousand dollar deal. Or maybe a bigger deal than that. Oh, surely bigger than that, come to think of it. At least a half a million dollars, *como no?*

So he plastered his little farm with a two thousand dollar mortgage. The rest of the story can be told in a line or two. The dream ship sank with Jesús on board, the mortgage sharks gobbled up the thirteen acres, his children all died and he is living on acorns up in a mountain cañon with his ancient mother. She is one hundred and three years old and he, her first born, is eighty at this writing. The blow was not a deadly one, apparently, but it ought to be a lesson to them for the future!

After the boom had "busted" a prominent San Francisco newspaper was reviewing the rascally course of the real estate excitement in Southern California; the ruin it had wrought, the desolation in its wake, the blighted hopes, the broken families, the desolated homes. It arraigned the press of Los Angeles and San Diego and the boom press generally. For every boom town had had a daily paper with paid editors whipping up excitement. This San Francisco paper wound up its editorial with the statement: "There is only one man in Los Angeles that kept himself clean from this unholy thing and that man is Horace Bell, who combated it with his paper."

A recital of the various forms of rascality perpetrated by the boomers would fill a volume. But the one greatest piece of rascality of all, to my mind, was the desecration of one of the city graveyards. It was a small pioneer graveyard covering ten acres.* Some of the most honored California pioneers and officers of the army were interred here, but it was no longer used for burials. The city allowed promoters to map it, cut it up and sell it off in small building lots. In building streets through it human remains were excavated and scattered and to-day wagons rattle through streets built up over buried human bodies. Houses stand on graves. The city of Los Angeles sold, or conveyed to the promoters, this cemetery plot, a municipal burying ground, without pretending to remove and re-inter elsewhere the bodies resting there. Boom insanity blighted not only people's good judgment but their humanity and sense of justice.

* The author refers to a plot of ground on the northwest corner of Figueroa and Ninth streets.

CHAPTER 25

"Kings of the Commonwealth"

It is wonderful how far the average man's vanity will carry him in the expenditure of money to see his name lauded in print and his face limned in publication. This biography business is one of the greatest industries of the age. It has flourished in Southern California with particular virility. The fad began here in '86 or '87 and it has grown until it is almost equal in importance to the oil industry and far ahead of Belgian hares.

Every man that publishes a paper goes into the biography business and some publishers have no other excuse for publishing except the biography business. One of these publishers goes to a groceryman, for instance, and solicits the privilege of publishing his photograph and history. Possibly the grocer, an old-timer, expresses surprise that there is anything to tell about him that the community doesn't already know. "Why, of course the old-timers all know about you," replies the solicitor patronizingly, "but they've never seen you lauded in print. That's what counts. And think of the newcomers arriving in town every day who are ignorant of your honorable history. Now, your life has been so eventful and your virtues are so great that we won't charge you for anything but the engraving of your picture."

But the subjects of the biographical sketches all pay exorbitantly, as a matter of fact. For an engraving costing a dollar the victim will be charged ten or fifteen dollars. Some as high as twenty dollars.

And what curiosities these biographies are. Summed up they generally amount to this:

JOHN JONES: He was born and he cried. He lived and he died.

I have been referring especially to the small weeklies. The big dailies are in the business on a franker scale. They usually get out New Year editions and for months previous to publication their representatives canvass the workshops of lawyers, doctors, bankers, ironmongers, soapmakers and woodcarvers, including carpenters (always designated as contractors), offering "write-ups" for from twenty to two hundred dollars.

Thus do inkslingers and typesetters draw revenue from Vanity Fair.

In 1887 or '88, during the big boom times in Southern California, a very talented literary lady called on me with a letter from the publishers of *The Golden Era,* a pioneer magazine of San Francisco. The letter requested her to solicit Major Bell's biography for the publication in question and called attention to the fact that the Major had been one of the earliest contributors to its pages; that *The Golden Era* had been publishing biographical sketches of its notable early contributors such as Mark Twain, Bret Harte, Joaquín Miller *et cetera* and that the editors greatly desired to add him to this list of high renown.

Said the lady, full of confidence and enthused over her assignment: "Just write your sketch yourself and I will enlarge upon it and embellish it to your guaranteed satisfaction. Remember, there is no charge."

I dashed the lady's high hopes by declining to be biographed along this plan which was one applied, I knew, only to lesser literary lights than Mark Twain and the others named, but she was such a lovely lady and such a really brilliant writer in need of a job that I offered her a helpful suggestion.

"Madame," said I, "it is with real regret that I have disappointed you, but if you will allow me I can give you a piece of advice that will put you in the way of making some money."

"For goodness' sake tell me," she replied eagerly. "I certainly need some money."

"Well," said I, "you write to your magazine and get authority to biograph the leading men of Los Angeles. The ones that claim to be, I mean. Get a fixed price to quote and I will give you a list of forty fools. Or more, if you need them."

In due course of time the lady received sanction from the publishers to go ahead on the new basis. Each citizen biographed and depicted was to pay a certain sum "for engraving" and to buy at least twenty copies of the magazine at twenty-five cents per copy. The lady herself, beside regular commission, was to get what she could out of each customer for putting the literary flourishes of her own pen to the stirring biographical sketches.

I gave the lady a list of forty persons whose vanity I felt sure would induce them to be liberal. The first one on that list was ex-Governor John G. Downey, then a millionaire and recently married a second time.

He subscribed and she took his story directly from his dictation. Much elated, the lady submitted the typewritten pages of the Downey sketch to me. It was extravagant and we laughed over it. I knew how extravagant it was because I was as familiar with the history of Downey as I was with anything else in the world.

"If it isn't sufficiently laudatory perhaps you can add to it," laughed the lady.

"Yes, I can," was my answer, and I did. When that biography was published there appeared in history for the first time the news that Governor Downey was a lineal descendant of Brian Boru, King of Munster; that the former governor of California was born in a castle in Ireland built by Boru himself and that the castle still belonged to the illustrious family of Downey.

This was all the merest fiction, my own invention. I wanted to see how far the man's vanity would carry him, so I had her take the additions to the sketch back to her customer for his inspection before sending them to the publisher.

"Why," exclaimed Downey, "how did you learn this? Oh, from Major Bell? Yes, I told that to the Major in confidence years ago. I never cared to parade myself as a descendant of royalty but as long as the facts are out go ahead and use them."

When the special edition of biographical sketches appeared it caused a great sensation; that is, among the subjects of the sketches. That all were pleased is putting it mildly. The lady biographist was invited to dine at the home of the ex-governor and found a hundred dollar bill under her napkin—the most extravagant piece of generosity ever known of this particular host. The other subjects of the biographies paid her twenty dollars a head.

There was one, a sort of clodhopper, who thought himself of particular importance. His dictated story about himself was submitted to me along with the others before publication. This sketch of the clodhopper was especially laudatory; such a luminary as it described simply had never existed in our town. It was too good not to be made better.

"Why," said I to the agent when she had finished reading it to me, "why, you have left out the main thing."

"What is that?"

"You haven't given the hero an ancestry."

"Give him one yourself," she laughed.

"All right. Don't you see that the name is French, or a corruption of the original Norman French? Why, this clodhopper's illustrious ancestor was one of the leaders in the army of William the Conqueror who crossed over on that great filibustering expedition from Normandy to England. This ancestor distinguished himself at the Battle of Hastings and the name has come in English history associated with deeds of valor. Somewhat changed it has come to the United States, has grown and flourished here and like a meteor it has flashed from the frigid shores of Maine to the golden sands of California. Why, of course, the subject of this sketch is the modern shining light of a most illustrious line."

This idea was duly interpolated in the sketch, was shown to the subject and met with his unqualified approval. He added a ten dollar gratuity to the quoted price in token of appreciation.

I forgot to say that after the lady writer had worked up my idea she resubmitted the sketch to me before taking it to the citizen most concerned. While she was reading the revised edition aloud in my office the "Baron of Casteca," Bill Jenkins, dropped in.

"Why," said he, "you certainly left something out that ought to go in."

"For heaven's sake, let me know what it is," exclaimed the lady. "Let's get it all in."

"Well, here it is," replied Bill Jenkins. "The honorable gentleman's father never washed himself during the twenty years he lived in Los Angeles. He never wore socks and his pantaloons never came within six inches of his shoetops. There's more if you have room for it."

"Mr. Jenkins, I'm writing for money," replied the lady austerely. "I won't have room for *any* of that." And she left with the sketch as it stood.

In this manner the little lady who needed money and knew an idea when it was pointed out to her went through the Forty Fools with a profit of more than a thousand dollars to herself.

She wound up her solicitations with Col. Robert S. Baker. I don't know how Baker became a colonel but I do know that he was a pretty decent fellow. He began life in California as a sheepherder. Finally sheep made him rich and he married the wealthy widow of Don Abel Stearns, one of the most successful of the Americans that settled here in Mexican days. I repeat that Baker was a decent fellow for I do not want to be misunderstood as casting any aspersions on him because he began life as a sheepherder. It was he himself who first told me he had begun life that way, roaming the hills and plains with his frying pan and blankets on his back. He was not ashamed of his early career and he was *not* one of my Forty Fools.

It was the lady biography collector's own idea to call on Colonel Baker. He politely declined to become one of the biographied. The lady persisted.

"Why, Colonel," she wheedled, "just look over this list, this galaxy of prominence, all ready signed up for biographies and pictures, and decide for yourself how well you would look among them. All for twenty dollars!"

Colonel Baker looked over the list, stuck his hand in his pocket and handed his caller twenty dollars. With the sweetest of smiles she received the money and said: "Now, Colonel, will you write it yourself or shall I assist you?"

"Write what?" inquired the Colonel in apparent surprise.

"Why, your biography of course."

"KINGS OF COMMONWEALTH"

"Oh!" exclaimed the Colonel, "did you think I gave you the twenty dollars to include me in that publication?"

"Certainly, Colonel."

"Oh, no! I gave you the twenty dollars to leave me out."

Col. R. S. Baker, honored be your memory as an exception to the generality of vainglorious citizenry! Green be your grave!

Hubert Howe Bancroft grew great in the biography business. He was the top of the biographical graft. He began compilation of a work to be called "Kings of the Commonwealth." Think of it—Kings of the Commonwealth! Any one could be a king of this commonwealth by paying from one thousand to five thousand dollars. Every old gambler in San Francisco, every old stockbroker, every shoddy real estate man and all of the sand-hill lords caught at the bait.

But it was in Los Angeles that the promotion of "Kings of the Commonwealth" began. A certain Doctor Fowler was the canvassing agent for Bancroft down here, the angler for kings. He found some here, too, the principal of whom was former Governor Downey. Doctor Fowler took Downey's biography as Downey dictated it to him, and after adding some literary flourishes submitted the manuscript to the ex-governor of California for his approval. Downey proudly showed it to Count O'Reilly.

This distinguished Count O'Reilly was a gentleman, and let it be said here that an Irish gentleman is the finest gentleman in the world. He was a Catholic count, that is a count of the Pope's creation, and let me say that the Pope greatly honored himself and the Church when he conferred this title upon Sarsfield O'Reilly.

Now, this Count O'Reilly related to me the discussion between himself and ex-Governor Downey over the biography prepared by Bancroft's agent. Said he: "Downey and I grew up in the same place in Ireland. We dug turf out of the same pit. We lived in mud houses not remote from each other and reached man's estate by the same humble but honest route followed by other village Irishmen. When I came to read about this castle and King Brian Boru and all that sort of nonsense I said to Downey, 'Why, John, what in the devil possessed you to get up such infernal lies? You will make yourself the laughing stock of all your friends. Why, I am astonished at you, John, about to pay five thousand dollars to put this sort of stuff in a bogus book.'

"The ex-governor replied in substance: 'Well, Count, I'm rich. I have made a great fortune and I am going to spend as much of it in this way as I can. I would rather pay five thousand dollars to be lied about in this way than to leave the five thousand dollars for a lot of hungry Munsterians to fight over when I die.'"

In due course of time Doctor Fowler followed Downey to one of the latter's ranches where the latter used to go to rusticate and got his check for five thousand dollars on the First National Bank of Los Angeles. Spence, another Irishman, was president of this bank. When the Downey check was presented he was at the window and refused to honor it. "I am Downey's business agent," he said to the disgruntled book agent, "and if this is the sort of thing he is spending money for then he is incompetent to manage his own affairs."

It came to pass about this time that the San Francisco newspapers got after the "Kings of the Commonwealth" scheme. Names of subscribers were ascertained and all manner of ridicule was cast upon them. The consequence was that the subscribers began to take cover and when Bancroft came to collect his fees the "Kings" refused to pay.

Lawsuits followed, with the final result that Bancroft never brought out the intended publication.

When Hubert Howe Bancroft was in Los Angeles collecting material for his well known voluminous "History of California," he called upon me for historical data. I furnished a great deal of material for the Bancroft history of California, for which I was never given a line of credit. Bancroft published my writings and called them his writings. It was an easy method on his part to make it appear that he was a great historian. He not only used my manuscripts but republished page after page of my published work and claimed this as his original research.

Here is an instance of my experience with Bancroft: About the beginning of our National Centennial, 1876, a great calamity befell Los Angeles in the failure of the Temple and Workman Bank. Temple and Workman were rich ranchers, owners with the Rowland family, of the great Rancho Puente of eleven leagues, and proprietors of the Rancho Merced, El Potrero de Felipe Lugo and other famous Southern California properties aggregating sixty thousand acres abundantly watered. Workman* was an Englishman by birth, a most excellent gentleman of rural manners, a pioneer who came to California with the Rowland-Workman party from New Mexico prior to the American occupation. Temple was a young Massachusetts man who came to Los Angeles soon after the occupation, a well-educated man of great industry, indomitable energy and a good generous heart.[1]

These ranchers were deluded into starting a bank and succeeded in filling its vaults with much good honest coin

---

*William Workman arrived in Los Angeles in 1841, with the party from Taos and Santa Fé that included Benj. D. Wilson and John Rowland.

of the realm. Then they became the victims of sharpers, to whom they loaned money without security. It was claimed on behalf of the bankers that the sharpers on the outside conspired with the bank manager on the inside who was in collusion with them and left Temple and Workman in ignorance of where and how the money had gone until the heavens fell and crushed them out of existence. Literally out of existence, for one blew his brains out after the revelation and the other died of a broken heart.

Well, when the bank suspended Mr. Temple went to San Francisco and borrowed eighty-five thousand dollars from Lucky Baldwin, a mere bagatelle compared to the exigency of the situation, but it reopened the bank for a short time. The interest on this loan from the benevolent Baldwin was 2 per cent. a month, secured by a mortgage on all the lands and other property owned by the novice bankers. All those magnificent ranch properties above named went as security for this eighty-five thousand dollars.

The bank's creditors finally threw Temple and Workman into the U. S. Bankruptcy Court and an assignee was appointed. First Dan Freeman and E. F. Spence served, then George E. Long. One day Long came to my office and said: "Major, I have been thinking over this Workman and Temple misfortune, and because you are prone to expose wrong-doing and rascality I want you to see the Temple and Workman books. I assure you that the books of that bank show more rascality than it is possible to imagine. If you will accept these books I will make a present of them to you for public use. You can do with them as you will."

At about this time Bancroft visited me in quest of material. I had recently published a book of reminiscences which had been well received and was editing a paper. Believing then that Bancroft was preparing a history that would be

The Porcupine.

FEARLESS, FAITHFUL AND FREE

VOL VI.   LOS ANGELES: SATURDAY, FEBRUARY 20, 1886.   No. 16.

PERKINS vs. BALDWIN.

LIKE MASTER, LIKE MAN.

We write on Wednesday morning, the testimony having been concluded on Tuesday evening, thirteen days of hard, patient work having been consumed in this most celebrated trial. Papers far and wide complain of the disgustingly filthy character of the testimony and the publication thereof by the daily press of Los Angeles. Let us examine and see how this came about. Baldwin was sued by Miss Perkins for the breach of a simple contract, a promise to marry her, and the only legitimate subject matter of inquiry should have been, was such a promise made and broken? On her part the affirmative was proven positively, and then what? Baldwin's defense was, that no such promise was made, and could not have been for the reason that Miss Perkins had been from the time she was eleven years of age, and during the time she was a member of the Baldwin family and friend, companion and concubine of the innocent little daughter of the beast, and ever since and now, a low, lascivious and drunken prostitute of the most degraded character, and that she for the time was simply hired by Baldwin as he might hire any other woman of similar conditions.

That sort of filth is Baldwin's style, in perfect harmony with his beauty, in stincts, and Mr. G. Wiley Wells, the main pillar of the Methodist church, was his leading lawyer and got up this filthy defense. The filthy part of the testimony was all hired perjury, pronounced so by

HISTORY OF THE CASE.

Miss Louise Perkins is nineteen years old, born in California, her parents being

"Is dat you, massa Wiley"

AN UNEASY SEAT.

impeach it, and so emphatic were they that the setters up thereof did not dare use the article of their own production. How came that infamy to be published in

OUR TRIBUTE TO CHINA.

The people of Los Angeles, over 30,000 inhabitants, a low estimate of our perma-

THE BEGINNING OF THE END.

The Seattle affair which occurred last week is a small beginning of that which is sure to follow unless Congress, now in session, enacts prompt and effective legislation as to the removal of the Chinese nuisance. Had there been an understanding and concert of action, as the Porcupine long ago recommended, and had Los Angeles, San Diego and the intermediate towns and cities one consent moved in concert the Chinese question would have been settled in a day, and in a month's time, the last Chinaman would have gone from us forever. The Seattle people didn't want the Chinamen, so they just went to work and were in a fair way to get rid of them when a foolish Government or disturbe the peaceful business of the day and four citizens are murdered. As we understand it there was no violence whatever offered the Chinese at Seattle. They were just required to go on board a steamer and depart, and the fares of those who had no money were paid by the citizens on a general collection for that purpose. Now comes in a Judge and issues his habeas corpus, brings the Chinese, already on board a steamer, before him and tells them to go where they please, to remain or go away. This not suspected the citizens who had the work in hand, the militia fired on them and a useless sacrifice of life followed. If Congress does not relieve us of the Chinese nuisance, there will be a Seattle movement on an extended scale, and so powerful will it be that all the troops and militia on the coast will be powerless to prevent the expul-

Courtesy Los Angeles County Museum Library

Half page of *The Porcupine* during the time of Major Bell's campaign against Lucky Baldwin and the latter's lawyer, J. Wiley Wells

an honor to California and that the truth of the Temple-Workman affair could find the widest publicity in his annals of Los Angeles County, I gave the Temple and Workman Bank books into the possession of Mr. Bancroft.

When the Bancroft volume containing the local annals appeared there was not a mention of the truth as contained in the bank's books. Not a mention of the revelations of the books at all. Not a reference to the fact that the notes of some of our supposedly leading citizens had been sold for ten cents on the dollar on the courthouse steps. Not a single actual rascal was recorded. But somehow it seemed that about every rascal that should have been named, every rascal of prominence participating in the ruin of Temple and Workman, every sharper whose hands were stained with their blood, became a subscriber to the absurd Bancroft history at two hundred and eighty-four dollars the set of volumes.

Luís Rubidox

CHAPTER 26

In Praise of the Mormons

IT would not be fair to write about the American beginnings of California without saying something about the Mormons. Really the Mormons were the true pioneers of the Golden State. There were other Americans here ahead of them, clear back through Mexican days even into the Spanish régime, but these individuals do not come under the head of pioneers as we use the classification in connection with the settlement of the Pacific Coast states. They were adventurers in the more personal sense—sailors cast adrift on these distant shores, or taking a fancy to the land and deserting their ships to marry native women and surrender their nationality for their own gain. Or they were hunters, trappers, traders that drifted in overland, some attached to exploring parties, others adventuring by themselves. Or here and there a Yankee shipping agent that had come to the coast to represent his firm and had remained permanently.

But the organized pioneers came after the acquisition of California by the United States, or more correctly they began coming westward from the date of the outbreak of the Mexican War. The principal movement was started by the gold rush of '49, but the Mormons came before that, along with the army that took and held California under the Stars and Stripes. They came on a purely patriotic and self-sacrificing errand—at least these first of them—to advance the interests of the very government that was opposed to their religious beliefs. In Southern California we have a community—the thriving city of San Bernardino, first American settlement in this part of the state—that was founded by Mormons.[1] For years San Bernardino was a Mormon stronghold, blood relative to Nauvoo, where the Mormon Exodus began.

In 1846 when American volunteers were mustering for the invasion of Mexico the Mormons were starting westward from Nauvoo, Illinois, to escape persecution and to found an empire of their own in the wilderness. It was their famous Exodus. Their first winter was passed at Cainesville, on the Missouri River. In the spring of '47 they started to open the way to the new Zion. Brigham Young was at the head of that band of pioneers. With an advance force of one hundred or so followers, Young pushed ahead and opened the way to Salt Lake, founded the new Zion and in the next year the main body followed. The result of their labors in the wilderness is the great commonwealth of Utah to-day.

But it is the young Mormons that turned aside from the purpose of their dream and the goal of their elders to help the United States government fight the war with Mexico, that concern Californians of to-day, and especially those of us of the south where the famous Mormon Battalion was principally stationed. The world has seldom listened to a story more fraught with hardship, peril and self-sacrifice than the story of the Mormon Battalion. The five hundred odd young men that composed this battalion were mustered into the service of the United States July 16, 1846. They bid farewell to their elders, their friends and relatives of the Exodus for this purpose and were started for California under command of Col. James Allen. They enlisted voluntarily to protect with their lives that flag under which they had been denied protection.

The battalion started on a march of three thousand miles, much of it through an unknown country, without as much provisions as a modern company of infantry would consume in one day. Their whole equipment was of the poorest sort, their mules and horses hardly alive; they suffered terribly from a quack doctor, or an ignorant one, assigned to their outfit whose prescriptions killed oftener than they cured; their distress was increased by the death of Colonel Allen, an excellent army officer, soon after they began their march. The command devolved temporarily upon Lieut. A. J. Smith, about whom the less said the better.

When Santa Fé was reached Lieut.-Col. P. St. George Cooke, U.S.A., was placed in command. He conducted himself as an officer and a gentleman and his published account of early experiences in California is well known to students of our Western history. The march to the Coast was resumed at Santa Fé October 14, 1846, and after a series of unspeakable hardships, with death and distress stalking them every mile, the command emerged from the desert and encamped at Warner's Ranch above San Diego. Here at the home of Jonathan Trumbull Warner, a Connecticut Yankee who had come to the country in the '30s with a trapping party and had settled, the young Mormons saw their first house in California.[2]

In the meantime the ship *Brooklyn* had sailed from New York conveying a party of Mormon colonizers that planned to penetrate inland from San Francisco. At the head of this company of Saints was Samuel Brannan, a name destined to become famous in the early American annals of San Francisco. Brannan brought ashore with him a printing press and immediately began the publication of a newspaper, and this paper later played an important part in disseminating the news of the gold discovery, as I shall describe.

On arrival at Warner's Ranch the Mormon Battalion was ordered by General Kearny to proceed to San Diego for station. Later the battalion was moved back to the vicinity of Warner's and quartered in the old San Luís Rey Mission. After a month here spent in intensive drill and discipline the command was moved to Los Angeles, then considered a hot bed of possible trouble. Los Angeles was then an old Spanish-Mexican town inhabited by restless, resentful Californians and lawless characters from other races. In these unfavorable surroundings, with vice and violence flaunting on every side, the young Mormon soldiers maintained a moral dignity that should be emblazoned in lustrous letters on their record. They respected the rights of property even when hunger was gnawing at their vitals, both on the long march and after arrival; they kept clear of the saloons, brothels and cock fights and by minding their own business they avoided unnecessary quarrels with the populace. However, when quarrels were forced upon them they sustained themselves valiantly as many a whipped "bad man" of that day could testify.

As the year of their original enlistment drew to a close and California was safely under the Stars and Stripes the young Mormons expressed their desire to rejoin the main body of their fellows, now establishing the new Zion. The army officers in charge in Los Angeles used every effort to induce the Mormon volunteers to reënlist, for they had found them good and useful soldiers, but the majority decided to be on its way. It was very much feared that the disbandment of the battalion would be followed by a fresh revolt on the part of the Spanish Californians. Enough reënlistments were secured from the battalion to maintain one company, which remained in Los Angeles. The rest

Rush for the gold regions.

Sutter's Mill.

Don Juan Bandini and daughter Margarita. Don. Juan originally held the great grant of Jurupa where is found now the famed Riverside orange growing district. Margarita later became Mrs. J. B. Winston.

A beauty of the old regime, Antonia de Bandini. Popularly known as "Mrs. Captain José."

of the Mormons were mustered out July 16, 1847, and began to push northward in a body.

On August 26 these ex-soldiers camped on the banks of the America River near where the city of Sacramento now stands. Soon they moved on to Sutter's Fort and on the offer of employment by Capt. Johann Sutter a number of them decided to remain here until the following summer. In charge of one of his men, James Marshall, Sutter sent forty or fifty of the Mormons to a point known now as Coloma to construct a sawmill. It was due to the construction of this mill that gold was discovered January 24, 1848. The construction of the mill would have been impossible at the time but for the aid of the former members of the Mormon Battalion, who alone among the immigrants had a sufficient force of millwrights, carpenters and other mechanics to carry on the work.

It was the twenty-fourth day of January that the eye of James Marshall was attracted to the bed of the millrace by glittering yellow substance. He scooped some up and declared to his companion, James C. Brown of the Mormons, that it was gold. Brown was sceptical but when the next morning Marshall came to him with an unmistakable supply of the yellow metal Brown seized up a handful and cried, "Gold, boys, gold!"

The exciting news was soon carried to San Francisco and was first published to the world in Sam Brannan's paper —the paper issued by the Mormons that had come on the *Brooklyn*. At first the story was ridiculed but when evidence of its truth was laid before the eyes of the world there began that wild delirium of gold hunting when men forsook their usual pursuits and ran madly toward the setting sun.

In the light of these events it seems but fair to affirm that but for the Mormon volunteers in the war with Mexico there might have been no discovery of gold in California for decades after that memorable January day in 1848.

It was in 1851 that an offshoot of the Mormon colony in Utah was founded at San Bernardino, sixty-five miles east of Los Angeles. The agricultural wealth that has accrued to the state from the introduction by these Mormons of their system of irrigation can scarcely be estimated and is a far greater contribution on their part than their assistance in the discovery of gold. It was my fortune to visit San Bernardino often in its early days and I became well acquainted with those pioneer Mormons. I was stationed at old Fort Jurupa for a time, close to the present site of Riverside, and as Quartermaster Smith of the post purchased a lot of supplies from the near-by Mormons there was much friendly intercourse between Jurupa and San Bernardino.

I was then a very young man, and as I look back now I can see that I was benefited by my contact with those serious, rugged people. They set good examples for youth. There were no gamblers tolerated at San Bernardino, no rum sellers, no lewd characters offering vice for sale. There were no drones there. Persistent industry, intensive husbandry were the impressive features of life there. The colony purchased its lands from the princely holdings of the celebrated Lugo family, whose grants came from the King of Spain and the Republic of Mexico. The first thing the Mormons did was to build a stockade about a quarter of a mile square with two great gates leading into it. Inside they placed their dwellings, shops and stores. Every night the gates were barred and a sentry kept vigilant watch from the walls against surprise by marauding bands of "bronco" or wild Indians from the mountains and desert. The desert lies just over the mountains, through the Cajon Pass, where the Santa Fé Railroad now enters the San Bernardino Valley. The next thing they did was to plant crops. Just one year from the time they purchased the land these settlers were harvesting good crops of wheat, barley and corn. A flour mill was erected and was soon furnishing breadstuffs not only for the colony but for Los Angeles as well, entering into active competition with the supply that had been coming to us largely from Chile and Peru. A sawmill was added and shakes were turned out to be sent in great caravans of ox carts all over Southern California to roof new buildings that Americans were erecting. Many of the roads still found leading into apparently inaccessible cañons of the San Bernardino Mountains were built by the Mormons in the '50s for their lumbering operations. They had their recreations, too—their picnics and dances, at which the stranger from the outside was welcomed. If he was well behaved he was treated with utmost hospitality.

The seed wheat from which was raised the first crop for the Salt Lake establishment, that is, the crop of 1848, was bought from the stock remaining on hand at the old Franciscan missions in what became Los Angeles County and was carried eight hundred miles across the desert by some former soldiers of the Mormon Battalion that went directly from Los Angeles to Salt Lake. From their wages as soldiers they purchased mules and Mexican-style packsaddles and transported the wheat to the Salt Lake Valley without wagons.*

Speaking of San Bernardino and its Mormon beginning in 1851 has prompted me to check over in my mind the settlements in Los Angeles County in 1852, the year I arrived

* See "The March of the Mormon Battalion. Taken from the Journal of Henry Standage by F. A. Golder." Century Company, New York, 1928.

in Los Angeles from the mines in the north. From the present-day viewpoint it is almost impossible to believe that the country was so sparsely settled at that time and that under the heading of "settlements" we counted private ranchos as if each represented a town. Wherever there was a ranch house with its accompaniment of quarters for Indian laborers and their families, it was counted on the map as a community. And each one was indeed important to the traveler for here could be found hospitable entertainment, food, drink, fresh horses and new raiment if necessary, for a pittance or for nothing. More than one can expect from the modern city unless one is a millionaire and pays his way fabulously. Starting from the Pueblo de los Angeles as a focal point we had as our most prominent settlements the Mission San Fernando, Mission San Gabriél, Mission Vieja,[3] Mission San Juan Capistrano and the port of San Pedro, then consisting of three adobe houses, a liberty pole and Dead Man's Island.

Of the ranch houses we had first, going eastward, La Puente. Then Chino, Jurupa, and the Mormons at San Bernardino. Toward San Diego we had first Rancho Santa Gertrudis, then the Yorba Rancho at the crossing of the Santa Ana River, the San Joaquín Rancho beyond the Santa Ana and El Aliso near Mission San Juan Capistrano. Going toward San Pedro we had Rancho de los Cuervos, the Domínguez or Rancho San Pedro and the Rancho Palos Verdes. In the rear of the present city of Long Beach was the Rancho de los Cerritos and further down the coast the Rancho de los Alamitos. Journeying toward Santa Monica we came to the Rancho Paso de las Tijeras.* Adjoining it to the southward was the Centinela. Then the Rancho Ballona, populated by the Machados and their kinsfolk.

* "Scissors Pass."

Further on was the San Vicente and adjoining it the Bocas de Santa Monica.

Along the southern base of the Cahuenga hills we had first the Rancho la Brea, then the Rancho Rodeo de las Aguas, Rancho Rincon de los Bueyes and Rancho de los Buenos Ayres. Crossing the range and following its northern base we found the little Rancho Cahuenga, the Rancho Encino and farther on Las Vírgines: then the Conejo, the Triúnfo and the great Malibu, the latter bordering the seacoast westward and stretching back into the mountains.

North from Los Angeles the first big ranch was the San Rafael, ancestral domain of the Verdugos. Then northeastward was the San Pascual where the rich and beautiful city of Pasadena now stands. Right here the author might pause to say that when he attained his twenty-first birthday he was offered the twenty thousand acres of Rancho San Pascual as a birthday gift. He chose instead a horse and saddle. This sounds like tall talk but it is true. His uncle, Alexander Bell, ran his sheep over this old property of the Ábila and Gárfias families and could have bought it for a pittance had I elected to marry into a California family and settle down, as Uncle Alec desired me to do. But the horse appealed more to my boyish imagination. Indeed, with the five thousand dollars' worth of finest carved-leather, silver-mounted saddle and bridle that went with the steed it was reasonable to believe at the time that this gift was worth more than the San Pascual acres could ever be worth.

Following the base of the Sierra Madre toward San Fernando from the San Pascual brought one to the Rancho Tejunga. Southward from this were the properties known as La Providencia * and Los Feliz, both lying along the Los

---
* Location of the present town of Burbank.

Angeles River, the Feliz extending to within a short distance of the Pueblo. Continuing on west from the Tejunga we passed the properties formerly belonging to the Mission San Fernando that went into the hands of Pico and his friends after the secularization, and on the western margin of the San Fernando Valley we struck the Rancho el Escorpión, formerly a great Indian village site. Wonderful medicinal springs rise out of the ground here; they played a large part in the Indian life and were patronized by the padres of the Mission San Fernando.

Other ranchos which I can recall were the San Antonio, a Lugo property extending from the Los Angeles River to the San Gabriél and from the Mission Hills to the Rancho Cerritos; and the San Francisquito on which are now located the towns of Newhall and Saugus. Outside of Los Angeles these ranch houses, with the little settlements around the decaying Missions, were the centers of population of the vast county of Los Angeles as it was constituted when California first became an American state. Over the wide wilderness stretches between roamed ten of thousands of cattle and horses, the current wealth of the country. Los Angeles itself was a little flat-roofed town surrounded by orchards and vineyards of considerable extent. Wine-making was the big industry of the metropolis. Outside the cultivated area of the Pueblo the only cultivated plots of any extent were around the Missions, mementoes from the industrious Franciscans. In these vicinities grain was still planted and harvested by most primitive methods. Wheat was cut with the small hand scythe, piled onto rawhides in a native carreta, a cart with two solid wheels and wooden axles, hauled by oxen to circular corrals and there threshed out under the feet of horses driven 'round and 'round. The grain was tossed into the air from baskets by women and children to be winnowed by the bonny zephyrs from the Pacific.

Methods and crops have changed mightily since then, but we have suffered some very expensive experiences in our efforts to arrive at a more toney type of agriculture, or rather to graduate from plain agriculture to aristocratic horticulture. Viticulture and wine making were just becoming staple activities yielding large remuneration when we all got it into our heads that oranges were the hope of the future and orange growing became so popular that a man without an orange grove was considered as plebeian as a man without negroes in slave times down South. Good old orchards of staple deciduous fruits and acres of vineyards were grubbed out and reset with tiny orange trees that cost several dollars per tree. Ten thousand dollars a year, they said, could be made off a few acres of oranges. So the vineyardist mortgaged his land and bought orange trees.

Those that launched the orange craze and supplied the seedlings made fortunes immediately. I remember a certain citizen, a busy, bustling little fellow who was summoned into court one day to serve as juror, and while I was in the courtroom he was drawn for service. He put up a voluble protest to the judge for allowing his business to be interfered with.

"Your Honor," said he, "my time is worth a hundred dollars a minute and I can't afford to be detained here."

"A hundred dollars a minute!" exclaimed the Judge. "How do you make that much?"

"Out of my orange nursery, sir. My income now is five thousand dollars a day and I want the Court to understand that I can't afford to be detained here at two dollars a day."

This little man made a great fortune out of some thirty

acres of orange nursery, but, alas, he fell into the hands of sharpers who convinced him he had great political possibilities. They induced him to put up money to found a newspaper that was to boost him into high political circles in Washington. He built a lavish mansion and practised the social amenities to be ready for his Washington début. But he never got there and the last I heard of him he was selling bouquets on a street corner to eke out an existence.

As the orange boom grew the enthusiasm of its devotees led them to make more and more extravagant claims. From ten thousand dollars off an acre they began to talk about twenty-five thousand dollars off one acre. This is the way they talked:

"We will have railroad communication with every city in the United States by the time our orange groves mature. Every family in the United States will buy at least five boxes of oranges. A box of oranges in any market in the world is worth at least five dollars. An acre of orange trees will produce five thousand boxes of oranges. Five times five is twenty-five. Twenty-five thousand dollars an acre from your oranges."

Whoop and hurrah!

Just as everybody had torn every other sort of fruit tree out and planted oranges on borrowed money and often on tracts of land that couldn't be irrigated, we all heard of a better thing to plant, a surer thing, a more remunerative thing, without shadow of doubt. Ah, the Mexican lime was that thing! The Mexican lime would produce in three years from the seed, less than half the time required by the orange, and, oh my, the profit there was in Mexican limes! A Mexican lime tree would support a man when it was in full bearing. All a newly married couple would need would be two Mexican lime trees. As the family increased, plant a lime tree for each increase and let the increase go on indefinitely. Lots of fun and nothing to worry about. Just call in a Chinaman to pick the limes and presto they were sold at great profit in San Francisco, New York, Boston, London. The whole world was dying for limes, and nowhere else could they be grown so well as around Los Angeles. So the dirt flew as holes were dug for lime trees, while those who had gone in heavily for orange trees tore their hair.

About this time the silk craze struck us. Everybody was going to become immensely rich on silk worms. The man that could procure an armful of mulberry cuttings and find room to plant them on land that wasn't cluttered up with mere orange and lime trees was on the sure road to wealth. The man that didn't go in for mulberry cuttings simply was a has-been.

Then came the great real estate boom and most of the orange and lime groves were grubbed up to make town lots. We have already talked about the boom and will not dwell on the subject again. But following the orange craze, the lime craze, the silk craze, the real estate craze, when everybody was mortgaged up to the hilt, along came a great blessing in disguise.

The Belgian hare came to our rescue! More mortgages were slapped onto property, where possible, and Belgian hares were purchased feverishly.

You could get a good Belgian hare for one hundred dollars. A better one for two hundred. An extra special imported hare for a thousand dollars. Now, it was the man that didn't have a pedigreed Belgian hare that was the plebeian. A man that did own pedigreed Belgian hares drove around in a fine carriage and pair behind a coachman. He held his head high and looked with scorn upon his hare-less neighbor. You ought to have seen the rabbitries! The elegance of them! Why, a rosewood piano was no match for the elegance of the accommodations for some of these hare-ems.

How they pampered the leading bucks! Lord Lurgan, for instance. Didn't you ever hear of Lord Lurgan, dear reader? Why, Lord Lurgan was said to be worth three thousand dollars. He was a big rabbit, a beautiful, prolific rabbit, was Lord Lurgan. I confess that I once drove several miles to feast my eyes on Lord Lurgan. Lord Lurgan had his reception days, when his rich owner would dress himself up in evening costume and receive distinguished visitors. They would peer into the palatial hutch and expatiate on the beauty, the virility and the worth of Lord Lurgan. As a mark of friendship to some particular visitor the proud owner would agree to dispose of one of Lord Lurgan's progeny to him for one hundred dollars, or two hundred dollars, or five hundred dollars, according to the hump on the progeny's back. Big hump big price.

Lord Lurgan's master used to profit as much as a thousand dollars a day, 'tis said, for the use of Lord Lurgan. That is, for allowing him to visit around, the owner receiving a certain proportion of the resultant progeny, I believe. That is a high figure but Lord Lurgan was a hare of parts. But alas, one day Lord Lurgan over-did himself and died. This was at home in his own hare-em and a lot of Lady Lurgans grieved themselves to death. Then a cat got in and killed off most of the little Lurgans, and a draught of air slipped through and gave the rest fatal colds. The rabbit business slumped all in a few hours for one great owner. The same sort of thing happened to a great many owners as time went on. Belgian hares began to be worth about ten cents apiece.

The Belgian hare blessing was turning into a curse

when the oil boom struck and despair was again dispelled. Every lot owner in Los Angeles was sure he had an oil well in his back yard. Instances of fortunes made by a handful proved tempting bait in the hands of greedy promoters. In the course of a few months incorporated oil companies, ranging from the modest ten thousand to ten million capitalization were as thick in Los Angeles as blackbirds in a newly-plowed field. Golden-worded pleas were issuing from almost every office in the city urging suckers to hustle and pay their money in before stock went to par. The more enterprising of these thieves trekked to New York and Chicago and there sold millions of dollars in stock not worth the paper upon which the certificates were printed. The worst feature was not the parting of fools from their money but the deplorable effect it had on the budding oil industry which of course had a legitimate basis and a tremendous future, as has since been proven. But this subject is all such recent history that I need not discuss it further.

All I will say is, the Lord save us from further booms of any kind. They clog the wheels of true progress. Los Angeles has reached an imperial position as a city and as a county, one already absolutely impregnable, but she has done so in spite of the choicest collection of booms that ever selected one locality in which to explode.

CHAPTER 1

[1] A military post. These grew into pueblos in course of time but they were distinct from those communities founded by royal decree as civil pueblos intended to develop into cities. The only three civil settlements founded by Spain in California were Los Angeles, San José and Villa Branciforte. The latter was on the site of the present city of Santa Cruz. It was abandoned after a few years and its lands reverted to the Mission Santa Cruz.

[2] The author's uncle. In the early 50's this building was known as Bell's Row. Later it passed into the hands of the Mellus family, to which Alexander Bell became related by a second marriage, and was known as Mellus Row. The two-story construction with galleries all around and a walled garden in the rear gave this adobe a marked distinction. It was the capitol building during Frémont's brief term as governor of California. The building was long since destroyed. Commodore Stockton is said to have lodged a short time in the Bell mansion but his better known headquarters, the Avila House, is still standing, in part, on Olvera Street just north of the Plaza. This, the early home of one of the leading Spanish families, was a center of the social life of Los Angeles from 1818 down to some years after the American occupation. A movement is now afoot to preserve the Avila adobe as a public monument.

[3] Abel Stearns was a Massachusetts Yankee who came to California in 1830 and settled in Los Angeles in 1834. He married Arcadia, daughter of Don Juan Bandini, a Chilean of Italian parentage and Mexican nationality. She was fourteen years old at the time of the marriage and reputed to be the most beautiful girl in California. Don Abel was probably the most influential and the richest man in the province during the latter years of the Mexican period. His home, known as El Palacio de Don Abel, on what is now North Main Street at Arcadia Street, where the old Baker Block stands, was known far and wide for elegance and hospitality. He held municipal offices at various times, was a delegate to the first Constitutional Convention that met in Monterey in 1849, and made the first improvements at San Pedro, now Los Angeles Harbor, where he erected the first warehouse. Don Abel

died in 1867, after undergoing financial reverses following two successive years of drought that devastated his vast cattle ranges. Rancho los Alamitos was one of these properties. His widow married Col. R. S. Baker, a wealthy American. In 1877 the celebrated *palacio* was torn away and the Baker Block erected on its site. This was the first building in Los Angeles in which iron framework was used. The upper story was occupied by the Bakers as a home. After the death of Mrs. Stearns-Baker this quaint structure was for some years the haunt of the Bohemian artists' colony of the city. It is now in the heart of one of the most populous Mexican quarters of Los Angeles. The combined Mexican colonies of this city are said now to comprise a population second only to the population of Mexico City. In other words, Los Angeles is the second largest Mexican city. This is an interesting fact when we remember that it represents the return of a race to a city once entirely its own.

[4] The treaty between the United States and Mexico signed February 2, 1848, whereby California and the rest of the territory acquired by the United States as a result of the Mexican War passed permanently into American possession.

CHAPTER 2

[1] Authorities differ as to the date of Carpenter's arrival in Los Angeles. C. D. Willard in his "History of Los Angeles," says he came with a party of trappers in 1832 or '33. Harris Newmark in his "Sixty Years in Southern California," says he came with the Wilson-Workman-Rowland party from New Mexico in 1841. His first property was a little rancho called La Jabonería (The Soap Factory) on the west bank of the Río San Gabriél near El Monte. The locality is still known by this name. Here Carpenter manufactured soap and made enough money from it to acquire a large part of the great Nietos family grant known as Rancho Santa Gertrudis, which stretched away on the opposite bank of the river across the region where are now the towns of Downey, Rivera and Los Nietos.

[2] Rancho Aguaje de la Centinela, site of the present town of Inglewood and its surrounding oil fields between Los Angeles and Redondo. This estimate of a mere million dollars was made, of course, some thirty years ago.

[3] Stages connected Los Angeles with the port of San Pedro, now

Los Angeles Harbor, where passengers were lightered out to coastwise steamers anchored off Deadman's Island. During 1929 this island was entirely removed by the United States government to widen the entrance to the inner harbor. Here were buried, in 1846, the American marines of the *Savannah,* Captain Mervine, killed during the encounter with the California forces in the Battle of Dominguez, in an unsuccessful attempt to march on Los Angeles.

[4] Phineas Banning operated the principal stage line between Los Angeles and San Pedro and had a home near the upper reaches of the inner harbor. In this locality he laid out, in 1872, the town of Wilmington, named after the city in his native Delaware. The Banning family early acquired ownership of Santa Catalina Island and controlled that famous resort until its purchase by William Wrigley, Jr., in 1919.

[5] This may have been either of two cousins who were important land owners—José Loreto Sepúlveda, holder of the Rancho Palos Verdes, thirty-one thousand acres fronting on and stretching westward from the Bay of San Pedro, or José Andrés Sepúlveda, grantee of the Rancho San Joaquín, 48,808 acres lying east of Tustin, Orange County, now incorporated in the great property known as the Irvine Ranch. The Agustín Machado mentioned was owner of Rancho la Ballona, on a corner of which now stands Culver City, home of several celebrated movie studios. Juan Avila (or Abila) held the neighboring grant of Las Ciénegas.

CHAPTER 3

[1] John Rowland was an American who came to California in 1841 in company with William Workman, a British subject, and others who had been engaged in the Santa Fé trade in New Mexico. To Rowland and Workman was granted Rancho la Puente, of almost forty-nine thousand acres of rich land eighteen miles east of Los Angeles. This little gift was said to have been made to them because of their aid to Pico's political cause in the movement that expelled Governor Micheltorena from the province.

[2] One of the earliest American settlements in Southern California, on the Río San Gabriél about fifteen miles east of Los Angeles. It was settled largely by rough-and-readies from Texas and the "El Monte Boys" were long celebrated for their proclivity to seek out trouble and to add to it. One of the stage stations on the famous Butterfield transcontinental route between St. Louis and San Francisco, the longest ever operated, was located at El Monte.

CHAPTER 4

[1] The celebrated Broderick-Terry duel was the outcome of political differences between Senator David C. Broderick and Judge David S. Terry of the State Supreme Court. Senator Broderick made certain charges against Judge Terry which resulted in the duel with pistols at thirty paces on the morning of September 13, 1859, in the hills of Marin County. It is said that Broderick already had a record of two duels fought with political adversaries.

[2] *Misión San Cárlos Borroméo del Cármelo de Monterey* just outside of Monterey. It was the second mission founded in Alta California (1770). Here Junípero Serra, the great Franciscan pioneer, made his headquarters, died and is buried.

[3] The First Regiment of New York Volunteers was organized in New York City by Col. Jonathan D. Stevenson, a militia officer and politician of that day. It was transported in six vessels around the Horn to California, the first three vessels sailing in September, 1846. The voyage took 180 days. Company E, commanded by Capt. Nelson Taylor, and Company G, commanded by Capt. Matthew R. Stevenson, a son of Colonel Stevenson, were stationed in Los Angeles until Sept. 18, 1848, when the regiment was mustered out. Company E was recruited in the New York East Side, and is said to have given the little old pueblo of Los Angeles a lively introduction to New York "tough" life. Colonel Stevenson was given command of the southern military district of California with headquarters in Los Angeles, and it was he who first read publically in the Pueblo the American Declaration of Independence, at the dedication of Fort Moore on the hill behind the old Plaza Church, July 4, 1847. This was a grand ceremony, according to the accounts of the time, with Companies E and G of the New York Volunteers, a detachment of the First Regiment United States Dragoons and the Mormon Battalion drawn up in a hollow square around the tall flagpole, which had been cut for the occasion in the San Bernardino mountains, a hundred miles eastward, and transported to the Pueblo on crude carts with the assistance of Indian workmen. The band played and the cannon roared a salute. Following Colonel Stevenson's reading of the Declaration in English it was read in Spanish by Stephen C. Foster, who had come west from Santa Fé as interpreter with the Mormon Battalion and later became prominent in the civic life of Los Angeles. Old Fort Moore, named for Captain Moore, U. S. Dragoons, killed in the Battle of San Pascual, San Diego

County, when General Kearny's small force was beset by the Californians under Andrés Pico, was located on top of the hill under which the Broadway tunnel now passes, and the site is marked by a tall flagpole and a tablet. A portion of the First Regiment of New York Volunteers occupied and held the southern extremity of the peninsula of Lower California during the Mexican War.

⁴ William Walker, a San Francisco newspaper man and native of Tennessee, often called "the little gray-eyed man of Destiny," sailed from San Francisco, May 4, 1855, with fifty-six followers to take possession of Nicaragua on the pretext that his assistance had been asked by the revolutionary party there in its attempt to free the country from its then alleged despotic government. The original expedition was followed by reënforcements, as recounted by the author, who was in command of one of these shipments of recruits. The Walker filibuster was at first successful, and after gaining command of the country General Walker appointed Patricio Rivas, of the revolutionary party, provisional president of Nicaragua. However, Walker, backed by his army, remained the real ruler. The Walker-Rivas government was actually recognized May 20, 1856, by the United States, under the administration of President Pierce. But fortune soon turned against the daring, silent, cold-blooded little Tennessean. Costa Rican forces, backed largely by Commodore Vanderbilt's Trans-Isthmian transportation interests, whose displeasure Walker had incurred, pressed him to the point where he had to surrender to a United States gunboat in a Nicaraguan harbor to save his life. Returning to the United States he organized another filibuster, this time against Honduras. There he was captured and executed by a firing squad Sept. 12, 1860. Previous to his Nicaraguan adventure Walker had invaded Lower California with the avowed intention of "liberating" it from the Mexican government and setting up an independent republic. He intended then to do the same for Sonora, but his expedition fell to pieces after his proclamation of the Republic of Lower California. This proclamation was issued and the government officers from president down actually named on the spot on Todos Santos Bay where the town of Ensenada, well-known to American week-enders below the border, now stands. The Battle of La Grulla, between Walker's forces and the Lower Californians, took place not far from here.

⁵ Judge Terry of the State Supreme Court was in disfavor with the Vigilance Committee because of his opposition to its methods. At a mass meeting in Portsmouth Square, San Francisco, his re-

NOTES

marks led to a personal quarrel during which Judge Terry stabbed his opponent. Judge Terry was arrested by the Vigilance forces and imprisoned in Fort Gunnybags, where his fate was debated. It was decided that the execution of a justice of the Supreme Court would be impolitic, and that it would be better to expel him from the country. However, the Judge's victim recovered, public excitement cooled and the Judge was finally released.

CHAPTER 7

[1] This road led to the Pueblo across Rancho la Brea by way of the same *brea* or asphaltum tar pools in which was discovered some years ago the great collection of prehistoric animal skeletons now housed in the Los Angeles County Museum at Exposition Park. These animals became entangled in the treacherous tar in the Pleistocene period while hunting and preying on other animals thus entangled and their bones were perfectly preserved beneath the oily mass. It is the greatest discovery of the kind ever made. From these pits have been taken to date the remains of 2,000 dire wolves, 1,500 sabertooth tigers, twenty imperial elephants and mastodons, seventy-five horses, thirty-five camels, one hundred and fifty prehistoric buffalo, thirteen ground sloths, sixty giant sloths, twenty lions and numberless lesser animals and fowls. From the surface crust of these springs the inhabitants of Los Angeles in the Spanish and Mexican régimes took the *brea* used in roofing the flat-topped type of adobe dwelling. The pits are now in the city limits of Los Angeles just off Wilshire Boulevard, and are in a producing oil field. The old "brea pits road" to the Pueblo came around the lower end of the Arroyo de los Reyes, now occupied by Westlake Park, along about what is now Ninth Street and then angled northeastward into town, joining Spring Street at about First Street across the property where the old Nadeau Hotel stands.

[2] Ferdinand Maximilian, Emperor of Mexico, second son of Archduke Francis Charles and brother of Emperor Francis Joseph of Austria. In 1863 he was offered the crown of Mexico by a party of Mexican exiles led by clericals opposed to the recent secularization of the Church by President Benito Juárez. France had long had designs on Mexico and Napoleon III backed up Maximilian with thirty thousand French soldiers in his pretensions to the throne. Renouncing his imperial rights in Austria Maximilian entered Mexico City in June, 1864, and became Emperor. He was accompanied by

his young wife, Princess Charlotte of Belgium, who became Empress Carlota of Mexico. The President of Mexico, Benito Juárez, aroused the patriotic portion of the population to a frenzy of resistance, but in spite of his efforts the French drove him back almost to the United States border. In 1865 Secretary of State Seward of the United States delivered an ultimatum to Napoleon III demanding withdrawal of French troops from the American continent as a violation of the Monroe Doctrine. Napoleon was forced to yield and began the withdrawal in 1866. The Empress Carlota made a hasty trip to France to plead against the desertion of Maximilian but to no avail and her distress was so great over the probable fate of her husband that she lost her mind. The forces of Juárez prevailed over Maximilian supporters after the withdrawal of the French and the Austrian was captured at Querétaro. After courtmartial he was shot June 19, 1867. The ex-Empress Carlota lived until January 19, 1927, dying in the Château de Bouchout near Brussels, in her native Belgium, without having regained her normal mind. The whole world had regarded the Empress Carlota with a sympathetic feeling ever since the tragedy that shattered her bright hopes so early, and she died one of the widely known figures of history.

CHAPTER 8

[1] Mission San Juan Capistrano was then in Los Angeles County. The present Orange and San Bernardino counties and parts of Riverside and Kern counties were included in the original county of Los Angeles. San Bernardino County to-day, with an area of 20,235 square miles, is the largest county in the United States. Therefore the huge area of Los Angeles County as originally constituted may be imagined.

[2] At one time *zanjero*, or water overseer, of the city of Los Angeles, when water was distributed in open *zanjas* or ditches. A brother of the Bill Jenkins, "Baron of Alcatraz and Casteca," mentioned elsewhere by the author. "Charley," ninety-one years old, is still living in Los Angeles (March, 1930).

[3] At Wilmington, Los Angeles Harbor. Of the original buildings there remain the officers' quarters, the powder magazine, the ruins of the guardhouse and a part of the camel caravan depot. The first-mentioned building has been well preserved by the present owner, Thomas F. Keaveny, a member of the Southern California Historical Society and locally well known as a historian of the harbor

district. The Keaveny family occupies the fine old Colonial style frame house. Embowered in flowering vines it presents a charming picture of the '60's. On its front is a bronze plaque inscribed as follows: "Officers' Quarters Drum Barracks, 1862-1868. Supply Depot Department of the Southwest, U. S. Army. In Memory of the Historic Past of This Building and the Importance of Its Association with Early American History in California, Rudecinda Parlor No. 230, Native Daughters of the Golden West, Placed This Tablet Oct. 2, 1927." The structure is said to be the first ready-cut house ever set up in the state. It was cut in Massachusetts in 1861, brought around the Horn and put together on its present site by the Army. Drum Barracks was established to hold down the strong Secessionist element in Southern California during the Civil War and to deny the possible use of San Pedro harbor to Confederate privateers that might invade the Pacific. For fear of the latter a post was also established on Santa Catalina Island, at the location known as The Isthmus. A portion of the island barracks still remains intact, though renovated for modern uses. The location of Drum Barracks was known as Newtown to distinguish it from Oldtown, or San Pedro proper. The post was the western terminus of the picturesque camel caravans operated by the U. S. Army from the harbor to posts on the Colorado and Mojave deserts with commissary supplies brought round the Horn. The caravans also plied northward through Los Angeles to Fort Tejon and camel camps on the Plaza of the old Pueblo were a common sight from 1858 to about the end of the Civil War when this style of transportation, introduced by Jefferson Davis while Secretary of War, was abandoned. In 1868 the troops still remaining at Drum Barracks were sent up into the present Inyo County to suppress an outbreak of the Paiute Indians and allied tribes and founded Fort Independence in the Owens River Valley. The government acquired the Drum Barracks site from Phineas Banning who is said to have bought, along with David Alexander, partner in his shipping and stage line interests, 2,400 acres of the San Pedro grant from Manuel Domínguez in 1858 at $1.10 per acre. If this is the price he paid it was high, for the neighboring Rancho los Cerritos is said to have been bought by the Bixbys from Don Juan Temple for seventy-five cents an acre at a little later date. In 1872 Banning reacquired the Drum Barracks site and laid out the town of Wilmington. During its life as military headquarters for the Southwest, Drum Barracks housed many young officers afterward famous, among them Phil Sheridan, Winfield Scott Hancock, John Magruder,

George Stoneman (later governor of California), and Lieutenant Hunt, first husband of Helen Hunt Jackson, author of "Ramona." Wilmington and San Pedro are now included in the municipality of Los Angeles.

[4] The old Pío Pico country home, El Ranchito, has been saved from total ruin by the efforts of the club women of Whittier, the community which now includes this property in its city limits. The two-story adobe has been somewhat restored and is open to the public on certain days. It lies on the right hand side of Whittier Boulevard, just after crossing the Río San Gabriél as one drives southward on the main highway to San Diego. Pío Pico was born at Mission San Gabriél, May 5, 1801. His father was José María Pico, corporal of the guard at the mission. The ex-governor died in Los Angeles Sept. 11, 1894, at the age of ninety-three.

CHAPTER 9

[1] Rancho de los Feliz, now comprising Griffith Park and eastern Hollywood. Los Feliz may mean "the Felizes" or "the Feliz family," as we would say, or may be translated "the happy ones," but should be spelled, in the plural, *felices*. The family name was originally Félix, the first grantee of the rancho being José Vicente Félix, a soldier with the Anza expedition of 1775-6 that brought colonists overland from Sonora for the founding of San Francisco. In 1787 this Corporal Félix was made *comisionado* or direct representative of the Spanish governor, Pedro Fages, in the newly founded Los Angeles, and the grant of Rancho Félix was accorded him possibly as early as 1802. (See Eldredge's *Beginnings of San Francisco*, note on page 302, Vol. 1. Also Bancroft's *History of California*, page 461, Vol. 1, and same, page 352, Vol. 2, showing early map of Los Angeles district. Also Richman's *California Under Spain and Mexico*, page 498.) However, "Los Feliz" has become firmly fixed in local usage and is the name of a prominent boulevard from Hollywood to Glendale, running along the southerly line of the grant. The old ranch house stood down by the river near the present municipal golf links in Griffith Park. The hills and cañons of this great park are known to the eyes of the world because for years the region has been a favorite location for filming "westerns." A large Greek theater is under course of construction in one of the beautiful cañons, a gift to the city provided for in the will of the late Col. Griffith J. Griffith, donor of the three-thousand-acre tract.

NOTES

[2] Helen Hunt Jackson visited with the Coronel family in the fine old adobe home at Seventh and Alameda streets, Los Angeles, while gathering material for her novel, "Ramona," and is said to have written much of the book in this house. Don Antonio Franco Coronel was long a prominent citizen of the city both before and after American occupation. He was one of the early mayors of Los Angeles after admission of California to statehood and was the first assessor of Los Angeles County. He was the author of the manuscript concerning the early events and customs of his province, "Cosas de California," quoted by the historian Hubert Howe Bancroft and now a part of the celebrated Bancroft Library of the University of California. The valuable Coronel Collection of early-day relics in the History Room of the Los Angeles County Museum is well known. Don Antonio's father, Don Ygnácio, an educated man who came to California from Mexico City, taught the only school in Los Angeles from 1838 to 1844, in his home on Los Angeles Street near the present Arcadia Street. (See C. D. Willard's "History of Los Angeles.")

CHAPTER 10

[1] Benjamin Davis Wilson, a native of Tennessee, widely and affectionately known as Don Benito among the Californians, came to Los Angeles in 1841 via Taos and Santa Fé, New Mexico, where he had engaged in trading. He took for his first wife Ramona Yorba, daughter of one of the most prominent old land-holding families of colonial California. Mount Wilson, back of Pasadena, famous now as the site of the astronomical observatory of the Carnegie Institution and home of the largest telescope in the world, was named for him. He built the first trail up the mountain for the purpose of cutting timber suitable to make casks for the wines from his famous Lake Vineyard property, located in the district of Pasadena now known as Oak Knoll and in the adjoining little municipality of San Marino where is located the great Henry E. Huntington Library and Art Gallery. The Wilson property, overlooking the old grist mill built by the padres of Mission San Gabriél in 1812 and now remodeled into a residence, has long remained intact in the center of intensive real estate development, but announcement has just been made in the public press (November, 1929) that it is at last to be subdivided and placed on the market. Of late years it has been known as the Patton Place, the property having passed

to Mrs. George S. Patton, a daughter of Don Benito Wilson, and from her to her son and daughter, Captain George S. Patton, Jr., U.S.A., and Anne Patton. Don Benito Wilson was the first United States Indian Agent for Southern California and the first clerk of Los Angeles County. He also served as State Senator.

CHAPTER 11

[1] Both families still well known in Southern California. The old Covarrúbias house in Santa Bárbara is one of the choice relics of Spanish days pointed out in that charming old community which retains such an intelligent regard for its romantic past. Leo Carrillo, the well-known actor, comes from the old Carrillo line so admired by Major Bell. Santa Catalina Island was granted by the Mexican administration to José María Covarrúbias in 1846, just a few days before the American seizure of Monterey. This *documento* is said to bear the latest date of any grant recognized as valid by the United States government. In other words it was the last of those last-minute Pico grants that "got by" in the American courts. The island was purchased from the Covarrúbias interests by James Lick, the early San Francisco capitalist, and has come down through several owners to William Wrigley, Jr. José María Covarrúbias served in the California State Legislature. His son, "Nick," served several terms as sheriff of Santa Bárbara County and one term as United States Marshal. The latter was a famous horseman and a familiar figure in all the fiestas and parades of Southern California down to a recent date, for advancing age did not unhorse him until the very end.

CHAPTER 12

[1] John Rains married María Merced Williams, daughter of Julian Isaac Williams and granddaughter of the celebrated land-owner, Don Antonio María Lugo. Williams came from Santa Fé in 1831, adopted Mexican nationality, married a daughter of Lugo and through his marriage came into possession of the Rancho Cucamonga and the Rancho Santa Ana del Chino, the latter a property of 22,000 acres granted to Lugo in 1841. The main portion of the Lugo, afterwards the Williams adobe ranch house, is still intact and, with additions, is known as Los Serranos Club resort, near the town of Chino, Los Angeles County. The Cucamonga country is

famous for its vineyards of wine grapes and in the old days was distinguished by a huge old adobe winery, the remains of which are still visible from the highway. A sister of Mrs. Rains, Francisca Williams, married Robert Carlisle, whose violent death Major Bell mentions. Afterwards she married Dr. F. A. McDougall, mayor of Los Angeles in 1877-78. The fine old ranch house of Isaac Williams, on the Santa Ana del Chino, was attacked in September, 1846, by a body of Californians and twenty-five Americans defending it were taken prisoner, among them Don Benito Wilson. The place was completely sacked. All prisoners were released after the signing of the Treaty of Cahuenga between Colonel Frémont and General Andrés Pico following the second occupation of Los Angeles by the American forces.

[2] General Carrillo was a delegate to the first Constitutional Convention at Monterey in 1849, although in the early stages of the American invasion he had been bitterly anti-gringo. For another account of the amusing incident concerning General Carrillo and the Mormon officer see *Los Angeles on the Eve of the Gold Rush*, by Stephen C. Foster in "Touring Topics," (Los Angeles) for August, 1929. This is the second installment published in "Touring Topics" of a manuscript in the Bancroft Library of the University of California, dictated in 1877 by Foster to Thomas Savage for the use of Hubert Howe Bancroft, the historian. In it Foster claims to have been the interpreter and go-between in the meetings at the Pryor home. He names Colonel Stevenson of the New York Volunteers as the superior officer who presided over the meetings at Pryor's.

[3] The present Central Station, used by the trains of the Union Pacific and Southern Pacific railroads, is on the site of the old Wolfskill home. William Wolfskill was the first to grow oranges in California on a successful commercial scale. The Franciscan missionaries planted the first oranges in California, notably at San Gabriél and San Buenaventura, but the fruit was used locally.

[4] Lieut. W. W. Emory, U. S. Topographical Engineers, was on the staff of Gen. Stephen W. Kearny on the march from Santa Fé to San Diego and Los Angeles and was the historian of the expedition. He figured prominently in the Battle of San Pascual when the American forces suffered severe losses at the hands of the Californians under Gen. Andrés Pico. Later, as major, he was a member of the U. S. Boundary Survey.

[5] Local magistrates sometimes rendered decisions by old Mexican codes of law and procedure, even after statehood. This practice had become established during the years of American military occu-

pation preceding statehood when the people were allowed to continue to exercise civil authority according to their customs under officials of their own election.

CHAPTER 14

[1] Descendants of the survivors of this party now living in California hold a picnic and reunion February 4 every year on the San Francisquito Rancho in memory of the rescue. The larger portion of the Death Valley emigrants that suffered so terribly during the crossing in 1849-50 is generally known as the Jayhawker Party. (See Manly's "Death Valley in '49.")

[2] Mountain Meadow, Utah, where a train of gentile emigrants was set upon by Indians September 7, 1857, and thirty-six killed. The Indians were led against the whites by a Mormon named Lee and the belief throughout the non-Mormon portion of the population of the United States that the Mormon Church had instigated the massacre aroused great bitterness. It seems never to have been proved, however, that the Mormons as an organization had anything to do with the attack.

[3] Of recent years two winter resorts have been opened in Death Valley. There are also several ranches where water has been developed, the best-known property being that of Walter Scott ("Death Valley Scotty"), an old-time prospector who has built a bizarre group of stone castles said to have cost a million or more dollars. His wealth is popularly supposed to come from a mine the location of which he alone knows, but recent developments tend to prove that he is financed from more practical sources. The lowest point on the floor of Death Valley is the lowest point on the continent, three hundred feet below sea level. Not far away is the highest point in the continental United States, Mount Whitney, 14,502 feet above sea level. Manly in his "Death Valley in '49" claims his party gave the region its sinister name.

[4] The pass through which the Atchison, Topeka & Santa Fé Railroad crosses the San Bernardino Mountains from the desert to the San Bernardino Valley. It is about seventy-five miles east of Los Angeles.

CHAPTER 15

[1] Now a cheap lodging house for Mexicans on North Main at the Plaza. It was erected by ex-Gov. Pío Pico in 1869 and was for some time thereafter the finest hotel south of San Francisco.

For a decade it was the center of the social life of the city and its once beautiful central court, with fountain and tropical foliage, was the scene of many a notable entertainment and was familiar to travelers from various parts of the world. In front of the Pico House portals the stages arrived and departed amid much noise, excitement and show of horsemanship, after the new hotel had dimmed the doubtful glory of the old Bella Union, the St. Charles and the Lafayette.

[2] Henry A. Crabb, a Stockton lawyer who married into a Spanish family. He was a Tennessean, a schoolmate of William Walker of the Nicaragua filibuster, and came to California in the same year, 1849. In 1857 he raised a force of adventurers in San Francisco to invade Sonora for the ostensible purpose of aiding the revolutionists there under Pesquiera against Governor Gandara. Annexation of Sonora to the United States was the ultimate purpose. The Crabb expedition came south on the steamer *Sea Bird*, landed at San Pedro January 24 and marched inland to El Monte, east of Los Angeles, where the party was provisioned, equipped and augmented before proceeding on the terrific march to Sonoita, Sonora. Instead of welcoming these deliverers Pesquiera turned on them, joined forces with Governor Gandara and helped to capture the entire outfit, some hundred all told. They were shot in the plaza at Sonoita, only one escaping, it is claimed. He was a Los Angeles boy named Charles Evans. Crabb's head was cut off and preserved in mescal and later sent back across the border with the compliments of the Mexicans. (See Cleland's "History of California: The American Period." Also Bancroft's "History of California.")

CHAPTER 16

[1] General Mariano Guadalupe Vallejo is often referred to as "the grand old man" of California, intelligent, reasonable and genial though rugged and determined in his opinions once they were formed. As a landowner he was vastly wealthy, while socially and politically none was more influential. He was the uncle of General José Castro, the military commander of California at the time of the American occupation, but he was far-seeing enough to anticipate the benefits of the American ownership of California in preference to ownership by England or Russia, which he foresaw as a possibility. In spite of his friendly attitude toward the United States he was seized in his own home by the Bear Flag party and

conveyed to Frémont's camp a prisoner, where he was held until the seizure of Monterey by Commodore Sloat put an end to further plans of the American trappers and settlers, backed by their ally, Frémont, for an independent California Republic. Gen. Vallejo made valuable manuscript contributions to the Bancroft historical collection and was always ardently interested in keeping alive the facts and traditions of the past. The Vallejo stronghold was at Sonoma and the family dominated the whole area north and northeast from San Francisco Bay to the Russian zone. The sites of the present town of Vallejo and of the Mare Island Navy Yard, on the Straits of Carquínez, were part of the Vallejo and Castro domains.

[2] Gilroy was the first permanent foreign settler in the Spanish province of California. In January, 1814, the armed British merchantman *Isaac Todd* anchored in Monterey Bay and landed three sailors sick with scurvy. One of these was a boy of twenty called John Gilroy. He was nursed back to health by Señora María Teodora Peralta de Bernal, who took him to her father's Rancho San Antonio in Alameda County, where the city of Oakland is now located. The boy was Scotch and his real name is said to have been John Cameron. He had run away to sea and changed his name. He became a favorite with his California friends and in 1819, on application of Capt. José de la Guerra, was given permission by the viceroy of New Spain to remain in California. (There was a law prohibiting permanent settlement by foreigners.) He was baptized into the Roman Catholic faith in the Mission San Cárlos and was married March 2, 1821, in the Mission San Juan Bautísta to María ·Clara Ortega, granddaughter of the Sergeant Ortega who discovered the bay of San Francisco in 1769. (See "The Beginnings of San Francisco," by Z. S. Eldredge, Vol 1, pp. 246-247.)

CHAPTER 17

[1] John Ross Browne, author of "Yusef: or The Journey of the Frangi" (1853); "Crusoe's Island: a Ramble in the Footsteps of Alexander Selkirk, with Sketches of Adventures in California and Washoe" (1864); "Adventures in the Apache Country" (1868); "An American Family in Germany" (1871); "Resources of the Pacific Slope" (1875).

[2] This terrible massacre was the first big explosion of the anti-Chinese campaign in California that finally led to the passing of the Chinese Exclusion Act by our national government. It riveted national attention on the troubled subject of Chinese influence on

NOTES

the Pacific Coast and succeeded the great Chicago fire as the topic of general discussion throughout the United States. From it grew a new political party supposedly represented by Denis Kearney and his howling San Francisco sand-lotters, and the new state constitution of 1879, dictated by the workingmen.

[3] Judge Wilson Hugh Gray, who came to California from Kentucky in 1852, following his brother, Franklin Gray, a prominent early property owner in San Francisco, who came in 1849. Judge Gray was much respected by the Chinese and on the night of the massacre a number took refuge, both men and women, in the cellar of his home located in a vineyard where the Lankershim Hotel now stands, at Broadway and Seventh Street. Among those who thus escaped the wrath of the mob was Yo Hing. For years afterward, until the Judge's death, he and his family were the recipients of costly silks, porcelains and teas from China every New Year, left at the house anonymously so as not to cause him embarrassment in his judicial position.

[4] John Schumacher, a native of Württemberg, came to Los Angeles as a soldier in Stevenson's New York Volunteers and afterwards conducted a grocery and bar on the west side of Spring Street just north of First where the old Schumacher Block stands (1930). Over his bar was sold the first lager beer dispensed in Los Angeles and he was the inventor of the famous drink of those times, *Peach and Honey*. While gold hunting on Sutter's Creek he found a nugget worth $800 with which he bought in 1853 the property—almost a whole block—on which the building bearing his name is located. (See Newmark's "Sixty Years in Southern California," pp. 39-40.)

[5] This building is still standing (1930). In the days of the ill-starred Harper municipal régime, in the early 1900's, when Los Angeles was still a "wide open" town, the famous White House was owned by a city councilman and was a red light resort.

CHAPTER 18

[1] Calabasas is familiar to present-day motorists going north from Hollywood via Ventura Boulevard and the Coast Highway. In early American days it was famed as a tough place and the region was the scene of numerous stage coach hold-ups. Now a favorite region for moving picture "locations," and rapidly being brought within the zone of urban development. The old settlement and stage station of Calabasas lie just beyond the new Studio City, an extension of the motion picture settlement of North Hollywood.

CHAPTER 20

[1] The city's first hotel and the capitol building of California during Governor Pico's final term of office. Los Angeles was named officially the capital of California by the Mexican Congress in 1835, but governors prior to Pico had refused to move the seat of government from Monterey except for a six months' period during the administration of Micheltorena, when the latter took up his official residence in the south. Other governors, however, spent much time personally in the southern end of the province, notably Echeandía, who preferred San Diego as a place of residence. The old hotel was remodeled somewhat in the '60's and renamed the St. Charles. It still stands, on the east side of Main Street, diagonally across from the Federal building.

[2] General Micheltorena, newly appointed governor of California, was at Los Angeles on his way north from Mexico when the first American seizure of Monterey took place. He immediately issued a furious proclamation to his "cholo" army, calling upon his soldiers to shed the last drop of their blood, and pledging the last drop of his own, in defense of the sacred soil of the province. But he cooled off when he received a letter of regret from Commodore Jones and an offer to meet and talk things over. The meeting was arranged. Commodore Jones brought his fleet into San Pedro and made his way up to the Pueblo with his staff, observing the pomp and panoply appropriate to the momentous occasion. Micheltorena demanded of the American commander a donation of fifty uniforms, a full set of band instruments and fifteen thousand dollars cash as a salve to Mexico's wounded feelings. The Commodore shrugged his shoulders and said that was a matter the two governments would have to settle through other channels; all he could do was to offer an apology for his mistake. After a proper amount of bluster and pouting the Governor of California said all right, let's have a grand ball and get some fun out of the affair, somehow, or words to that effect; and forthwith the grandest *baile* in the history of the south was held in the *palacio* of Don Abel Stearns, at which Micheltorena appeared, tradition says, in his imported American light wagon drawn by his own soldiers in harness. During the evening Commodore Jones, U.S.N., offered suitable apologies to General Micheltorena, *jefe político y militar de California*, following which the delightful festivities were redoubled.

[3] In the valley of the Gila River near Florence, Ariz. These ruins

were probably seen by Coronado's expedition in search of the Seven Cities of Cíbola in 1540, but their discovery is first definitely recorded by Padre Kino, the Jesuit missionary, in 1694. In 1892 Congress set aside the area covered by the ruins as a public monument.

CHAPTER 21

[1] Sanford Avenue is named after him. The boilers of the *Ada Hancock* of the Banning fleet exploded April 27, 1863, while the tug was conveying passengers to the steamer *Senator*, and twenty-six lives were lost. Among the dead was Albert Sidney Johnston, Jr., son of the commander of the Department of the Pacific, U.S.A., at the outbreak of the Civil War, afterwards a Confederate general killed at Shiloh. Gold to the amount of forty thousand dollars is said to have been lost on the muddy bottom of the upper bay, off Wilmington, ten thousand of it in a Wells, Fargo shipment and thirty thousand from the person of Fred E. Kerlin who was leaving California with his hard-won gains. Another victim was Captain Thomas W. Seeley of the *Senator*, California's celebrated poker-playing skipper. The mother of Albert Sidney Johnston, Jr., was a sister of Dr. J. S. Griffin, the army surgeon attached to the staff of Colonel (later General) Stephen W. Kearny on the march from Santa Fé to San Diego and Los Angeles during the Mexican War. He is said to have been the second American doctor to practice in Los Angeles. Griffin Avenue is named after him. He acquired Rancho San Pascual, sold a part of it to Don Benito Wilson and the latter sold a portion to Mrs. Johnston, who erected a home where she lived while her husband was engaged in the Civil War. She named the estate Fair Oaks and from it one of Pasadena's prominent thoroughfares takes its name. Fair Oaks Avenue was formerly a road that led to the Johnston home.

CHAPTER 22

[1] The first American alcalde of Los Angeles and referred to in a previous note as official interpreter for the army during the American military occupation of the city. He was appointed by Colonel Mason, military governor of California, in 1848. Abel Stearns served with him in the office of *síndico* or treasurer. In 1854 and 1856 Foster was elected mayor. In 1849 he was a delegate to the convention in Monterey which framed the first constitution for the

state of California. From 1850 to 1853 he was a state senator. He lived in Los Angeles until his death in 1898.

[2] Under the Spanish plan title to all land in California was vested in the King. When a pueblo was founded by royal decree four square leagues of land was set aside for the community. Each settler was apportioned a town lot on which to build his home and a field of a certain size to cultivate. These parcels became his and were assignable to his heirs if at the end of five years he had complied with all requirement of the regulation and had reimbursed the government for its advance of agricultural implements, seeds, live stock and the necessities of life required until he could support himself from the land. He could not sell or mortgage these properties and if he or his heirs failed to comply with requirements at any time during their tenancy the land reverted to the Crown. The unassigned portion of the four square leagues, with the exception of pieces reserved for government, ecclesiastical or communal use, belonged to the pueblo or municipality to be distributed, with the approval of provincial and royal authorities, as increase of population should suggest. These lands were called *própios*. When the Mexican Republic succeeded the Spanish Crown the right to sell his land was accorded the individual but the public land belonging to the pueblo governments was not alienated, and the titles thereto were affirmed by the United States when it came into possession of California. The municipality of Los Angeles, therefore, during its early American years, owned a great acreage of unimproved land.

CHAPTER 23

[1] John B. Frisbie, a native of New York who came to California in 1847 as captain of Company H, First Regiment of New York Volunteers (Stevenson's) and later became a prominent figure socially and financially in the Bay region. He was candidate for lieutenant-governor in the first state election in 1849 and in 1860 sent the first cargo of wheat from California to Europe, inaugurating a trade which grew to tremendous proportions. Died in Mexico City in recent years.

[2] Some of these grants made by Pío Pico are even yet under dispute, despite favorable court action years ago. As late as April, 1929, the United States Senate sent a subcommittee of the Senate Public Lands Committee to Los Angeles to hear evidence of fraud which certain individuals and squatters' organizations claimed to

have unearthed concerning land titles that have their origin in Spanish and Mexican land grants. An attempt was made to reach a final decision as to what further action is necessary, if any is necessary, to quiet these titles once and for all after eighty years of agitation concerning them. The Senate committee consisted of the following senators: Dale of Vermont, Nye of North Dakota, and Bratton of New Mexico. One squatters' organization represented some eight hundred individuals who believed they had the right to file on parcels of land now included in city developments and enormously valuable, because they considered the original titles fraudulent, in which case the land would be public domain. A lot of California history was brought out at these hearings from the mouths of old natives brought in from valley and cañon to testify, as well as from the briefs of lawyers and title experts. Since returning to Washington the senators have submitted a report unfavorable to the claims of the squatters.

CHAPTER 24

[1] Named for the Rancho Sauzal Redondo ("round willow thicket"), a grant of 22,468 acres to Antonio Ygnácio Abila which had an ocean frontage of ten miles. The town of Redondo is just over the southern edge of this grant. This and the neighboring ranchos, La Ballona of Antonio Machado, Aguaje de la Centinela of Bernardino (Bruno) Abila, Las Ciénegas of Juan Abila and Rodeo de las Aguas of the Valdez family were famous places for hunting wild fowl in the early American days—jacksnipe, wild geese and every species of duck known to the western coast. The quaintly named Rodeo de las Aguas—"round-up of the waters" or "gathering place of the waters"—took its designation from a remarkable cluster of springs about where Sherman, lately called West Hollywood, is now located. The name also expresses, it is said, the early-day custom of holding rodeos here for all the surrounding ranches, the central location of the property with reference to a cluster of comparatively small ranchos from the Cahuengas to the sea, and the famous springs, making it a popular choice for the festivities associated with the round-up. The Beverly Hills district is included in this property.

[2] This is now a highly developed horticultural region covered with lemon, orange, olive and avocado groves and florists' rose and seed farms. The San Fernando Valley was transformed in recent years by the Los Angeles Aqueduct, bringing water from the Owens River

Valley two hundred and thirty miles away, across deserts and mountains. Across the mouth of Pacoima Cañon there was completed in 1928 one of the highest dams in the world to control and store winter flood waters.

CHAPTER 25

[1] According to other authorities the author seems to have mistaken the date of F. P. F. Temple's arrival. "Templito," as he was known to the natives on account of his five feet four inches of stature, was a brother of the better-known Don Juan Temple who came to Los Angeles as early as 1829 and opened the first general merchandise store in the Pueblo. This was at the present junction of North Main and Temple streets, afterwards the site of the Downey Block and now of the Federal Building. "Templito" came around the Horn from Massachusetts in 1841, entered business with his brother John and, in 1845, married Antonia Margarita Workman. His principal rancho was La Merced, in the San Gabriél Valley, where his great adobe 70 x 110 feet was notable among the ranch houses of the day. The oldest building razed to make way for the construction of the new City Hall, begun in 1928, was the Temple Block, the southern portion of which was erected by John Temple in 1857, diagonally across from the location of his original store. John married Rafaela Cota, an heir of the Rancho Santa Gertrudis, one of the earliest grants on record, made to the Nieto family in 1784. Rancho los Cerritos, now part of the site of the city of Long Beach (Rancho los Alamitos of Don Abel Stearns being the other part) was the home ranch of Don Juan Temple. A part of the immense old adobe house is still preserved on the grounds of the Virginia Country Club, Long Beach. Don Juan died in 1866 and his wife and daughter moved permanently to Paris.

CHAPTER 26

[1] A rancho of the Mission San Gabriél was established in the San Bernardino Valley as early as 1810. A few years later a chapel was built by the padres, with attendant temporal structures, fourteen in all. The ruins of this group, located on high ground between the present cities of San Bernardino and Redlands, towards the San Gorgonio Pass, are now (1930) in process of restoration by the county of San Bernardino, to be preserved as a public monu-

ment. San Bernardino's historical background is a unique blend of Catholicism and Mormonism. After the Franciscan missionaries were dispossessed by the Mexican government most of the San Bernardino property was granted to the Lugo family, from which the Mormons purchased. In 1851 a Mormon bishop, Nathan C. Tenney, and his wife were living in the old Franciscan chapel, where Mrs. Tenney conducted a Mormon school. (See *Last of the Missions*, by Maurice S. Sullivan in "Touring Topics" for October, 1929.) This mission outpost was on the road that wound its course, mostly over deserts, from Los Angeles to Sonora, Mexico.

[2] This Connecticut Yankee, better known to the natives as Don Juan José Warner, or Juan Largo—"Long John," on account of his height of six feet four inches—came to California from New Mexico in 1831 with Ewing Young's trapping expedition and, after various adventures, settled in Los Angeles in 1834. He was associated for a time with Don Abel Stearns and Don Juan Temple, and then went into the mercantile business with Henry Mellus. Their store was on Main Street about half a block north of the present Temple Street. Warner became a Mexican citizen and in 1844 was granted the Valle de San José, a property lying among the mountains midway between the Mission San Diego de Alcalá and the Mission San Luís Rey de Francia. It is still known as Warner's Ranch or Warner Hot Springs. In 1853 the house was attacked by Indians and sacked and Warner permanently removed his family to Los Angeles, where he lived on a site now occupied by the Burbank Theatre, Main Street near Sixth. A large adobe house under oak trees in an arroyo on the old stage road east of the main valley is often mistakenly pointed out as the Warner ranch house. Judge Benjamin Hayes, who camped near the house in 1850 and visited Warner in it, distinctly says it stood out alone *on a bare knoll* where the road forked toward San Diego on the south and Los Angeles on the north. Apparently no vestige of the old thatched adobe that was the haven for so many weary travelers remains. (See "Pioneer Notes from the Diary of Judge Benjamin Hayes." Privately printed, Los Angeles, 1929. Also "History of Warner's Ranch and Environs," by J. J. Hill. Privately printed, Los Angeles, 1927.)

[3] "Old Mission." The original location of the Mission San Gabriél above Montebello on the San Gabriél River (originally called the Río San Miguel). Here the mission was founded in 1771, but the site was flooded from the river during the winter rains and the padres moved to the present location of the establishment, on high ground near the base of the mountains nine miles east of Los Angeles.

THE HISTORIES OF MR.

(From Old

MR. BROWN'S STORY

Jones & Brown Landing

Brown stick to it

THE CONCLUSION OF MR. B.'S STORY WILL BE FOUND ON THE BACK END-SHEET

BROWN AND MR. JONES
(Engravings)

MR. JONES' STORY

Jones dont like hard Work

Trys a fast way to make money

MR. J.'S STORY IS ALSO CONTINUED AT THE END OF THIS VOLUME

THE HISTORIES OF MR.
(From Old

MR. BROWN'S STORY—(Continued)

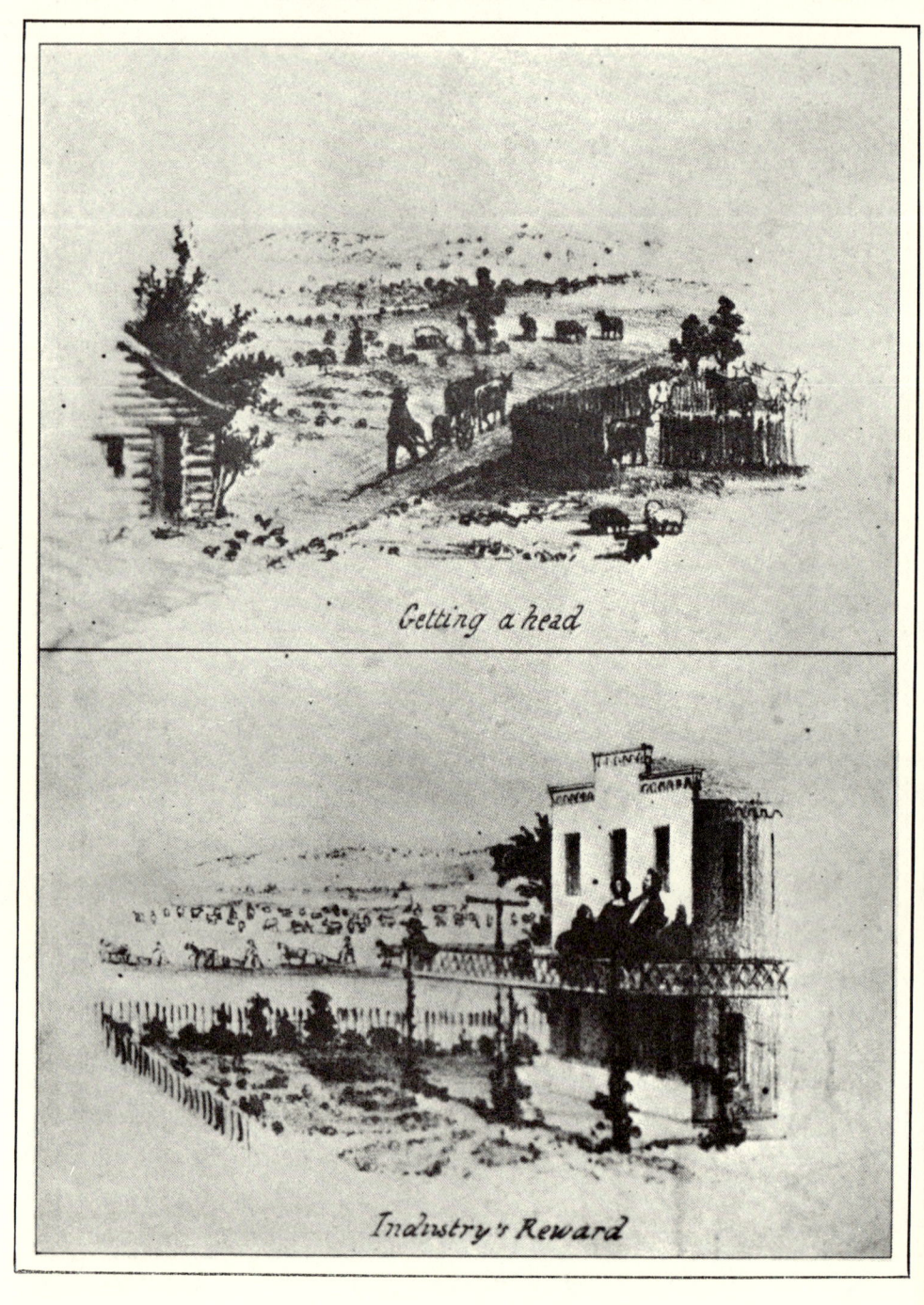

Getting ahead

Industry's Reward

BROWN AND MR. JONES
Engravings)

MR. JONES' STORY—(Continued)

Wommen and Wine

Ruin and the Gutter

Index

Abila, see Avila
Adobe houses, 3
Aerolite, excitement on Rancho Rodeo de las Aguas over a falling star, 238
Africa, 164
Agricultural Park, 178
Alabama, 220
Alameda Street, Los Angeles, 117, 190
Alaska, 250
Aliso Street, Los Angeles, 3, 117
Allen, Gabe, 165
Allen, James, 294, 295
Allen, O. H., 80
Alvitre, murderer, 241, 242
American flag at Monterey, first raised, 207, 210
American River, 297
Amphibious monster, Elizabeth Lake, 204
Andersonville, 80
Apaches, 28
Arcadia Hall, 179
Arcadia Hotel, Santa Monica, 97
Arcadia Street, Los Angeles, 179
Arizona, 69, 114, 151, 204, 205, 211, 213, 214, 265, 266
Arguello family, 4
Arguello, Sergeant, 195, 198
Arkansas, 218, 219
Arkansas Colony, 22
Arkansas River, 99
Arnold, Benedict, 244
Ashe, Richard P., 38
Associated Press, 232, 233, 265
Australia, 270
Avila, Bruno, 12, 13
Avila, Doña Luisa de, 116
Avila family, 301
Avila, Juan, 16

Baker Block, 4
Baker, Robert S., 286
Baldwin, John M., 91, 174
Baldwin, Leon, 90, 96
Baldwin, Lucky, 290
Ball, Frank, 259, 260
Ballona, 75
Bancroft, Hubert H., 168, 171, 287, 288, 289, 290, 292; —'s History of California, 289
Banks, Calabasas squatter, 184, 185, 186
Banning, Phineas, 16, 235
Barcelona, 70
Barter, George W., 172, 173
Barton, James R., 72; massacre of sheriff's posse, 74; —, 99, 100, 101; — War, 243
Bayley, Bill, 100
Baxter, Captain, 139
Bean brothers (Los Frijoles), 236
Bean, Joshua, 224
Bean, Samuel, 224
Bean, Roy (The Law West of the Pecos), personality and career of a celebrated character, 223 to 236
Bear River, 144
Beaudry, Prudent, 277
Belgian hare craze, 305, 306

Bell, Alexander, 3, 150, 263, 301
Bell, Jacob, 178, 179, 180
Bella Union Hotel, Los Angeles, 137, 164, 208, 235, 249
Bell's Addition, first realty boom in Los Angeles, 84
Berry, Jim ("Doctor"), 15
Bettis, Lige, 25, 28, 104
Bilderrain, Jesús, 172
Biographies, ridicule of a vanity still practiced in California, 281 to 292
Bill el Molacho, 234
Bill el Tuerto, 234
Blackfoot Indians, 145
Bland, Rev. Adam, 150
Boru, Brian, 8, 284, 288
Boston, 118, 119, 207, 305; — hide droghers, 236
Botello, General, 173, 174
Branscomb, Harvey, Calabasas squatter, 192, 193
Brannan, Samuel, 295, 297
Brea pits, 63
Brent, John L., 74, 75
Brewer, Margaret (Doña Margarita), 46
Bridger, John, 139
Brier, Rev. J. W., 136, 140, 150
Brier, Mrs. J. W., 143
Brierly, John, 203
Broderick, David C., duel with Judge Terry, 32, 36
Brodie, journalist, 84
Brooklyn, ship, 295, 297
Brown, Dave, 240, 241, 242, 244
Brown, James C., 297
Brown, Sam, 219
Browne, J. Ross, 164, 165
Buckner, Simon B., 75
Bullfights, 258
Butterfield stage line, 157

Cahuenga, 249; — Pass, 63, 64, 69, 70, 249; — Hills, 301
Cainesville, 294
Cajon Pass, 145, 298
Calabasas, sanguinary history of, 181 to 193; — stage road, 249
California, aspects under Spain and Mexico, 1, 2, 3, 4; presidios and pueblos, 2, 3; ceded by Mexico, 6; early day court procedure, amusing incidents, 121 to 126 and 153, 154, 155; early day tax collecting, amusing incidents at Gilroy, 156 to 163; American flag first raised, 207, 210; modernism imposed on medievalism, 264; gold discovered, 297
California Home Guard, 81
California Hundred, 81
California Volunteers, 75
Californians, customs and characteristics, difference from Mexicans, 1, 2, 3, 4; hospitality, 26; loss of great possessions, 5, 6, 7, 8, 10, 18; marriage of native girls with foreigners, 255 to 259
Campeche Bay, 43
Canby, E. R. S., 75, 151, 152, 228

330

INDEX

Cape Gerardeau, 264
Cape Horn, 118, 236, 237, 259
Carlisle, Robert (Bob), 235
Carlos III, 250
Carpenter, Lemuel, 10, 11, 12
Carrillo family, 4, 116, 199
Carrillo, José A., his famous apology to a Mormon officer, 116, 117, 118
Carrillo, Judge, his unusual education and remarkable judicial decisions, 118 to 126
Carrillo, Pedro, 199
Carrillo, Ramón, 106, 107, 114, 115, 116
Carrillo, Señora de, 119
Carroll, Frank, 224
Carson, Kit, 139
Casa Grande, 211, 212
Central America, 37, 127, 129
Chagres River, 53
Cherokee, 99
Chihuahua, 224
Chile, 299
China, 258, 270, 271
Chinameca, 42, 43, 46, 47, 48, 52
Chinamecans, 47, 48, 49
Chinatown, Los Angeles, 168 to 176
Chinese, massacre of, at Los Angeles, 166 to 177; —, 208, 209, 229, 230
Chiripo River, 130, 133
Choy, Ah, 170, 171, 176
Ciénega Creek, 29
City Guards, San Francisco, 37
City of the Angels, 70, 146, 164, 176
Clay Street, San Francisco, 32
Clifford, Pinkney, 241
Coatzacoalcos, 42
Coatzacoalcos River, 43, 44, 45
Cockfights, 258
Colorado Desert, 26, 138
Coloma, 297
Colombia, 57
Coleman, Norman J., 129
Commercial Street, Los Angeles, 3, 76, 81, 174, 179, 251, 252
Compton, 116
Confederate Army, 228
Conkling, Roscoe, 213
Cook, Grove C., 161, 162
Cooke, P. St. George, 295
Coronel, Antonio F., 85, 86, 87, 88, 90, 95, 96
Correa, Gumisindo, 64, 69, 70
Cortéz, steamship, 37, 38, 39
Cortéz, Hernando, 43, 46, 52
Cosaleacaca, 47
Cosaleacacans, 48
Costa Rica, 66
Cota, Leonardo, 71
Covarrúbias, José M., 106
Crabb, Henry A., 151
Creighton, editor, 82
Crocker, Charles, 168, 213
Cruz, Jesús L., 83
Cucamonga, 103, 114
Cunningham, James (Jim), 40

Dana, Richard H., 236
Dávila, Captain, 68
Davis, Calabasas squatter, 187, 190, 191
Davis, Jefferson, 82
Dead Man's Island, 300
Death Valley, 136, 137, 138, 140, 142, 143, 150
Death Valley Party, 136
Del Norte, 187
Devil's Turnpike, The, 195
Diamond Springs, 145
Díaz, Porfirio, 116

Digger Indians, 143
Domínguez, battle of, 116; Rancho-, 300
Donner Party, 136, 138, 139
Dowes, James, 37
Downey, 212
Downey Block, 79
Downey, John G., 9, 283, 284, 287, 288
Dragons, 203
Drought, starvation of California herds, 9, 18, 82
Drum Barracks, 75
Duane, Charles P., 38
Ducommon Street, Los Angeles, 76
Duffy, James, 37
Dummer, Samuel R., 147, 149, 150
Dyches, George, 103
Dye, Joe, 81

Eama, brig, 208
El Basquo Grande, 182, 184, 188, 191, 192, 202, 204
El Boticario, examples of money lending, 5 to 17
El Carpintero, example of a ranchero ruined, 10, 11, 12
El Dorado Bar, first American saloon in Los Angeles transformed into first Protestant church, 148, 149, 150
El Jarabe, 92
El Monte, 31, 76, 77, 78, 100, 181, 241, 247, 248
El Molacho, 234
El Paso, 228, 231
El Tuerto, 234
El Ranchito, 84
Elizabeth Lake, tales of its hellish origin and its fabulous monster, 198 to 206
Ellington, victim of Alvitre, 241
Embustero, Guillermo, 198
Embustero y Mentiroso, Guillermo, 194, 202, 206
Emory, W. W., 117
Encino Valley, 106
England, rumored political designs on California, 210, 262
Epitaph, The, 204
Eschrich, a Wurttemberger, 258
Eschrich, Doña Carlota de, 258
Estudillo family, 4
Estudillo, Guadalupe, 226
Etchepare, tavernkeeper, 64, 70
Evertson, Evert, 235
Evertson, Laura, 235
Etchemende, Jean, 190

Fandango, 19
Farragut, David W., 57
Feliz, Antonio, 85, 86, 92, 95, 96
Feliz, Doña Soledad, 86, 87, 90
Feliz Springs, 96
Figueroa Street, Los Angeles, 83, 144
First Artillery, U.S.A., 147
First National Bank, Los Angeles, 288
First Texas Cavalry, 219
Fisk, James (Jim) Jr., 58, 59
Flores, Juan, origin of Flores Revolution, 72, 73; —, 99, 243
Fontes, Andrés, 73
Fort Hall, 144
Fort Jurupa, 298, 300
Forty Fools, The, 281
Forty Mile Cañon, 140
Forty Thieves, The, 228
Foster, Stephen C., colorful career of a Maine Yankee and Yale graduate, 240 to 245

INDEX

Fowler, Doctor, 287, 288
Franciscans, their trade with Yankee ships, 236; seed for first crop of Mormon wheat in Utah derived from California missions, 299
Fredericksburg, 219
Free Rovers, The, 228
Freeman, Dan, 12, 290
Frémont Battalion, 208
Frémont, John C., 3, 139
Frisbie, John B., 256

Galesburg, 138, 139; — Party, 141, 144
Gallardo, Félix, 81
Gárfias family, 301
Gárfias, Manuel, 116
Garnier, ranchero, 188
Georgia Bell Street, Los Angeles, 60
Georgians, 141
Gilroy, 157, 158
Gilroy, John, 157
Gilroy, Nicodemus, 159, 160, 161
Gilroy, Señora de, 160, 161
Gilroy Township, 158
Gold discovered in California, 297
Golden Era, The, 282
Goller, John, 136, 137, 138
Goller Mine, 137, 138
González, Juan, 243
Goyeneche, Jean, 188
Graff, Johann, 144
Granada, 66
Grand Avenue, Los Angeles, 83
Granger, Louis C., 144
Grant, Ulysses S., 57
Gray, Wilson H., 170, 174, 176
Greytown, 130, 131
Griffith, Griffith J., 91 to 98
Griffith, Mrs. Griffith J., 98
Griffith Park, 97, 98
Grizzly bears, characteristics, bear-and-bull fight at Pala described, 106 to 113
Guadalupe Hidalgo, Treaty of, 6
Guichicovans, 45

Halleck, H. W., 57
Hangtown, 9, 145
Hansen, George, 251
Harathzy, John (Count), 225, 226, 227
Harper's Weekly, 164
Harris, Emil, 170, 171, 174, 176
Harry, negro slave boy on the Trinity, 21, 22, 27
Harte, Bret, 282
Hayes, Bob, 38
Hayes, Jack, 38
Hawaii, 207
Headquarters Saloon, The, 223, 224, 228, 235
Hell's Home Stretch, 31
Henderson, William (Billy), haunted by Murrieta's ghost, 35, 36
Heningsen, General, 66
Hick's Store, Los Angeles, 174
Hide trade of early California, 236
Hing, Yo. 170, 171, 176, 177
Hippogriffes, 203
Holmes, James (Jim), 55, 56
Hollywood, 98
Honduras, 43, 131
Honolulu, 297
Hooker, Joseph, 57
Hopkins, Mark, 168
Houghton, S. O., 33
Houston, Sam, 220
Howard, James G., 176

Howard, Volney E., 191
Huachuca Mountains, 204
Hughes, Archbishop, 150
Hughes, John H., 149, 151
Hugo, Victor, 211
Hunt, Captain, 139, 144
Huntington, Collis P., 168, 213
Huntley, Sir Harry, 56

Ida Hancock, tugboat, 17, 224
Idaho, 137
Illinois, 138, 142, 264
Iowa City, 139
India, 164
Indian ranchería at Los Angeles, 73
Indian Territory, 21, 27
Indianola, 222
Ingersoll, Robert G., 213
Inocente, Don, 86
Ireland, 8, 284, 288
Irving, Washington, 211
Ishem, emigrant, 142

Jefferson Street, Los Angeles, 144
Jenkins, Charles N., 75, 80, 81
Jenkins, William W. (Bill), 13, 14, 15, 17, 101, 212, 215, 285
Jersey Lily Saloon, The, 228, 229, 230, 231, 236
Jesús María, town of, 224
Jim the Penman, 265, 266
Johnston, Albert S., 74
Jones, Ap Catesby, 210
Joshua trees, 269, 274
Journey of Death, The, 29
Juárez, Benito, 41
Jurupa, 298, 300

Kansas, 273
Kate Aubrey, packet, 130
Kearney, Denis, 208
Kearny, Stephen W., 117, 296
Kentucky, 80, 127, 130, 131, 133, 134
Kewen, E. J. C., 76, 176
King, A. J., 76, 170, 171
King of Hawaii, 207
King, Jack, 235
King of Munster, 284
King of Spain, 298
Kings of the Commonwealth, 287, 288
Knights Templars, 197, 198
Kramer's Store, Los Angeles, 76

Laguna del Diablo, 195, 200, 202
Lachenais, mob victim, 177, 178, 179, 180
La Ciénega, 28, 29
Land frauds, Peralta case, 211
Land grants, legality of those issued by Pico, 263, 264
Land holdings, 2
Langtry, 224, 228, 229, 231, 232, 233
Langtry, Lily, 228
La Nopalera, 70
Lawler, actor, 58
Lazzarovich, John, 191
Leandri, J. D., owner of a thousand ox-carts, 257
Leona River, 221
Leonis, Michel (Miguel), 182 to 193
Lick Observatory, 238
Lincoln, Abraham, 75
Little Salt Lake, 139
Lloyd, Reuben H., 213
Logan, Boone, 213
Logan, Jonathan, 21
Logan, Dick, 21

INDEX 333

London, 268, 305
Long, George E., 290
Long Beach, 300
Long Wharf, San Francisco, 40
López, Chico, 200, 202
Lord Lurgan, untimely end of a distinguished hare, 306
Los Angeles, pueblo and city of, 2, 3, 4, 9, 33, 34, 35, 38, 39, 60, 63, 64, 66, 70, 71, 72, 74, 75, 76, 77, 78, 79, 80, 81, 82, 83, 85, 87, 88, 89, 93, 94, 96, 98, 99, 101, 105, 106, 116, 121, 134, 136, 137, 144, 146, 147, 155, 164, 166, 168, 172, 174, 177, 179, 182, 184, 186, 187, 190, 194, 202, 205, 208, 214, 217, 218, 221, 222, 223, 224, 226, 228, 233, 234, 235, 238, 245, 256, 258, 259, 264, 265, 267, 268, 269, 270, 271, 272, 273, 274, 275, 276, 278, 300, 301, 302, 305, 307
Los Angeles City Water Co., 90
Los Angeles County, early mortgage records, 6, 17; —, 33, 73, 106, 114, 120, 127, 144, 177, 186, 187, 214, 240, 242, 254, 258, 292; list of towns and ranches in 1852, 299, 300, 301, 302; primitive agricultural methods, 302
Los Angeles News, The, 174, 175
Los Angeles River, 73, 85, 253, 302
Los Angeles Star, The, 172, 174, 175
Los Angeles Street, 3, 4, 172, 174, 179
Los Cuervos (Cuerbos), battle of, 116
Louisiana, 83, 151, 219
Louisiana-Tehuantepec Co., 45
Louisville, 130
Love, Harry, 32, 36
Lugo, Antonio M. (El Viejo), 240, 255, 256, 302
Lugo family, 240, 298
Lugo, José del Carmen, 9

Machado, Augustín, 16
Machado family, 300
Main Street, Los Angeles, 4, 79, 120, 147, 164, 251; Upper —, 275
Maine, 148, 240, 261, 285
Mac el Medico, 14
Mackay, John E., 213
Magee, Bill, 218, 219
Magruder, John B., well known army officer plays saloonkeeper, 147 to 152
Malay, 207, 215
Malcolm, Henry, 64, 66, 68, 69
Malinche, 43, 47, 52
Manila, 207, 258
Man-killers, California and Texas types contrasted, 218
Mansfield, J. K. F., 57
Mansfield, Josie, favorite of Jim Fisk, Jr., 58, 59
Mansfield, lieut.-gov. of California, 57
Marchessault, Damien, 246
Mare Island Navy Yard, 57
Marina, Doña, *see* Malinche
Marryat, Frederick, 211
Marshall, James, 297
Martínez, Jesús, 60, 64, 69
Mascarel, Joseph (José), 77, 244, 252
Mason Creek, 219
Massachusetts, 207, 289
Matanzas, great cattle slaughters, 237
Maximilian, Emperor, 149, 178
Maximilian War, 67
Mazatlán, 67, 68, 70
McGullion, miner, 21, 22, 27, 28
McLean, James (Jim), 55
McMullen, murder victim, 221, 222, 223

McNear, Wiley, 78, 79
Medicinal springs used by Indians and padres, 302
Mendocino, 214
Mendocino County, 213
Mervine, Captain, 116
Merriweather, Dave, 130
Mexico, 1, 2, 3, 6, 19, 30, 41, 43, 48, 52, 62, 67, 83, 106, 113, 116, 119, 149, 165, 178, 208, 210, 219, 228, 250, 257, 263, 294; — City, 256, 258; Republic of —, 51, 237, 298
Mexican War, 116, 139, 147, 244, 293, 294, 298
Mexican Joe, narrow escape on the Trinity, 22, 24; saves American emigrants from Murrieta's bandits in Arizona, 28, 29, 30, 31; victim of mob in San Gabriél, 99, 101, 102
Meza, Calabasas squatter, 191
Micheltorena Battalion, 116
Micheltorena, Manuel, 1, 263
Michigan, 139
Miles, Los Angeles store clerk, his famous loan, 16, 17
Miller, Joaquín, 182
Minatitlán, 46, 48, 49, 51
Miramon, Miguel, 41
Missions, trade with Yankee ships, secularization, reason for final great slaughter of cattle, 236, 237
Mission Carmel, 33, 34
Mission San Gabriél Arcángel, 19, 100, 198, 223, 224, 235, 236, 238, 300
Mission San Fernando Rey de España, 300, 302
Mission San José de Guadalupe, 33
Mission San Juan Capistrano, 264, 300
Mission San Luís Rey de Francia, 108, 296
Mission Vieja, 241, 300
Mobs, attempted lynching of Mexican Joe on the Trinity, 22, 24, 25; Vulvia and Senati hanged, 31; riotous scenes in Los Angeles during Civil War, 72 to 82; Mexican Joe victim of mistaken identity at San Gabriél, 100, 101; Zavalete lynched in Los Angeles, 163; great Chinese massacre in Los Angeles, 166 to 177; Methodist pastor heads mob to lynch Lachenais in Los Angeles, 179, 180; mayor of Los Angeles resigns to conduct hanging of Dave Brown, 242, 243; comments on mob rule, 244
Mojave Desert, 168, 194
Monterey, 33, 153, 157, 159, 207, 208, 210, 257, 262; — Bay, 155, 210
Monterey County, 33
Monterrey, Mex., 196
Moreno, Atanácio, 31
Moreno, Diego, 60, 63, 64
Mormons, their Exodus, importance of their part in American occupation of California, 293 to 299
Mormon Battalion, 116, 139; departure for California under Colonel Allen, hardships, loyalty, 294, 295, 296, 297, 298, 299
Mountain Meadow Massacre, 140
Murphy, John M., a sporting tax collector, 155 to 162
Murrieta, Joaquín, 19, 28, 29, 30; death of, head of, exhibited in San Francisco, 32; last escape of, famous portrait of, owned by author, 83, 84; head of, exhibited in New York museum, 84; ghost

of, haunts Billy Henderson, 35, 36; —, 215, 233, 235, 243

Napa County, 263
Napoleon, Louis, 178
Natchez, pistol expert, 32, 33, 34, 36, 38
Natchez's Arms Store and Pistol Gallery, San Francisco, 32
Natchez, town of, 32
Natchez-Under-the-Hill, 130
Natick House, Los Angeles, 79
National Centennial, 289
Nauvoo, 294
Negro Alley (Calle de los Negros), Los Angeles, 170, 171, 173, 190
Nelson, William, strange case of mind over matter, 221, 222, 223
Nevada, 140
New Constitution, The, 212
Newhall, 136, 302; — Ranch, 14, 31
New High Street, Los Angeles, 179
New Mexico, 213, 215, 228, 234, 289
New Orleans, 75, 130, 222, 246
New Spain, 212
New York, 3, 34, 35, 59, 152, 164, 271, 295, 305, 307
New York Volunteers, 256
Nicaragua, 37, 38, 39, 41, 64, 66, 83, 127
Nicaragua, Lake, 66
Nichols, John G., 144
Nigger Pete, 75, 76
Nieto, Diego, 233, 234
Nieto family, 233
Noriega family, 4
Normandy, 285
North Carolina, 220
North Fork, 22

Oakland, 209
Ocampo, Francisco (Pancho), his lurid matrimonial career, 257, 258, 260
Ocampo, Doña Francisca de, former widow of Leandri, 257, 258
Oil boom in So. California, 307
Old Town, San Diego, 225
Omaha, 138
O'Reilly, Sarsfield (Count), 287
Oregon, 144
Oriental Hotel, San Francisco, 57
Ortega family, 4
Osborne, Doctor, 101
Oury, Grant, 151

Pacheco Pass, 157
Pacoima, 272, 273; — Cañon, 272
Pala, 108
Palomar Mountain, 108
Panamá, American boy polices isthmus, 53, 54, 55, 56; —, 67
Paris, 3
Parisian journalists visit Los Angeles, amusing incident, 244, 245
Parnell, lion, 106
Pasadena, 116; author's refusal of site of city as birthday gift, 301
Pearson, General, 74
Pecos River, 228, 232
Peel, B. L., 177
Peg-Leg Mine, 137, 138
Peg-Leg Smith, 137, 139, 144, 145
Peralta Barony, 212, 214
Peralta, El Español, 214
Peraltaites, 211
Peralta land fraud, 211 to 215
Peralta, Miguel, 211, 213, 215
Peru, 299

Petaluma, 277
Petranilla, Doña, 87, 88, 89, 90, 96
Phillips, Chino, 105
Phœnix, 214
Pico, Andrés, 243, 264, 302
Pico, Antonio M., 4
Pico Heights, 273
Pico House, Los Angeles, 148
Pico, Lieutenant, 195, 196, 197, 198
Pico, Pío, last governor of California under Mexico, 4, 11, 12, 83; his ruin averted by a friend in Scotland, 84; —, 261; his origin, appearance and capabilities, early antipathy for Americans, 262, 263, 264
Pico Street, Los Angeles, 83
Piñacarte, musician, 249
Piños Altos, 228
Pitt River, 218
Pixley, 247
Placerville, 145
Plaza, Los Angeles, 168, 172
Plaza, San Francisco, 32
Polaski's Store, Los Angeles, 76, 77
Pomona, 99
Pope, The, 287
Potrero de los Feliz, 92
Potts, J. W. (Little), 78
Prehistoric reptiles, 206
Price, M., 36, 37, 38
Price, Sterling, 75
Protestant church, first in Los Angeles, 146
Providence Spring, 142
Providencia, battle of, 263
Pueblo lands, how Los Angeles is said to have been despoiled of its municipal heritage from the King of Spain, 250
Puta Creek, 263
Pyrenees, 64, 182
Python, 203, 204

Queen of the Angels, 164

Rains, John, murder of, 114; —, 115, 241, 256
Rancho Aguaje de la Centinela, 12, 13, 300
Rancho el Aliso, 300
Rancho de los Alamitos, 300
Rancho la Ballona, 300
Rancho Bocas de Santa Monica, 301
Rancho la Brea, 301
Rancho de los Buenos Aires, 301
Rancho Cahuenga, 301
Rancho de los Cerritos, 300, 302
Rancho del Chino, 256, 300
Rancho el Conejo, 301
Rancho de los Coyotes, 258
Rancho de los Cuervos (Cuerbos), 300
Rancho Cucamonga, 114, 256
Rancho el Encino, 183, 188, 301
Rancho el Escorpión, 183, 302
Rancho Feliz, 85, 91, 92, 301, 302
Rancho Gilroy, 157, 158
Rancho Jurupa, 300
Rancho el Malibu, 301
Rancho la Merced, 289
Rancho ex-Mission San Fernando, 183, 264, 302
Rancho de los Palos Verdes, 300
Rancho Paso de las Tijeras, 300
Rancho Potrero de Felipe Lugo, 289
Rancho la Providencia, 301
Rancho la Puente, 20, 263, 289, 300
Rancho Rincon de los Bueyes, 301
Rancho Rodeo de las Aguas, 236, 301
Rancho San Antonio, 302

INDEX

Rancho San Francisquito, 143, 302
Rancho San Joaquín, 300
Rancho San Pascual, 116, 301
Rancho San Pedro (Domínguez), 300
Rancho San Rafael, 301
Rancho San Vicente y Santa Monica, 301
Rancho Santa Gertrudis, 300
Rancho Tejunga, 301, 302
Rancho Temescal, 127
Rancho el Triúnfo, 301
Rancho de las Vírgenes, 301
Rancho Yorba (Santa Ana), 300
Ranchos, extent of, vast herds owned, 2; loss of, by native owners, 5, 6, 7, 8, 10, 18, 255, 256, 257, 258, 259
Rangers, 4, 19, 32, 38, 224, 233, 235
Real estate, great boom of the '80s in So. Cal., examples of the craze, 267 to 277
Reavis, James A. P., 212, 213, 214
Reavis, Señora de, 215
Redman, J. W., 153
Redman, R. A., 155
Redondo, 208, 268, 270, 271
Register of U. S. Land Office, his famous street fights, 12 to 16; his violent death, 102, 103
Reminiscences of a Ranger, 8, 31
Reynolds, William (Bill), remarkable origin and career, 207 to 217
Rezer family, 128, 129
Rezer, Rafe, 127, 130, 131, 133
Rhodes, Jack, 81
Río Grande, 29, 221, 228, 229, 236
Río Pecos, 228, 232
Rivera, Felipe, 203, 204
Riverside, 298
Robertson, William, 142
Roman, Richard, 38
Romero, Fraile, author's reverend companion in Mexican adventures, 41 to 51
Rosecrans, 247
Ross, Bill, 38
Rowland family, 289
Rowland, John (Don Juan), 20, 263
Rubottom, Uncle Bill, adventures of a well known Arkansan, 13, 21, 22, 24, 25, 31, 99, 100, 101; he kills Register of U. S. Land Office at Los Angeles, 102, 103; —, 104, 105, 114, 115, 116
Rubottom's Company, 21, 22, 25, 31
Runnels, Ran, 53, 54, 56
Russ House, San Francisco, 68

Sacramento, 40, 159, 160, 297
Sainsevain, Louis, 246
Salazar, José, 136
Salt Lake, 138, 139, 141, 144, 294, 299; — Valley, 299
Sánchez, Juan, 86
Sanford, William B., 224
Sansome, Elias, Calabasas squatter, 187, 191
Sansome, John (Johnny), 219, 220
Sansome Ranch, 219
Savannah, frigate, 116
San Antonio, 221, 222, 228
San Bernardino, 26, 115, 144; its Mormon origin, 294, 299; early Mormon life there, 298, 299; —, 300; — Mountains, 299; — Valley, 299
San Bruno, 61, 68
San Clemente Island, 80
San Diego, 2, 4, 147, 150, 187, 225, 226, 257, 295, 296, 300; — Bay, 147, 224; — County, 198, 225

San Fernando, 106, 272; — Mountains, 168; — Valley, 181, 183, 271, 302
San Francisco, 15, 32, 33, 35, 36, 37, 38, 40, 52, 55, 57, 58, 61, 67, 68, 69, 151, 208, 235, 257, 258, 259, 265, 279, 280, 282, 287, 288, 290, 295, 297; — Bay, 157, 277
San Gabriél, 21, 25, 100, 195, 196, 228, 233, 235, 236, 262, 302; — Valley, 236, 237, 238
San Jacinto, battle of, 219
San Joaquín Valley, 157
San José, 4, 33, 153, 155, 156, 157, 257, 260
San Juan Capistrano, 73
San Juan Guichicova, 44, 45
San Juan del Sur, 66
San Luís Obispo, 153
San Pascual, battle of, 243
San Pedro, 15, 17, 38, 116, 235, 300, 305
San Quentin, 55, 73, 78
Santa Ana River, 300
Santa Bárbara, presidio and pueblo of, 2, 3, 4, 106, 114, 118, 136, 208, 249
Santa Clara County, 155, 157; — River, 144
Santa Fé, 224, 295
Santa Fé Railroad, 299
Santa Monica, 97, 300
Santa Rosa, 277
Saugus, 302
Schumacher, John, 179
Scott, Jonathan R., 144
Second Illinois Cavalry, 81
Sells Brothers, 203, 204
Senati, bandit, 29, 30, 31
Sepúlveda, José, 16, 17
Sepúlveda, Judge, 177
Serra, Junípero, 195, 198
Serrano family, 26
Seward, William H., 248; visits Los Angeles, 249; —, 250
Shasta, 264
Shacklett family, 128, 129
Sherman, William T., 57
Shore, county clerk, 15
Shylocks, 5, 6, 7, 102, 221, 255, 259, 261
Sierra Madre, 301
Sierra Nevada, 262
Silk shawls, 258
Sinaloa, 67
Sipes, Jack, 218
Sloat, John D., 209
Smith, Captain, 139, 140
Smith, Eli, 103
Smith, Obed, 259, 260, 261, 262
Smith, Mrs. Obed, 262
Smith, Quartermaster, U.S.A., 298
Soap mines, 237, 238
Soda Springs, 144
Soledad Pass, 120, 168, 194, 195
Smoked Yankee, 217
Sonoita, 151
Sonoma, 2, 4, 225, 256
Sonora, 29, 31, 60, 224
Sonoratown, Los Angeles, 121, 245, 275
South America, 164, 270
South Sea Islands, 207
South Seas, 215
Southern California, 85, 181, 298; real estate and horticultural booms, 218, 221, 227, 233, 279, 281, 282, 289, 293; changes, amusing review of fads, 303; oil boom, 307
Southern Pacific Railroad, 99, 166, 168, 213, 228, 231, 232
Spadra, 99
Spain, 157, 182, 213, 214, 278

INDEX

Spanish Country, 137, 144, 145
Spanish Trail, 139, 144
Spence, E. F., 290
Spiritual Conquest of California, The, 194
Spring Street, Los Angeles, 13, 179
Squatter War, Calabasas, 182 to 192
St. Elmo Hotel, Los Angeles, 120
St. John, ex-governor of Kansas, 273
St. Louis, 152
St. Nicholas Hotel, San Francisco, 38
Stanford, Leland, 168
Stars and Stripes, 210, 293, 296
Steadman, General, 57
Stearns, Abel, 4, 148, 286
Stevenson's Pioneer Regiment, 33, 256, 258
Stock, gambler, 79
Stockton, 40, 59
Stockton, Robert F., 3, 57
Stokes, Ed. S., 213
Stoneman, George, 57
Sturgis, Doctor, 235
Sublette's Cut-off, 139
Suchiltepec, 44, 45
Sue, Eugene, 211
Supreme Court of California, 176, 241, 242
Surveyor General, 208
Sutter, Johann, 297; —'s Fort, 297

Tabor, John, 57
Tallow mines, 238
Tansy Bitters, 133, 134, 135
Tegucigalpa, 131, 132
Tehachepi Pass, 168
Tehuantepec, 41, 42, 44, 45, 51, 52
Tejunga Cañon, 89; Grand —, 92; — Mountains, 89, 90
Temescal, 21, 22, 25, 26, 31; — Creek, 26
Temple Block, 79, 178, 208
Temple, F. P. F. (Templito), 289, 290
Temple Street, Los Angeles, 179
Temple & Workman, bank failure and resultant tragedy, 289, 290, 291, 292
Tennessee, 220
Terry, David S., duel with Senator Broderick, 32, 33, 36; confined in Fort Gunnybags, 37; conspiracy to deport him, 38, 39
Texas, 149, 151, 218, 219, 220, 221, 222, 224, 228, 230
That Fine Young Señorita, song, 259 to 262
Thompson, policeman, 171, 172, 176
Three-Fingered-Jack, 32
Toler, William, 209
Tombs Prison, 152
Tombstone, 69, 204
Trafford, John, 188
Treasure trove, in Cahuenga Pass, 60 to 71; in Nicaragua, 66, 67; at San Gabriel, 236
Trinity County, 21, 22
Trinity Mountains, 21; — River, 218
Tucson, 28, 29, 30, 31, 151
Tulare, 150; — Valley, 32
Turner, Joel H., 244, 246, 248, 250, 251, 254
Twain, Mark, 282
Two Years Before the Mast, 236

Union Hotel, San Francisco, 260
United States, U. S. Government, 1, 6, 7, 37, 181, 186, 187, 208, 209, 210, 211, 213, 228, 244, 248, 250, 262, 263, 271, 285, 293, 294
U. S. Army, 222
U. S. Land Commission, 120, 263

U. S. Marshal, 37
U. S. Mint, San Francisco, 225, 226
U. S. Navy, 209
Utah, 294, 298

Valdez family, 238
Vallejo family, 156
Vallejo, Mariano G., 4, 157, 256; opposes Pico's anti-gringo attitude, 262
Valenzuela, Doña Juana, 86
Vanderbilt, Cornelius, 56, 66
Vásquez, Chico, 200
Vásquez, Tibúrcio, 200
Vega, Placido, 67, 68, 69
Ventura County, 181, 187
Verdugo family, 301
Victoria, 220
Vigilance Committee, San Francisco, plot to deport Judge Terry, 37, 38, 39; —, 40
Vignes, Jean L., 83
Virgin Bay, 66
Voltigeur Regiment, U.S.A., 147
Vulvia, Luís, 29, 30, 31

Walker's Cut-off, 139
Walker Filibuster, 64
Walker-Rivas Army, recruits sent from San Francisco to Nicaragua in command of author, 37
Walker War, 130
Walker, William, 38, 41, 66, 67, 127
War of the Rebellion, 219
Warner, Jonathan T. (Don Juan), 295
Warner's Ranch, 295, 296
Warren, William (Billy), 81
Wasatch Mountains, 139
Washington, D. C., 3, 244
Washington Street, Los Angeles, 60
Watermelon, George, 265, 266
Watkins, Lewis D., 37
Webster, Daniel, 208
Wells, Fargo, 55
West Virginia, 187
Widneyville, 268, 269, 270, 274
Wilkes, Charles, 207
Willey, Three-Legged, 219, 220
Williams, Isaac, 256
Wilmington, 75, 235
Wilmington Street, Los Angeles, 251
Wilson, Benjamin D. (Don Benito), 100, 150, 253
Winchester rifles, 204
Whimp family, 128, 129
White House, Los Angeles, 179
Whistler, Doctor, 78
Wolfskill, William, 117, 263
Wood, William S., 213
Woods, Annie, 58
Woodward's Ranch, 221
Woodward, Texas rancher, 221, 223
Workman, William (Billy), 79, 263, 289

Yale, 240
Yankee, Smoked, 217
Yankee trading ships, 236, 237
Yaqui Indians, 29
Yarnell, Jesse, 185, 237
Yorktown, 152
Young, Brigham, 294
Yuma, 26
Yung, Sam, 170, 171, 176

Zanja Madre, 190
Zavalete, mob victim, 164
Zion, 294, 296

THE CHICANO HERITAGE

An Arno Press Collection

Adams, Emma H. **To and Fro in Southern California.** 1887

Anderson, Henry P. **The Bracero Program in California.** 1961

Aviña, Rose Hollenbaugh. **Spanish and Mexican Land Grants in California.** 1976

Barker, Ruth Laughlin. **Caballeros.** 1932

Bell, Horace. **On the Old West Coast.** 1930

Biberman, Herbert. **Salt of the Earth.** 1965

Casteñeda, Carlos E., trans. **The Mexican Side of the Texas Revolution (1836).** 1928

Casteñeda, Carlos E. **Our Catholic Heritage in Texas, 1519-1936.** Seven volumes. 1936-1958

Colton, Walter. **Three Years in California.** 1850

Cooke, Philip St. George. **The Conquest of New Mexico and California.** 1878

Cue Canovas, Agustin. **Los Estados Unidos Y El Mexico Olvidado.** 1970

Curtin, L. S. M. **Healing Herbs of the Upper Rio Grande.** 1947

Fergusson, Harvey. **The Blood of the Conquerors.** 1921

Fernandez, Jose. **Cuarenta Años de Legislador:** Biografia del Senador Casimiro Barela. 1911

Francis, Jessie Davies. **An Economic and Social History of Mexican California** (1822-1846). Volume I: Chiefly Economic. Two vols. in one. 1976

Getty, Harry T. **Interethnic Relationships in the Community of Tucson.** 1976

Guzman, Ralph C. **The Political Socialization of the Mexican American People.** 1976

Harding, George L. **Don Agustin V. Zamorano.** 1934

Hayes, Benjamin. **Pioneer Notes from the Diaries of Judge Benjamin Hayes, 1849-1875.** 1929

Herrick, Robert. **Waste.** 1924

Jamieson, Stuart. **Labor Unionism in American Agriculture.** 1945

Landolt, Robert Garland. **The Mexican-American Workers of San Antonio, Texas.** 1976

Lane, Jr., John Hart. **Voluntary Associations Among Mexican Americans in San Antonio, Texas.** 1976

Livermore, Abiel Abbot. **The War with Mexico Reviewed.** 1850

Loyola, Mary. **The American Occupation of New Mexico, 1821-1852.** 1939

Macklin, Barbara June. **Structural Stability and Culture Change in a Mexican-American Community.** 1976

McWilliams, Carey. **Ill Fares the Land:** Migrants and Migratory Labor in the United States. 1942

Murray, Winifred. **A Socio-Cultural Study of 118 Mexican Families Living in a Low-Rent Public Housing Project in San Antonio, Texas.** 1954

Niggli, Josephina. **Mexican Folk Plays.** 1938

Parigi, Sam Frank. **A Case Study of Latin American Unionization in Austin, Texas.** 1976

Poldervaart, Arie W. **Black-Robed Justice.** 1948

Rayburn, John C. and Virginia Kemp Rayburn, eds. **Century of Conflict, 1821-1913.** Incidents in the Lives of William Neale and William A. Neale, Early Settlers in South Texas. 1966

Read, Benjamin. **Illustrated History of New Mexico.** 1912

Rodriguez, Jr., Eugene. **Henry B. Gonzalez.** 1976

Sanchez, Nellie Van de Grift. **Spanish and Indian Place Names of California.** 1930

Sanchez, Nellie Van de Grift. **Spanish Arcadia.** 1929

Shulman, Irving. **The Square Trap.** 1953

Tireman, L. S. **Teaching Spanish-Speaking Children.** 1948

Tireman, L. S. and Mary Watson. **A Community School in a Spanish-Speaking Village.** 1948

Twitchell, Ralph Emerson. **The History of the Military Occupation of the Territory of New Mexico.** 1909

Twitchell, Ralph Emerson. **The Spanish Archives of New Mexico.** Two vols. 1914

U. S. House of Representatives. **California and New Mexico:** Message from the President of the United States, January 21, 1850. 1850

Valdes y Tapia, Daniel. **Hispanos and American Politics.** 1976

West, Stanley A. **The Mexican Aztec Society.** 1976

Woods, Frances Jerome. **Mexican Ethnic Leadership in San Antonio, Texas.** 1949

Aspects of the Mexican American Experience. 1976

Mexicans in California After the U. S. Conquest. 1976

Hispanic Folklore Studies of Arthur L. Campa. 1976

Hispano Culture of New Mexico. 1976

Mexican California. 1976

The Mexican Experience in Arizona. 1976

The Mexican Experience in Texas. 1976

Mexican Migration to the United States. 1976

The United States Conquest of California. 1976

Northern Mexico On the Eve of the United States Invasion:
  Rare Imprints Concerning California, Arizona, New Mexico, and Texas, 1821-1846. Edited by David J. Weber. 1976